Ship
of
Death

EMIGRANTS AT DINNER.

THE TRAGEDY OF THE 'EMIGRANT'

Ship
of
Death

THE VOYAGE ■ THE QUARANTINE ■ THE AFTERMATH

JANE SMITH

INDEPENDENT INK

First published 2019 by Independent Ink
PO Box 1638, Carindale
Queensland 4152 Australia
independentink.com.au

Cover design by Maria Biaggini @ Independent Ink
Edited by Samantha Sainsbury
Internal design by Independent Ink
Typeset in 12/17 pt Minion Pro by Post Pre-press Group, Brisbane
Cover image: Photograph of ship by Jim Fenwick
Page ii image: Illustrated London News, 13 April 1844, p.299.

 A catalogue record for this
book is available from the
NATIONAL LIBRARY OF AUSTRALIA National Library of Australia

ISBN 978-0-6486503-0-0 (paperback)
ISBN 978-0-6486503-1-7 (epub)
ISBN 978-0-6486503-2-4 (kindle)

Contents

Many children of the *Emigrant* died prematurely – at sea, in quarantine, and in their adopted land. I find it hard to imagine how so many parents of the Victorian era bore the loss of so many of their children, and feel grateful every day that mine have made it to adulthood.

I dedicate this story to my children, Lucy and Eddie, who have grown into beautiful, creative and kind adults.

I also dedicate it to the memory of Mary Connor, the poor, young, illiterate, plucky and wise Irishwoman who took pity on six little orphans.

Foreword

By Kerry O'Brien

When I cooperated with an SBS television program called *Who Do You Think You Are* back in 2011, one of the things I learned for the first time about my Irish ancestors was that they had come to Australia in 1850 as refugees from the Great Potato Famine that killed a million people. The irony, given the pathetic help given to the Irish by the English during the famine, was that they sailed from an English port on an English bounty ship called the *Emigrant* to help solve the labour shortage on farms run mostly by English immigrants in what was to become Queensland.

We learned enough of the history of their voyage, with their fellow-travellers from England and Ireland, to put the basic story together for the program – and a wretched story it was. Of the crew and 276 passengers who sailed, 47 died, either at sea or in a makeshift quarantine camp on Stradbroke Island at the mouth of the Brisbane River, nearly all of them from typhus. Jane Smith, excellent historian that she is, has gone much further in fleshing out the saga of that 1850 voyage, and in doing so has added a rich vein to our understanding of the personal, individual legends of early white settlement in Queensland.

Smith has very carefully woven together the facts of the voyage and its participants, ascertained from all the available primary sources, with the broader historical knowledge of the times and circumstances to frame the whole as a genuine saga. She has captured the sense of purpose and stoicism they brought to the venture, the personal tragedies, the awfulness of the disease, the fear of what lay ahead. You feel the pathos with her of a tiny baby stitched into a piece of weighted canvas sliding off a plank of timber into the depths of the ocean, or the sacrifice of the selfless Moreton Bay doctor who died with his patients on Stradbroke. But then she has moved on from the voyage and the weeks of quarantine, and followed many of the survivors as they struggled to build new lives. Those survivors included my great-great grandparents and their two small children [Charles and Anne O'Brien of County Clare, with their children Mary (six) and John (an infant)].

In my schooling in Queensland through the fifties and early sixties, I was fed a dry and very limited diet of history. It was about names and places and dates, and bare detail of what took place, almost guaranteed to kill your natural interest in the big stories of human history rather than nourish it. Jane Smith's endeavour, a real labour of love but also a significant contribution to community revelation, reflects a vastly superior capacity for disciplined but accessible historical story-telling than my generation was raised on. This account of a handful of people crossing the ocean in a small ship over a few months 169 years ago is one of many that together make up a complete mosaic. In understanding one, we come closer to understanding them all – and maybe in the process, developing a little more compassion and understanding for those making similar voyages today.

Author's note

Most of what we know about 19th-century voyages comes from shipboard diaries and surgeons' logs. Unfortunately, no known diaries from the *Emigrant*'s passengers have survived. Journals of other voyages, however, show enough consistency to allow us to make reasonable assumptions. I do not *know*, for instance, that little William Frith's shrouded body was lain on a plank across the bulwark and tipped into the sea, that the ship's bell tolled and the passengers gathered on the deck to sing hymns at his funeral – but that is how a burial at sea was *normally* conducted, and was almost certainly conducted on this particular voyage. Likewise, only scant accounts exist of the course that typhus took in its victims on the *Emigrant*. Where I have described symptoms in particular sufferers, I have described the typical course of the disease. I hope the reader will forgive these assumptions, which I have made in the interests of bringing life to the story.

There are many aspects of shipboard life that we *can* be sure of: the cleaning procedures, the accommodation, the provisions, the mealtime routines, the duties of passengers, surgeon and crew, and the strict rules governing behaviour – these were all required by law. They are documented in countless primary and secondary sources of information about 19th-century emigration.

Only three known contemporaneous first-hand accounts of the voyage exist. One of these was written by Captain William Henry Kemp, and another by his wife, Frances Sarah Kemp; the former was published in the *Moreton Bay Courier* and the latter in *The Emigrants' Penny Magazine*. These letters outline the course of the epidemic and give us names and dates. The only other first-hand account written at the time – a letter penned by passenger Jane T. Cullen – is principally an expression of gratitude to the 'good and kind' Captain Kemp and his selfless wife. Other first- and second-hand accounts written decades after the voyage are reliable only in one particular: that the loss of life was great, and the suffering immeasurable.

The long quarantine at Dunwich has been documented more extensively than the voyage. Correspondence between the colonial secretary, the doctors and other authorities has been captured on microfilm and can be viewed at the State Library of Queensland. The correspondence is, for the most part, business-like and matter-of-fact; even so, the desperation in the emigrants' situation is evident. Much of the correspondence quoted in this text comes from those files.

I would like to add a short note regarding the accuracy and spelling of passengers' names. *Many* discrepancies have come to my attention during the course of my research, when comparing names recorded on embarkation lists, arrival lists, birth, death and marriage certificates, newspaper reports, letters and police records. This may be a result of a combination of clerical and transcription errors and illiteracy. I have tried to use the version I felt was most reliable or most frequently used by their owners. I hope that this causes no offence.

I would also like to clarify the matter of Mary Elizabeth Wade's name. In all correspondence and official documents except for her first baptism record, she is recorded simply as Elizabeth Wade. Confusingly, a stepsister who accompanied her on the voyage was also named Elizabeth Wade. To distinguish the two women, I have in most instances referred to the tragic 19-year-old as Elizabeth Wade and her stepsister as Elizabeth Matilda Wade.

The story of the *Emigrant* is a story of tragedy and extraordinary resilience. I find it remarkable that so many of the emigrants' families later sailed out to join them in Australia, even knowing first-hand as they did how easily the voyage could end in disaster. They must have believed that the risk was worth taking. Times were tough. These pioneers were desperate but they also showed courage and a sense of adventure. They contributed a great deal to the growth of Brisbane but also spread to New South Wales, Victoria and South Australia. Some had successful lives and some did not; all of them struggled. I hope I have done them justice.

There are too many stories to tell in one book. For more details about the fate of passengers not provided in this book, please see my website: *The Tragedy of the Emigrant*.

I acknowledge that much of this story took place on land that once belonged to Australia's First Peoples. I offer my deepest respects to the Quandamooka Peoples, the traditional owners of the lands and waters of Moreton Bay: the Nunukul, the Goenpul and the Nughi. I recognise their continuing connection to land, waters and culture, and pay my respects to their Elders past, present and emerging. I also thank the North Stradbroke Island Museum on Minjerribah.

A special note

Ship of Death tells the stories of 276 British people who sought to escape lives of endless struggle and build more prosperous lives in Australia. Many of the lucky ones achieved their goal. It must not be forgotten, however, that any good fortune our early European settlers experienced came at the expense of those who had lived in this land for tens of thousands of years: Australia's First Peoples. I would like to warn readers that this book contains quotes from 19th-century texts that reflect attitudes of the time and are offensive today.

Minjerribah (North Stradbroke Island) has been a home to the Nunukul and Goenpul people for at least 21,000 years: the Nunukul in the north, and the Goenpul in the south. Aboriginal people know Central and Southern Moreton Bay and the land and waters between the Brisbane and Logan Rivers as 'Quandamooka'. The Peoples of the Quandamooka include the Nunukul and Goenpul of Minjerribah and the Nughi of Moorgumpin (Moreton Island). (Please note that as a result of colonisation and the active suppression of Aboriginal languages, and due to differences in oral sources, the European spellings for places and nations varies.)

In 1823, the Quandamooka Peoples' lives – and the lives of the First Peoples of 'Meanjin' (Brisbane) and the district – were changed forever when Lieutenant John Oxley sailed north looking for a new place to send New South Wales' recidivist convicts. The decision to settle in the Moreton Bay region (as we now know it) had a monumental effect on the lives of the Indigenous population.

The impact on the Quandamooka Peoples was compounded two years later with the decision to build a depot and pilot station at 'Pulan' (Amity Point) to facilitate shipping, and then a small convict outstation with a military post and stores at 'Goompi' (Dunwich). According to oral history, the Quandamooka people initially welcomed the newcomers with food, shelter and care, believing at first they were Ancestors coming back to them. Before long, however, European intrusion caused suffering in many ways, starting off with dispossession of land and suppression of culture. Another big impact was loss of families from all the diseases that the newcomers brought with them. This was especially so on Minjerribah as the quarantine station was located there.

Ship of Death, however, focuses on the lives of the emigrants – their voyage, their experiences in quarantine, their fates – and the stories of others whose lives were closely connected with theirs during the ordeal. During their period of quarantine, the isolation of the quarantine station from the local population was enforced by guards and we have no record of any interactions between the people quarantined there in 1850 and the Indigenous Australians. For this reason, the story of Indigenous Australians has only a small place in my account of the *Emigrant* tragedy.

Of course, any lack of information about direct contact

between the emigrants and the Indigenous people does not mean the newcomers' presence was not felt. Far from it. European settlement of Moreton Bay – as in other parts of Australia – caused irrevocable disruption to Indigenous lives. After 1850, Brisbane grew and Europeans soon outnumbered the Indigenous people, taking over their land, disregarding their laws, and causing immeasurable damage to their culture, their health and their livelihood.

It is beyond the scope of this book to detail the effect of European immigration on the Aboriginal peoples of Moreton Bay and Brisbane. To gain a deeper understanding of Aboriginal history, politics, customs, laws and interactions with early white settlers, I urge you to read the profound and eye-opening *Warrior* by Libby Connors.

Part 1

Our parting sorrow

Emigrant's Farewell

Fare thee well dear Isle of Ocean,
All ye weeping friends farewell;
Oh, who can the wild emotion,
Of our parting sorrow tell?
Yet One above will safely guide,
Our passage through that swelling tide

Though we're called from home to sever,
And to tread a foreign land;
Though, dear Father, we for ever
Lose thy kind and guiding hand –
Parent and Guardian, staff and stay,
The Lord shall guard and guide our way.

And dear Mother, broken hearted,
When thy sheltering arms we leave;
If, when far from thee departed,
Even thou should'st cease to grieve –
Still, there is one who never yet
Absent, or distant, can forget.

Fare ye well, sweet sisters, nearest,
Both in kindred and in soul;
Fare ye well, kind brothers dearest,
Though the sea between us roll –
Yet One there is, who at our side,
Closer than brother will abide

May God save thee, Isle of Ocean!
Country of our birth, farewell!
Although waves in wild commotion
High around the vessel swell
The Lord shall keep his little band,
Safe in the Hollow of His hand.[1]

Chapter 1

Arriving at the gateway to a better life

Early April 1850

PLYMOUTH, DEVON, SOUTHWEST ENGLAND

An undercurrent of fear tempered the excitement as they converged upon Plymouth. They were farm hands and carpenters and servants; they were newlyweds and families and singles hoping to find a mate; there was even a bigamist amongst them. In their midst was a child who would become a Supreme Court Judge, a future wife-beater, a handful of mayors and alcoholics in the making, countless pioneers who would shape a new nation. There were unborn babies, children who would never be adults, and a half-dozen waifs who would become orphans. There were some who would lose their lives and others who would lose their minds.

They came from the eastern counties – Kent and Essex and Surrey – and from nearby Somerset and Devonshire; from London and Cambridge, and as far north as Lincolnshire. They came from Ireland: from Queen's County and Galway, Tipperary, Limerick and Clare. Whatever their origins, they were united in purpose.

Hope drove them on: hope for a better life in which hard work might lead to material gain. Their home lands offered little. They were poor workers – men, women and children – whose overcrowded and impoverished homes promised nothing but unending drudgery. There was hope in the colonies: a chance of prosperity. But there was also risk.

They came by rail and steam packet to the busy port town of Plymouth. They wove their way through the narrow, crooked streets, down steep inclines towards the harbour where the vessel that would transport them to new lives waited.

The town of Plymouth had been shaped by its proximity to the sea. It had begun as a fishing village and grown into a thriving place of trade. It was a bustling town: teeming with life and squalor, overcrowded and riddled with disease. The gateway to a better life. For these two hundred odd souls, it was the beginning of the adventure of a lifetime. For some, it was the last adventure they would ever have.

THE WADE/BALL FAMILY

A family of six made their way through the streets of Plymouth. They had travelled over two hundred miles from the slums of London's East End and were bound for the Baltic Wharf, where the Emigration Depot awaited them.

Unlike many of the bewildered emigrants whose paths would soon join theirs, they were accustomed to this flurry of city life. Joseph William Ball was a 44-year-old postman-turned-milkman, London born and bred. His wife, 41-year-old Mary, was at his side. With them were four daughters: four young women, just what the colony of New South Wales needed. They were respectable women of marriageable age. Virtuous women accompanied by parents who were themselves still young enough to supplement the colony's desperately under-supplied workforce.

To outward appearances, they were an average family: the working poor. An observer would never guess at the loss and trauma that had followed them so far, nor the heartbreak that was yet to come. No observer could imagine the secrets of this complex blended family, connected as they were by an intricate web of marriage, estrangement, death and re-marriage. The girls were daughters to three different fathers and three mothers. But they were united in this, the biggest adventure – the biggest gamble – of their lives: emigration.

Travellers from London typically came to Plymouth by train or steamer. If the family had travelled by sea, a barge would have conveyed them from their steamer directly to the wharf upon which the Emigration Depot sat. They would have clamoured from the barge up the slippery steps onto a wharf that was bustling with the comings and goings of fellow-travellers.

More likely, the Wade/Ball family had travelled here by steam train. Their journey would have begun at Paddington station and they would have travelled on the Great Western Railway to Exeter via Bristol in carriages set apart for emigrants. At Bristol, passengers changed to the South Devon Railway which chugged on to the newly-opened Plymouth Millbay station. The journey took seven or eight hours. By the time they reached Plymouth, they would have been dusty, stiff and tired. Unfolding themselves from their carriages and stepping out onto the platform, they would have been grateful to have been greeted by officials who conveyed them and their luggage, by hansom cab or horse-drawn omnibus, to the Emigration Depot.

The wharf was only a mile from the station. As the travellers rattled along closer to the harbour, the road wound downward and the neighbourhood became less savoury. Dotted with gaslights and lined with densely packed homes, the streets were shabby and unsanitary. Old houses built for the gentry had fallen into disrepair, the carved stonework of their facades now a sad reminder of better days. Tumbled-down walls, stained with damp, littered the backstreets and gave partial shelter to the homeless. Formerly grand homes had been subdivided to make room for the ever-growing population; Plymouth's overcrowding problem was dire.

The travellers would have passed beneath laundry that fluttered damply from the poles protruding from layer upon layer of tenement windows. In the back streets, narrow lanes opened to communal courtyards dense with the stench of shared privies and poor drainage. Disease was a constant threat. The previous year, cholera had killed over 2000 of Plymouth's population of some 50,000. The town would soon be described as 'one of the most unhealthy (because uncleanly) towns in the kingdom'.[2]

None of this mattered to Joseph Ball and his family. They were headed to a new and spacious land: Australia. Where the sun was fierce but the air was fresh and free of the insidious and inescapable dankness of England. Where they hoped to put privation and loss behind them and make a life in the land of opportunity.

The Emigration Depot sat on the Baltic Wharf behind Fisher's Nose, a headland that extended from the western side of Sutton Pool into the deep inlet of Plymouth Sound. A long, 70-foot high fortification of limestone and granite, known as 'The Citadel', hugged the coastline and towered above the wharf. Below it, overlooking the majestic sound, lay the Emigration Depot.

The party was escorted into the depot. Here they would stay for a few days of preparation before boarding; they would undergo final checks for eligibility and learn the rules and routines of shipboard life. With beds for up to 700, the three-storey building was a lively place. On the basement floor were two large apartments, one of which served as a kitchen, wash house and laundry. The other was a storeroom for the travellers' luggage. In here, Joseph Ball's family deposited their modest belongings, each item clearly marked in large letters with its owner's name.

The newcomers were greeted by the aptly named super-intendent Mr William J. Seaward (or Seward) and his wife Mary. The warmth of the Seawards' greeting was balm to tired and anxious travellers. Their hosts revived the family with refresh-ments: meat and potatoes, plentiful and nutritious. The emigrants took heart from the Seawards' kindness and were reassured by the cleanliness and well-ordered routines of the establishment.

Joseph and Mary Ball were newlyweds. They had married at Saint Peters in Stepney, on 13 November 1849 – only five months earlier. But they had known each other a long time, having lodged together for at least eight years.

Both parties had been married before; this was his second marriage and her third. Hidden in Mary's past was a secret that had to be kept from the emigration authorities. It was a secret that would have scandalised Victorian society and jeopardised her chances of an assisted passage if it got out.

THE FREQUENTLY MARRIED MARY BALL

Mary was born in Scotland[3] in 1810 or 1811. Her parents were Thomas Shanks, a wood-turner, and his wife, Mary McDuggan. By the time she was about ten years old, Mary's family had left Scotland for the outskirts of London, where her brother William was born. In Greenwich in 1825, Mary Shanks married a journey-man carpenter named Frederick Whittenbury. Mary was only 14 or 15 years old and her husband at least 20 years her senior.

Mary gave birth to a daughter at the City of London Lying in Hospital, St Luke, on 8 June 1831. Mary and Fred Whittenbury named their daughter Mary Elizabeth, but the child was known by all as 'Elizabeth'. It was this daughter, now a young woman, who accompanied Mary on the great adventure of emigration. The girl had been the only constant in Mary's turbulent life.

Mary and Fred's marriage was not a success. Only a short time after the birth of their child, the couple parted ways. But the complex process and the cost of divorce put it beyond the reach of ordinary people like the Whittenburys. Better just to pretend that the marriage had never happened. This was a difficult thing to do, given the evidence in the form of a child.

Mary soon found a new husband who was prepared to take on a baby daughter. Mary's second husband was John Wade, a working-class widower – a reed-merchant from Essex with several children of his own: Ann, Charlotte, John, Elizabeth Matilda and Emma. The pair married on 27 May 1833 at St Dunstan's in Stepney, when little Elizabeth Whittenbury was two years old.

Mary passed herself off as a 'spinster' at her marriage. Whoever recorded the wedding in the parish register wasn't particular about checking details. He registered John as a 'bachelor', although he would have been more accurately described as a widower. But how much did Mary's new husband know of her life before they married? Did he really think that she was a spinster – a single, never married mother – or did she let him believe she was a widow? Did he know that she was already married – and that in marrying him she was, in fact, becoming a bigamist?

It seems likely that John knew of Mary's status; their marriage in Stepney took place not far from her previous marital home, and her former husband had remained in the area. But regardless of what he knew or didn't know, John Wade seems to have accepted the toddler Elizabeth and brought her up as a daughter.

Within a year of their marriage, John and Mary Wade had another child: a boy named William. He was baptised on 7 February 1834 at Rainham, Essex. The need to baptise their son may have been urgent. He may have been already sick and threatening to die, for only nine days after the ceremony, baby William was buried.

Later that year, the Wades celebrated another baptism. Perhaps little William's death had reminded them of the fragility of human life, and the need for insurance against damnation. John's daughter Emma was ten years old and had never been baptised. It may be that the matter of her baptism had been forgotten in the aftermath of her mother's death. In any case, after little William's death, the Wades decided that it was time to rectify the situation – and, at the same time, establish John as the legal father of Mary's daughter Elizabeth.

On 24 August 1834, both ten-year-old Emma and her stepsister, three-year-old (Mary) Elizabeth Wade, were baptised. History was rewritten. Mary Elizabeth, formerly Whittenbury, daughter of the journeyman carpenter Frederick, was officially declared to be Elizabeth, the child of John and Mary Wade. It was a complicated situation, given that Elizabeth Wade was also the name of her older stepsister.

The family celebrated another baptism the following year. John and Mary's second child together, Ellen, was baptised in Essex on 31 May, 1835.

The Wade marriage was brief but its effects far-reaching. Through it, Mary had acquired several stepchildren, and her daughter had secured a new name. But by 1841 it was all over. The child Ellen had vanished from the records and can only be presumed dead. John Wade had either died or deserted, leaving Mary alone again. But not for long.

By 1841, she and her ten-year-old daughter Elizabeth were living with Joseph William Ball at Bethnal Green. Joseph was a postman, and a poor but hardworking and good-hearted fellow. Mary worked as a 'mangler', daily forcing laundered clothes through a mangle to squeeze out the water: a tedious and physically demanding task.

Mary had taken none of her stepchildren with her to live in the poverty-stricken and crowded parish of Bethnal Green. By this time they were all – by the standards of the day – adults; the eldest, Ann – if still alive – was 25 and the youngest, Emma, about 16. But while the fates of Ann, John and Charlotte are unknown, it is clear that their younger sisters, Elizabeth Matilda and Emma, remained close to their stepmother. When Mary and Joseph married in 1849, Mary's stepdaughter Elizabeth Matilda Wade was a witness. By this time, Elizabeth Matilda was 26. Mary and Joseph gave their marital statuses as 'widow' and 'widower' respectively – ignoring the fact that, legally, Mary was still married to Frederick Whittenbury.

Frederick was still alive. He was living with another woman in Hackney – only a few miles from Mary's home – although he hadn't remarried. The couple was still together ten years later. Presumably Frederick had had nothing to do with his first wife or daughter since they'd parted. It's possible that Joseph Ball knew nothing about Mary's first husband. Quite likely that he never knew his wife was a bigamist. Possible, too, that Elizabeth knew nothing of her first father.

Joseph Ball had a daughter named Mary Ann, who was a few years older than his stepdaughter, Mary's daughter Elizabeth. By the time of Mary and Joseph's marriage in 1849, they had between them quite a brood of young women. They were not a wealthy family. In those tough and uncertain times, the question of their daughters' futures must have been a troubling one.

At 18, as she prepared to sail from Plymouth, Elizabeth Wade was a young woman on the brink of an exciting new life. Like her stepsisters, she was a domestic servant. Although she appears to have had some education – she could read and write – her prospects, if she had remained in England, were grim. The best she could have hoped for was either a lifetime of service or marriage to a working-class man: a labourer, perhaps. For the older girls, who at 25 and 27 were past their first flush of youth by Victorian standards, the chances of a good marriage in England were dwindling. Either way – married or in service – the future was bleak. Wages were low and jobs were hard to come by. Emigration to Australia, on the other hand, provided opportunities: a good marriage, land ownership, status and wealth. They had little to lose and much to gain.

Elizabeth had witnessed her mother's struggles first-hand. In her short life she had known three fathers and at least three different homes, and she had lost at least one sibling – but through all of the upheavals in her life, Elizabeth's mother Mary had been a constant presence. They must have been close. No wonder, then, that if one chose to emigrate, the other would follow. So it was that only months after their marriage, the blended Wade/Ball family launched into the process of applying to emigrate.

OPPORTUNITY BECKONS IN A NEW LAND

It was 1850: a time when that part of the far-distant British colony soon to be known as 'Queensland' was struggling to grow. Having begun its life as the New South Wales convict settlement of Moreton Bay in 1824, its development had foundered a decade later when transportation had ceased. The government had opened Moreton Bay to free settlers from 1842 but, as a huge and untamed part of the colony that was sparsely populated with Europeans, it lacked the economic clout that would generate real development. It needed shepherds, farm servants, agricultural labourers, rural tradesmen, miners and female domestic servants. Meantime, Britain suffered from overcrowding and a shortage of jobs. In short: Queensland sought more workers, while Britain needed to cast them out. Emigration was the perfect solution.

But Moreton Bay citizens were not interested in British undesirables. They didn't want the ex-convicts or the refuse from Britain's prisons and workhouses. Healthy, hardworking young people were what they needed: people who would contribute *and* reproduce. People who were strong in body and mind – who were courageous and able to withstand the rigours of life in the colonies. They were the middle-class farmers and merchants, the serving girls and labourers. Young women and families of good 'moral character' were favoured in the selection of immigrants to the colony that was anxious to shed its convict origin. Young single women were in particular demand in a land top-heavy with men.

The United Kingdom was in the grip of an emigration frenzy. Two decades earlier, emigration to the antipodes had been a daunting prospect. Australia was still regarded by its colonisers as a rough place, seething with felons and Aboriginal people, strange and threatening fauna and an unforgiving landscape. Rumours of lawlessness and godlessness deterred many 'decent' people from taking the risk. But as stories of colonists' prosperity began to trickle 'home', and as time and growth began to turn the new country into something that more closely resembled

Britain, reluctance to emigrate began to fade. There were clergy-men aplenty in the new land, potential emigrants were assured; education systems were developing, and the era of transportation of convicts was coming to an end. No longer was Australia seen as a frightening place, fit only for criminals and fearless pioneers. Australia, potential emigrants were assured, was just like England – only warmer and more prosperous.

In fact, in some circles, emigration was almost seen as a *duty*. To remove oneself to the colonies was to relieve England's unemployment problem, while at the same time developing a new market that would consume English goods and bolster its economy. Emigration would not only save the emigrant; it would save England. It was the *noble* thing to do. The poorer classes were encouraged to 'better' themselves by emigrating, and the wealthier classes to provide an example to their inferiors by showing a pioneering spirit.

The colonial governments were just as anxious to receive these immigrants as their home countries were to despatch them. So desperate were the colonial governments that they had operated a number of sponsorship schemes to entice immigrants since the 1830s.

In 1840, Britain's Colonial Office created the Colonial Land and Emigration Commission to provide free and assisted passages to Australia. Its role was to charter ships and select emigrants according to a strict set of criteria. The opening up of the northern reaches of New South Wales – the area later to be known as Queensland – was incentive for the government to encourage emigration with renewed vigour. The first government-assisted vessel to sail directly into Moreton Bay was the *Artemisia*, in December 1848. The vessel for which the Wade/Ball family was bound was about to become the second.

Candidates for an assisted passage had to show certification proving that they were 'sober, industrious, and of good moral character'. They had also to be 'in good health, free from all bodily and mental defects, and . . . in all respects capable of labour, and going out to work for wages'.[4]

Mary and Joseph had been living in the same lodgings for at least eight years before they married, though how their relationship had developed during that time is impossible to know. Perhaps it was the idea of emigration that had given them the incentive to marry. As a married couple, they improved their chances of being selected for government-assisted emigration. Single men were considered a risk; their tendency to run off to the goldfields was bad news for the workforce. Married men, on the other hand, were more likely to be tethered by family responsibilities to the kind of steady, productive work that would strengthen the colony. Their applications were viewed more favourably than those of their single counterparts. In their forties, Joseph and Mary could no longer be considered 'young', but they were capable of work. And what was more, with not one but *four* single daughters of marriageable age between them, they were just what the colony needed.

To promote emigration, the commission published an annual pamphlet that provided all the information a potential emigrant might need. Mary, Joseph and their daughters were poor but literate. Reading the pamphlet, they must have realised that as a family they were ideal candidates for government-assisted emigration. Widows and widowers with young children were ineligible, as were single mothers and unaccompanied children under 18. Single women who were pregnant were strictly barred. Joseph and Mary Ball were young and fit enough to work; they were no longer widowed, and their daughters were of an age to work and reproduce. As long as Mary's marital history remained undiscovered, the family stood every chance of securing a passage.

Through their local parish clergyman, they had applied to their emigration agent, one of a network of selecting agents assisting the commissioners throughout England. They had been required to show certificates of birth and marriage, and character references from members of society whose occupations identified them as 'respectable'. The emigration agent had studied these documents to determine their eligibility, and considering their ages, occupations, health and – most importantly – their moral characters, he had deemed the Balls and Wades to be suitable. Mary must have sighed with relief; her secret was safe. The first step had been completed.

Meanwhile Stephen Walcott, the secretary to the Colonial Land and Emigration Commission, had been considering applications from ship owners and brokers to convey emigrants to Moreton Bay. An application on behalf of ship owner John S. de Wolfe was given the commission's seal of approval.[5] The ship's name was *Emigrant*.

An advertisement for passage in the *Emigrant* had appeared in London's *Times* newspaper:

FOR MORETON BAY, New South Wales, calling at Plymouth to embark passengers, (under charter to Government, and will positively leave Deptford on 25th March) the remarkably fine and very fast sailing ship EMIGRANT, A1, 753 tons per register, coppered and copper-fastened, W.H.Kemp, Commander; lying in the West India Docks. Has a full poop, with superior accommodation, and presents a most desirable opportunity for passengers, having made her last passage to Sydney in 90 days. For freight or passage apply to Carter and Bonus, 11, Leadenhall Street.[6]

Now that the vessel had been settled upon, all selecting agents forwarded the applications from their local areas to the commissioner for processing. The Balls' and Wades' applications were duly submitted and approved.

The family had been waiting to hear when and from which port they would sail. There were two possibilities: London and Plymouth. It wasn't long before the Balls and Wades received their embarkation order. They would sail from Plymouth for Moreton Bay in April, on board the barque *Emigrant*. From this moment, it all happened quickly. Their old life had ended, and a new one begun.

Their agent had told them everything they needed to know: what clothing to pack and what to expect in Plymouth. Joseph had been ordered to pack six shirts, six pairs of stockings, two suits and two pairs of shoes. The women had each packed at least six shifts, two gowns, two flannel petticoats, six pairs of stockings and two pairs of shoes. The clothing had to be new and robust enough to last the voyage despite regular washing in saltwater. They packed enough sheets, towels and soap to last the voyage. The women had been advised to bring extra flannel, and the men two or three extra serge (twill) shirts. They packed carefully; their luggage space was limited but they would be facing extremes of temperature, from the sluggish heat of the tropics to the frigidity of the Southern Ocean.

Although their fare was subsidised, the passengers were asked to contribute a portion. For Joseph and Mary, who were over forty, the contribution was £6 each. This may have represented eight to twelve weeks' pay, for a labourer working near London could expect to earn 10 to 15 shillings per week. The four younger women, being of a demographic more sought after in the colonies, paid only £2 each. The expense was not insignificant, but the Wades and Balls could expect to recover their costs. In Australia, if Joseph found work as a farm labourer he might earn as much as £38 a year, and the women might make £21 or more as housemaids.

Once they had scraped together the funds for their supplies and their journey to Plymouth, they were able – to an extent – to relax. From the time of their arrival in Plymouth, the Colonial Land and Emigration Commission was in control. Their accommodation at the depot – where they would receive food, entertainment and advice – was supplied free of charge.

THE EMIGRATION DEPOT

The Balls and Wades were lucky. In 1850, a new era in emigration was beginning. The horrors of earlier times were still fresh: times when unscrupulous sea captains would ferry masses of desperate emigrants across the Atlantic to New York in crowded, unventilated 'coffin ships', and passengers would die in frightening numbers of starvation and disease. The Wade/Ball family was also lucky to have access to government accommodation at the depot. It had only been operating for less than eight years; prior to that, emigrants had to fend for themselves – as they still did in the northern port of Liverpool.

For those less fortunate emigrants, the days prior to departure were the beginning of a long nightmare. Lodging houses were crowded, dirty and disease-ridden, and the emigrants were at the mercy of their often dishonest landlords. These unregulated and morally questionable places were especially hazardous for young single women. Many emigrants came from rural homes and were both psychologically and physiologically unused to crowds; in the dirty lodging houses of Liverpool they were as vulnerable to disease as to exploitation. Not so in the south. The depot at Plymouth was clean, well ordered and safe.

The depot was a large building at Lambhay (on the Baltic Wharf) that had formerly served as a royal victualling yard for the Ordnance Board. It had been operating as an emigration depot since 1842. By the time the Wade/Ball family arrived at its door, the depot was well established and running smoothly under the superintendence of Mr William J. Seaward and his wife.

One of the great benefits for emigrants departing from Plymouth was that, unlike their counterparts in Liverpool who were scattered amongst seedy rooming-houses in alleys and back lanes, they were housed together under strictly monitored conditions. Any potential emigrants who were sick upon arrival at the depot were immediately placed in quarantine. Standards of hygiene were high. The depot boasted 'every facility for washing the Emigrants and for Purifying their Clothes'.[7] In the basement apartment there were troughs and plenty of fresh hot water; here, even before being shown to their sleeping quarters, the emigrants stripped off and scrubbed themselves with soap and water. There were no baths in situ, but should the state of an emigrant's cleanliness be too dire to rectify with a sponging down, portable baths were brought in.

Most likely, the ladies went first: Mary Ball, her daughter Elizabeth Wade, and Mary's three stepdaughters. After they had finished washing off the grime from their long journey from London, Mary's husband Joseph would have been obliged to go through the same process.

Mrs Seaward typically inspected the emigrants' clothing, including the items they had packed into boxes for the journey. She saw to it that all the clothing was washed in fresh water from the river and dried. She was on the lookout for fleas and lice; if any items were suspect she would arrange for them to be 'purified' in ovens specially set aside for the purpose.

These measures were weapons against the spread of disease. While the causes of most diseases were still unknown, it was understood that they flourished in conditions of poor hygiene. And in an age that could provide few cures, prevention was everything. Emigrants were commonly the poor: people who had been made weak and vulnerable to disease by inadequate nutrition and a limited understanding of hygiene. Diseases such as measles, whooping cough and scarlet fever were constant threats on a long voyage, where passengers were confined together in close quarters, and fresh air was limited. A passenger carrying typhus spelled disaster for everyone.

Considering the large numbers of people gathered at the depot at any given time, the potential for epidemic was frightening. But the Plymouth depot's record was good. In 1852 – two years after our story begins – it was reported that in the previous five years the depot had seen only 25 deaths. More than 36,000 emigrants had passed through the depot in that time. Emigrants had the high standards of sanitation to thank for the facility's excellent health record.

Once she'd been scrubbed clean and her clothing had been inspected, the 18-year-old Elizabeth Wade would have packed the items she'd need in the first weeks of the journey into a canvas bag supplied by the commission. To these supplies, she would have added a new mattress, bolster, blankets and counterpane, also provided by the commission. She would keep this bag in her berth on board the ship where she had ready access to it. The remaining supplies, she would have packed into a box to be stored in the hold and retrieved only when she needed to swap her worn clothing for fresh items.

Elizabeth was taken to the second storey of the depot with her stepsisters to the quarters set aside for unmarried women. These sleeping quarters led off from the superintendent's office and access to them was strictly forbidden to anyone but the single females. The dormitory was light and clean, and as comfortable as any place that the young woman might yet have known. It was lined with berths, stacked two high, like those in which she would sleep on board.

Her mother and stepfather slept in quarters reserved for married couples, just as they would on the ship. It was here in the dormitories that they would all learn to adapt to communal living.

The time for second thoughts was almost past; soon there would be no going back. It was a time of excitement and dread; joy and sadness; hope and fear.

THE IRISH – THE MAUNSELL FAMILY

It was April; the chill mantle of winter was beginning to lift and a light breeze nipped the salty air. Tufts of cloud blew in, frothing the sky like sea-foam. A tide of Irish drifted in to the depot; they were a sorry lot, wretched with poverty. The English working poor were struggling, but their Irish counterparts were desperate. For Catherine Maunsell and her brother Patrick, the chance to go to Australia wasn't just an opportunity; it was a godsend.

The long and dreadful years of the Famine were not yet behind them. Only four years earlier – in 1846 – potato blight had destroyed the crop upon which so many of the people depended. For the second year running, the crop that provided sustenance and a livelihood for some of the poorest people in the western world had failed. The Irish had been suffering privation and misery for decades, but for many, the potato blight was the final straw.

The system had been stacked against them for years. Much of Irish land was owned by the English aristocracy or Irish Protestants of English heritage: wealthy men whose ancestors had wrested the titles to their land from the Irish Catholics in centuries past. For the most part, they were absentee landlords who hired agents to manage their estates. Although these estates were vast, the 'middlemen' subdivided them into pitifully small holdings that they let out to tenant farmers.

These middlemen, who were usually Protestant, held the Catholic tenant farmers to ransom. They could evict their tenants as they pleased – and they often did – and they charged exorbitant rents that impoverished the farmers but lined the already plush pockets of the landlords back in England. Except in Ulster, any improvements that farmers made to the estate would become the property of the landlord when the lease expired. This removed any incentive to improve their living conditions, and tenant farmers lived in squalor.

The subdivisions were often less than ten acres: barely large enough to support a family, let alone provide an income. The plots were too small for livestock. The only crop that would sustain a family on land of such inadequate size was the potato, for it grew in poor soil and was rich with nutrients.

The tenant farmers, impoverished as they were, were not at the bottom of the socio-economic scale. Even more desperate were the cottiers – the landless labourers – whom some farmers allowed to live on their land and provide labour in lieu of rent. Cottiers built small cabins on the land and grew their own potatoes to feed their families. Both tenant farmers and the cottiers depended upon the potato.

In 1845, disaster struck. The leaves of the potato plants withered, and dismayed farmers dug up their potatoes only to find that they had blackened and rotted in the ground. Almost half of that year's crop was inedible due to this strange disease. This 'potato blight' only added to the hardship that the farmers already suffered. Prices rose as the disease spread throughout Ireland.

The blight had never been seen before in Ireland and, hoping that it was a one-off problem, the farmers planted more potatoes the following spring. But the next harvest was worse: the blight destroyed almost the entire crop.

Over the following years, starvation and disease devastated the country. A slight improvement in 1847 was followed by further crop failure in the next two consecutive years. Then in 1849 cholera struck down a population already weakened by malnutrition. They were dark and dreadful times during which around a million people perished. For many of the survivors, emigration was the only chance to rise above poverty and despair. Between 1845 and 1855, close to two million people would flee the misery of Ireland for more hopeful shores.

Of these refugees from the Great Famine, Catherine Maunsell was one. Like some 209,000 others, she left her home and family in Ireland during the year of 1850 in the hope of a better future abroad.

Catherine's father, James Maunsell, was a farmer on the estate of the Earl of Clare in the county of Limerick. Their home was in the townland of Richhill, near the town of Castleconnell. On the eastern bank of the Shannon River, the town was known for the healing waters of its spa. Most of the fertile land was used for agriculture and most of the inhabitants were farmers or turf-cutters.

The Maunsells were in a slightly better position than some of their compatriots. Their landlord was John Fitzgibbon, the second Earl of Clare, whose home was the grand and stylish Mountshannon House: one of the finest in the south of Ireland.

Fitzgibbon had inherited the house from his father, the first earl: a man whose name was reviled in much of Ireland.

The first earl, also John Fitzgibbon, was a lawyer who had had a controversial political career. He was of Irish Catholic heritage, although *his* father before him had converted to Protestantism in order to study law – a career out of reach for Catholics. John Fitzgibbon the elder was well educated, rich and imperious. In the early days of his political career, he spoke out in favour of Irish liberty and legislative independence from English government. He succeeded: legislative freedom was granted in 1782 and Fitzgibbon became attorney-general the following year. This 'freedom' was an illusion, however; the King's nominated representative in Ireland turned out to be more or less a British puppet. True parliamentary reform that would benefit the Irish people had not been achieved.

Fitzgibbon's ideals soon gave way to personal ambition. His allegiance appeared to switch to England; he opposed reform and turned his back on his early supporters. Hated by the Irish, he was rewarded for his loyalty to Britain by promotions through the ranks: from High Sheriff of County Limerick to Lord Chancellor and Earl of Clare.

Fitzgibbon, the first earl, was known for his anti-Catholic stance. He opposed Catholic emancipation in Parliament and reforms to the tithe system that would have brought relief to millions of Catholics.

This man was the owner of Mountshannon, the estate on which the Catholic James Maunsell grew up. James was employed by Fitzgibbon from a young age and remained in service to the family for most of his life. When Fitzgibbon died in 1802, the second earl – also John Fitzgibbon – succeeded him, becoming the Maunsells' landlord for the rest of James' working life.

Although the younger Fitzgibbon inherited his father's title and property, he appears to have acquired neither his incendiary political position nor his anti-Catholic views. Indeed, he was said to have built a school for the children of his estate workers, where boys learned to read and write, and girls were taught needlework. There were parochial schools and an infants' school in the district; there was even a school for girls at Mountshannon. James Maunsell was literate and so were his children – even the girls. They may have attended one of the schools supported by the Fitzgibbons.

James Maunsell saw himself as a 'faithful servant' to his landlord.[8] But while the second earl may have been a more congenial landlord than his father, he enjoyed great wealth only through the exploitation of men like Maunsell. It must have been galling to live in a tiny, damp and squalid cabin, plagued by lice and fleas and subsisting on potatoes, while watching the extravagant comings and goings of the master. Most of Limerick's farmers lived in mud, thatched-roof cottages, the best of which were equipped with chimneys and consisted of two or three small rooms of six by eight feet each. These dark and 'indescribably wretched' cabins had no windows; the only light came from the door. The occupants slept on bog-rushes or straw.[9]

Mountshannon House, on the other hand, was an impressive building with a grand gabled portico held up by four fine Ionic columns. It was said that the entrance hall was so wide that one could drive a coach through it; and that the house boasted 365 windows: one for each day of the year. The mansion was full of bronzes and paintings that the earl had brought back from his travels, and its 900 acres of land were beautifully landscaped.

But while the earl got rich on the rents from his 10,316 acres of estates in Limerick and 3,178 in Tipperary, James Maunsell scraped out a living for himself, his wife and a multitude of children on just a little over two acres. Modest as it was, James' plot was larger than most of his neighbours'. He was better off than some; he could read and write, and he was in a secure enough financial position to lend money to a neighbour. But life was a struggle nevertheless.

In 1850 James' eldest son, Stephen, was around 24 years of age. Next in line was Patrick, a 23-year-old gardener, and then Catherine, a domestic servant of 22. Their younger siblings were James (aged 19), Ellen (17), Honora (16), John (11 or 12), Bridget (eight or nine) and Margaret (five or six). These were the children of James and his second wife, also named Catherine. James also had three more grown children by his first wife.

Feeding, housing and clothing this brood on two acres of land was a formidable task. While his eldest children may have had work, their prospects were grim. And if the potatoes continued to fail, what then? What would become of the younger ones?

Emigration was the only answer. The Maunsells had heard of the opportunities available in Australia. The older children Patrick and Catherine would go first and test the water. They would find work, marry well and prosper, and in time they would earn the funds to sponsor the emigration of their siblings and parents. Patrick was young, strong and ambitious; he was a capable man and a hard worker. He would protect his sister against the perils facing young women alone on the high seas.

So it was that Catherine Maunsell and her brother Patrick bade farewell to the only home they had ever known: their village on the banks of the beautiful Shannon, with its abundant trout and salmon and its glorious waterfalls. Farewell to the crowded and vermin-infested cottage that lay under the shadow of the imposing Mountshannon House, and farewell to their mother and father and ten siblings and to a wretched cycle of poverty and oppression.

To get to Plymouth the two siblings had first to travel overland to one of Ireland's port towns: Cork or Dublin. Cork, 60 miles away, was the closer, and probably the departure point that they chose. From there they would have caught a steam packet to Plymouth.

Until now such a journey would have been beyond their wildest dreams; the cost was prohibitive. But the plight of the Irish had become so desperate that the British Government had realised they had to act. The Land and Emigration Commission agreed to pay the passage from Cork or Dublin to Plymouth for those Irish emigrants who met the selection criteria of the colonial governments. From Plymouth, they might take advantage of the assisted emigration scheme like their English fellows. This was a stroke of luck for Catherine and Patrick.

The passage was free but it was harrowing. The Irish Sea was notoriously rough and the passengers had little shelter; for 48 hours they endured an icy, windy drenching on the crowded deck of the steamer. Weak with malnutrition even before they even boarded, Irish emigrants typically arrived in Plymouth 'in a state that no language can describe'.[10] And that was before the real journey had even begun.

AT THE EMIGRATION DEPOT: PREPARATION FOR DEPARTURE

The day of departure drew nearer and the uncertain sky cleared and clouded, cleared and clouded again. Rain fell in sporadic gusts. In the few days leading up to their embarkation, more emigrants trickled in. In the depot, their emotions ranged as widely as their accents. There was sorrow; most of the emigrants had already farewelled their loved ones and many had little hope of ever seeing them again. And there was fear: fear of the unknown land for which they were bound, and dread of the voyage, for the risks on such a journey were very real. But for the most part, calm hopefulness prevailed.

For many, the decision to emigrate had been made on the recommendation of friends or family already in Australia. These friends had sent back stories of their improved situation in life: stories of abundant work and good wages. Patrick Maunsell may have recounted the stories he'd heard to the other young men, buoying them all with promises of good fortune. The children chattered, excited by the sense that a grand adventure lay ahead. During the periods of respite from the rain, they played on the green yard beneath the cannon of The Citadel.

Catherine Maunsell and the Wade girls would have kept busy with needlework and washing and tending to the children. Like the men, their hopes were high; their voices broke out now and then into joyful song. Although strictly separated at night, the single men and women were allowed to mingle by day. As one wit pronounced: 'no kissing was allowed on any pretence whatever. If a young man wanted to kiss a young woman for her mother, he would have to get a special order from the Emigration Commissioners in London. A moderate amount of hand squeezing was permitted, but if the young woman cried "oh!" the young man must drop it at once. A married man was permitted to flirt with his wife as much as he liked between the hours of 10am and 4pm, but no man was allowed to kiss another man's wife; and that was the reason so many poor wives never got kissed at all.'[11]

While Elizabeth Wade and her sisters may have dreamed of matrimony, they would have expected the odds of meeting a potential husband on board to be slim. From start to finish, propriety on the voyage was just as important as physical cleanliness; a lady's virtue was considered as much in need of protection as her health. And the long voyage to Australia – which could last up to four months – left young women open to the perils of idleness. To safeguard her purity, no effort was spared.

It was the role of the newly created British Ladies Female Emigration Society (BLFES) to look after the interests of young women venturing to the colonies. Their first annual meeting was held on 16 April 1850, as *The Emigrant* lay awaiting departure in Plymouth Sound. The society's stated aim was:

> ... to improve the social and moral condition of those who have determined to emigrate, by providing suitable persons to act as matrons during the voyage, by providing employment for the women, by visiting the ships at the several ports, and by establishing committees at the Australian ports to visit the emigrants on their arrival.[12]

The BLFES had evolved from the Emigrant Employment Society (EES), which had been formed in the previous year for the same purpose. The ladies of the society were industrious. These benevolent souls visited countless emigrant ships on the brink of departure, issuing advice, reading material and supplies to keep the young ladies busy with worthy pursuits. They championed the cause of 'those unprotected females, who are launched on the waves of a troubled world, and exposed to more fearful perils than any they may have to encounter on the stormy deep they are about to cross'. Understanding that the benefits of emigration outweighed the potential evils that young women might face on the voyage, the EES sought to advise them on how to make their leisure time on the journey 'profitable', to 'elevate the character of those who are leaving their native country' and to provide an 'agency for the moral improvement of Emigrants'.[13]

The ladies of the EES (and later the BLFES) distributed publications like *The Emigrants' Penny Magazine* to the passengers. This was a monthly periodical full of advice and encouragement for those taking the great gamble of emigration. It included reports from those who had already made the journey, as well as prayers and hymns for emigrants, advice on recreation, health and provisions, and information on what to expect in their new homes: the type of employment they might find, the wages and costs of living and opportunities that awaited them.

The ladies also provided, when needed, help of a more tangible nature. Emigrants had to bring their own supplies for the journey: changes of clothing, soap, sheets and towels to last three months or more. Upon their arrival at the depot, their luggage was inspected and if the necessary items were lacking, they were ordered to buy them. Some of the poorer passengers – people like Catherine and Patrick Maunsell, perhaps – did not have the means. In such cases, the EES would furnish the passengers with these items; without the charity of these generous ladies, these desperate people would not have been allowed to board.

The spiritual welfare of the emigrants was always of utmost concern. Like most of the English passengers, the Ball/Wade family were members of the Church of England. Many an anxious emigrant derived strength from the visits of Rev. Mr T. C. Childs to the depot; the hardworking clergyman took great interest in the welfare of emigrants.

Religious societies exhorted the emigrants to thank God for the opportunities that awaited them. They were not to reflect with bitterness on the circumstances that had driven them from their stricken lands, but to remember with gratitude the generosity of God and government, who had made departure to the colonies possible. They should not think only of 'bettering their earthly lot', but give themselves up to God's service, for He had given each of them a commission 'to do something for Him in Australia'. Emigrant tracts advised parents to read their Bibles regularly and to encourage others to do the same; to thank God before every meal; to be patient, considerate and forbearing; to 'cherish purity of heart and action' and to join together every evening for worship. They urged family men to guard young women against impropriety, and *never* to allow themselves to 'breathe an indecent joke, or utter an improper word'. Emigrants were warned that if they ignored the Christian life and thought only of 'temporal prosperity', God's blessing would escape them, and their children would spread vice around the country.[14]

At the depot, Elizabeth Wade and her family were introduced to the strict routines that would regulate their lives for the next few months. Breakfast was at eight, dinner at one, and the evening meal at six. Food was plentiful and good: beef or mutton, bread, potatoes or other vegetables, tea, sugar, butter and salt. Many of the poor Irish ate better at the depot than they ever had before. Catherine and Patrick Maunsell must have marvelled at the feasts served up to them. Even their different habits and tastes were accommodated; the Irish had the choice of oatmeal and molasses instead of tea, sugar and butter if they preferred it. The hearty food boosted their health and their spirits; it was a foretaste of the bountiful life ahead.

Mealtimes ran to order. The emigrants were allocated to 'messes', six to nine adults in each. Each mess was given two large oval tin dishes – one for meat, and the other for potatoes – a round tin butter dish, two teapots, a sugar canister and a bread basket. Elizabeth, like every other emigrant, collected one plate, a knife, fork and teaspoon, and a drinking mug. These were hers to keep for the journey. If she lost an item, she would somehow have to manage without.

Here at the depot, Elizabeth and the others in her mess learned how to manage at sea: how to cook, how to set up their berths, how to organise their cleaning routines as a group. They learned skills to keep themselves occupied during the long days ahead – skills useful to pioneers in the colonies like rope making, bag making and basket weaving.

They also learned about hygiene. The emigrants who came from far-flung regions – the poor Irish and the Scottish Highlanders – were less robust than their English counterparts, and more prone to disease. They understood little about personal hygiene. The ladies of the EES taught them how to wash and how to keep their living quarters clean and tidy. How to use cutlery and what to eat. How to use a water closet.

On many emigrant ships, the Irish were scorned by their English counterparts. Most likely, Elizabeth Wade and Catherine Maunsell were wary of each other at first. The English generally regarded the Irish as dirty and ill-mannered. Prejudices caused friction between the Catholics and the Protestants. Whether the passengers awaiting embarkation on the *Emigrant* would show such prejudices remained to be seen; at the outset, they seemed a harmonious group. Many of the married couples were 'pious and intelligent', the young men 'orderly' and the single women 'modest and industrious'.[15] Their futures promised to be bright.

The hour of departure drew near. Elizabeth Wade had made it so far over a range of hurdles: the selection process, the scraping together of funds, the acquisition of supplies, the journey to Plymouth. There was one more obstacle to overcome. This was, perhaps, the most crucial: the final inspection. Even at this late stage, she might be refused a passage.

Joseph, Mary and the girls lined up for their interviews with an official from the Emigration Commission. A list had been prepared of all the lucky souls who had been selected for assisted emigration, and it was time for the official to check their particulars against this list. Nervously they provided their records of birth and marriage and the references from their local clergy. In the case of married couples and families with young children, only the 'head' of the family was recorded on the list. The official took down Joseph's name and recorded his occupation as 'Milkman'. He noted that Joseph was accompanied by a wife and grown daughter Mary Ann, and recorded his age, his marital status and the county from which he had been selected. He registered the Wade girls – Elizabeth, Elizabeth Matilda and Emma – separately as single women.

One by one, the hopeful emigrants lined up for inspection. They were middle-aged married couples like Mary and Joseph; scores of young single women and unmarried men, like Catherine and Patrick; and of course families with children in tow. While the selecting agents favoured families, the rules were strict about the number of very young children. The New South Wales Government wanted its new workforce to arrive alive. Infants, with their tendency to attract and spread disease, were a liability. Children carried not only a much greater risk of death themselves but threatened the health of the other passengers. Families with more than three children under the age of ten, or two under seven, were rejected.

Then the travellers' luggage was checked to ensure they had the requisite items for the journey, and that they were *not* carrying any prohibited items like liquor or firearms.

Before they could embark, Elizabeth and her family had to present themselves for a medical check. This was their first encounter with a man who would figure largely in their lives over the coming months: the ship's surgeon-superintendent. His name was Dr George Mitchell. He was a young man, Irish-born and educated at Edinburgh. He was only 25 years of age, and the weight of responsibility upon his shoulders was colossal. It was up to him to ensure that the passengers survived seasickness, exposure to extreme heat and cold, confinement in crowded quarters, and limited access to fresh food and exercise for three to four months, and that they arrived in good health and fit for work. If they were unfit on arrival, the surgeon was at risk of dismissal. And his responsibility began right here in the depot. He would take the emigrants' medical histories, examine them, and vaccinate them against smallpox if necessary. If he observed symptoms of infection in anyone, he would leave them behind. Dr Mitchell's word on this matter was final.

Despite his youth, George Mitchell was up to the task. He was qualified, experienced and robust, kind and conscientious. He examined Elizabeth Wade and her mother, her stepfather and sisters, and found them all in good health. Likewise, he examined Catherine and Patrick Maunsell and more than two hundred others.

Then it was done; they were ready to embark.

Chapter 2

The 'remarkably fine
and very fast sailing ship'

April 1850

PLYMOUTH SOUND

The morning of 14 April began calmly, with a breath of west-south-westerly breeze and scattered puffs of white drifting across the horizon.

Elizabeth Wade and her family gathered with the other travellers in the basement of the depot, where doors opened out onto the quay. The granite waters of Plymouth Sound, dotted with sails of vessels large and small, lay before them. Some two miles out from the quay, the *Emigrant* was waiting.

The time for misgivings was past. The wharf bustled with activity; travellers crowded upon it, busy and buoyant, gazing hopefully out to sea. Rowing boats and dinghies with sails fluttering scuttled back and forth between the dock and the larger vessels out in the sound. Local seamen plied their trade, eager to pick up a few coins by ferrying anxious passengers to their waiting ships. Clasping their canvas bags, the *Emigrant*'s passengers filed onto the lighters and sailboats that nudged the quay. When they had settled themselves amongst the bags and boxes, the sailors grasped the oars or eased the sails, and the vessels groaned away from the wharf. Across the sound, with its deep still waters, its labyrinth of bays and inlets and its skyline spiked with the masts of scores of boats, the crews guided the vessels. Past the fortressed hump of Drake's Island they glided, and the steep shoreline of Plymouth receded behind them.

The wind gathered momentum. As the hour of embarkation loomed, the sky marbled over with cloud, and showery winds beset the harbour. Ahead, the waters of Plymouth Sound lapped against the timber hull of the *Emigrant*. She was a grand sight: a three-masted barque, her sails furled and waiting for release, her flags snapping sharply in the briny air. At 753 tons, she was larger than the average 19th-century emigrant ship. The ship was only five years old, and modern and well furnished.

Humans were not the *Emigrant*'s only cargo. She also carried mail to the people of the colonies who waited eagerly for news from 'home', and an assortment of exports for the businesses of Moreton Bay. Sundry supplies were needed for a settlement not yet strong enough to support itself from local production: food, clothing, drapery and machinery. The *Emigrant* carried countless cases and trunks of goods, including an engine and supplies of 'Marzetti's superior ale, porter and cider'.[16]

Periodically, little boats drew alongside the barque to deliver passengers and cargo. The crew sprang into action: with rope tackles, they hoisted and swung boxes of goods across to the waiting ship. The passengers milled about with quickening pulses, thrilled by the busyness and noise and activity. To the eyes of the emigrants, all was confusion: sailors darted here and there, shouting instructions and heaving bags and crates and trunks on board.

The emigrants clambered aboard, perhaps climbing a rope ladder or perhaps scrambling up a rudimentary wooden gangway that the crew had lowered for them. At last they were on the swaying deck amid a forest of ropes, boxes and packages, the deck unsteady beneath their feet, and the timbers creaking. Drizzling rain mingled sharply with sea spray. Sailors scurried to and fro, ferrying their cargo into the hold below.

Overseeing the business was the ship's captain: William Henry Kemp. The emigrants' lives would be lived according to his command for the months to come. Their health and wellbeing depended upon his competence and wisdom. Though they could not have known it, the emigrants would soon have cause to be grateful for Captain Kemp's kindness.

CAPTAIN KEMP

Captain Kemp was an experienced master mariner. Born in the port town of Chatham, Kent, which had a long history as a naval base and a centre for ship building, it is no wonder that the young Kemp took up the seafaring life. In this seaside town, in which all commerce related to shipping thrived and the dockyards bustled with life, William Henry Kemp learned to love the sea.

In his early twenties, Kemp was already at the helm of ocean-going ships. He left Kent for the north of England, where he furthered his career in the port towns of Hull and Liverpool. William married Frances Sarah Denny in Kingston upon Hull, Yorkshire, in June 1833. They were childless for 12 years, during which time Kemp commanded a good many merchant ships.

By 1845, the Kemps were settled in Liverpool where, at last, Sarah gave birth to a living child: a daughter they named Fanny Hannah. She was baptised in St James' Church and named after her mother (Frances Sarah) and William's mother (Hannah).

Thus Kemp began balancing his seafaring life with fatherhood. It was a life heavy with responsibility. During a time of mass emigration, his was an occupation in great demand. The horror years of emigration were not long past. During the late 18th and early 19th century, poverty, Highland clearances and unemployment drove the poor of Scotland, Ireland and England in hordes from their homes to foreign shores. In those days before the 1803 Passenger Vessels Act provided some protection – and the subsequent years, until the Act was enforced – unscrupulous ship owners and captains took advantage of their passengers' desperation and packed them into squalid, unseaworthy vessels. On those overcrowded voyages, where passengers were underfed and hygiene was disregarded, disease thrived. To board an emigrant ship was to gamble with one's life.

The ships that Kemp commanded were *not* of this ilk. By the time his career was at its peak, Acts of Parliament regulated conditions for emigrant ships. Captain William Henry Kemp complied willingly and conscientiously. He was proud of his record. He sailed two years in a row to Quebec – 1846 and 1847 – carrying 500 passengers during the worst days of a typhus epidemic that had devastated so many vessels crossing the Atlantic, and landed them safely.

In 1845 regulations had been introduced under which mariners could sit a voluntary exam to qualify them to take charge of ocean-going merchant vessels. In 1849, Kemp – who was already an experienced captain – sat the exam, passed it, and was awarded a first-class certificate at Liverpool, thereby gaining formal qualifications under the voluntary scheme to command a ship.

By 1850, the Kemps were based in Liverpool, the busy port of the north – the departure point for many long-distance voyages.

From there the captain sailed to Bombay; to St Helena; to South Africa; to New South Wales; and several times across the Atlantic to Quebec. He was in command of more than a dozen vessels. A competent commander and a good man, Kemp's services were sought after. He was able to provide well for his wife; they lived comfortably and enjoyed the attentions of at least one servant.

By the time he took charge of the *Emigrant,* the captain was 39 or 40 years old and had been in command of vessels for some 18 years. Sarah Kemp often accompanied him on his long sea voyages.

This 1850 voyage to Moreton Bay would be Kemp's third trip to Australia. His first had been in January 1842, when he sailed *Marchioness of Bute* into Sydney. The second was only a year before the start of this narrative: 1849. On that occasion, he had sailed into Port Jackson on 8 June in command of the *Emigrant* and in the company of his wife and young daughter, Fanny.

When Kemp set off this time for Moreton Bay, once again his beloved wife and five-year-old daughter were with him. This was not unusual. Given that a captain of an emigrant ship was responsible for protecting the reputations of the young single women amongst his charges, he was expected to be of unblemished character himself. A family man was preferred over a reckless youth. The presence of his wife and child on the voyage would reassure the authorities and the emigrants of the captain's solid, moral character.

A maidservant accompanied the Kemps.[17] The party would not have to share the dormitory-style steerage accommodation with the passengers, though they would be free to mingle with them on deck; the Kemps and their maid would enjoy the comfort of cabins, as would the ship's surgeon. The accommodation was – in contrast to the steerage quarters – private, airy, and equipped with comfortable beds. There were no other cabin passengers; the commissioner's ships provided strictly for steerage class only.

Captain Kemp was qualified and experienced, and as much at home on the sea as anywhere. The *Emigrant* was familiar to him and to his wife and child. He took charge of the barque once again, no doubt, with calm self-assurance, for Captain Kemp had confidence in his own abilities. During his many years in charge of ships, he avowed, he had been 'much of the time employed in conveying passengers, having crossed the seas ten different voyages, with ships full and crowded, two of which have been to Sydney . . . during the whole of which I never lost more than one adult on any passage, and two or three children.'[18] He had no reason to expect that this voyage would be any different.

EMBARKING

The spirited crowd gathered upon the deck. This ship was to be their home for the next three months; with great eagerness they must have surveyed their surroundings. There was nothing to cause alarm. The vessel was capacious and modern, her speed and manoeuvrability enhanced by her size. She had made the last passage to New South Wales in only 90 days.

The *Emigrant* was licensed to carry 235 passengers. On this voyage, some 276 embarked, though, inexplicably, no one questioned the extra few dozen. About 60 of the passengers who later arrived in Moreton Bay were not registered on the embarkation list created at Plymouth. It is likely that these extras were either paying or working for their passage.[19]

The scene may have seemed chaotic to the passengers, but there was method behind the madness. Every aspect of the voyage was regulated by law, down to the minutest detail. As the passengers gazed and wondered, the captain strode hither and thither, issuing orders, the surgeon conferred with commission officials regarding the parting muster of emigrants, and the sailors loaded the strictly regulated provisions.

Gone were the days when passengers had to provide for the journey themselves: days when, having been cheated by lodging-house landlords or forced by repeated delays in departure to dip into their supplies at the port of embarkation, emigrants would board woefully ill-equipped and starve to death during the voyage. These days the commission insisted that ship owners make adequate provision for the journey. Enough food, water and medical supplies had to be stocked to last twenty-two weeks in case – Heaven forbid – the voyage should take that long.

Crates of food were loaded onto the barque: 'ship's biscuit', salted pork, flour, sugar, oatmeal, potatoes and dried peas, preserved meat, tea and rice. Filtered water was brought aboard in great oak casks whose interiors had been charred to keep the water fresh and sweet and prevent putrefaction.

The surgeon was well supplied with all the medicines and trappings of 19th-century practice. His drug stores included opium, arsenic, lead, mercury, quinine and digitalis. He was well stocked with ointments, purgatives, 'prepared chalk' for diarrhoea and magnesia carbonate for upset stomachs. There was a generous supply of mineral lime and 'Collins Patent Powder' for disinfecting, and marine soap – soluble in salt water – for bathing and laundering.

The ship was required to carry two bedpans, 12 yards of flannel and 24 of calico, a set of splints, silk for sutures, an enema apparatus and a pair of scissors. Dr Mitchell had at his disposal instruments for extracting teeth, an amputating knife and saw and, most importantly, midwifery forceps. There were bandages, a 'bleeding porringer' and 50 leeches for bloodletting.

Foodstuffs and drink were stocked for medicinal purposes. Lemon juice would prevent scurvy during the months without fresh fruit and vegetables. Oatmeal, arrowroot, sago and tapioca were available for stomach upsets and diarrhoea, scarlet fever, sore throats and colic. Vinegar was used to treat just about anything. It was considered an antidote to poison; a whiff of it was thought to revive a patient from a faint, a dose to relieve gout; it could be mixed with a range of other substances to make ointments or potions for the treatment of haemorrhaging, coughs, fever, asthma, burns, nosebleeds, inflamed eyes – any number of disorders. It was used as a cooling agent with which to wash patients in the throes of a fever. The surgeon had access to preserved milk for young children, sugar, tins of preserved boiled beef and mutton, all of which were believed to have medicinal properties. Port wine, brandy and sherry were at hand, as was a supply of stout for nursing mothers.

Thus well provided for, the passengers milled about upon deck under darkening skies. They were joined by the ladies of the Emigrant Employment Society,[20] accompanied by Mr Allen of the Anglican Evangelical Church Pastoral Aid Society. The visitors mingled with the emigrants on deck, providing encouraging words, parting advice and prayers. They listened to the stories of the passengers, who were keen to share their histories and hopes. One young woman bubbled with enthusiasm. She kept within easy access a 'high testimonial to her good conduct' written by her former employer, the 'celebrated missionary' Rev. Joseph Wolff.[21] When the ladies engaged her in conversation, she proudly unfolded the reference to show them. They were impressed and told her so.

The ladies were, on the whole, tremendously satisfied with the calibre of the emigrants. 'It is such sons and daughters alone,' they wrote, 'who will do credit to the mother country, and prove of benefit to her colonies.'[22] The ladies gave the female passengers books and needlework, wool and knitting patterns. At the same time Mr Allen moved amongst the men, advising and cautioning as he saw fit. Prayer books and Holy Scriptures were given freely to the passengers, as were tracts and other books supplied by religious organisations. There was no shortage of instruction on how the emigrants might maintain their honour and reputations through the long journey ahead.

SETTLING IN

It was blustery and damp on deck; Elizabeth Wade and her peers would have wasted no time in going below to escape the weather. It was time to make themselves familiar with their accommodation.

The emigrants descended a ladder into the steerage quarters. They were clutching the canvas bags, supplied by the commissioners, that contained the clothing, linen and utensils they would need for the first few weeks. Because of the limited space in their quarters, the rest of their belongings had been packed into boxes and stored in the hold.

By the dim light of lamps, fired by sperm-whale oil and secured at regular intervals to the uprights between decks, they could just make out the layout of their accommodation.

A long table spanned the ship, from bow to stern. At each side of this table were fixed bench seats upon which the passengers would sit for their meals. Lining the hull on each side of the table were two tiers of shelving which would be their sleeping berths.

The living quarters were strictly segregated. Elizabeth and her sisters made their way to the single women's section at the stern. There they scanned the apartment for their names written on cards and nailed to the front of the berths to find the 18 inches of space that had been allocated to each of them. The berths were fitted with foot and head boards, a narrow bench at the end upon which the passengers could lodge their bags, and a railing for their water pots and utensils. Each berth was separated from its neighbour by a small partition or curtain, and furnished with a mattress of straw. The bottom layer of berths sat six inches or more from the floor and was fitted with boards that could be removed for cleaning. Above it, with only 30 inches or so between them, was the upper tier. The person on the lower bunk would need to learn quickly not to sit up in the night. 'There is just sufficient room for one to lay down all his length,' wrote one voyager, 'you must not try to pull up your knees or they will come into contact with the boards.'[23]

This was where all girls of 15 years or older, single women and wives travelling alone would sleep. Irish and Englishwomen, Catholics and Protestants – all confined together. The only official distinctions to be made between classes here were based on gender and marital status. But within their sections, emigrants were allocated berths, if possible, next to friends or family or others of a similar 'class' to themselves.

It was usual for the Irish and the English travellers to keep themselves apart. The English typically held the Irish in contempt, while the Irish regarded the English with resentment and suspicion. The English were inclined to view the Irish as ignorant and dirty, their habits uncouth and their children unruly. It was true that the poor Irish were often disadvantaged, being malnourished and unaccustomed to the diet and hygiene routines of shipboard life. They might also expect to face prejudice upon their arrival in Australia. But the Emigration Commission ruled that all passengers be treated equally, regardless of their origin. It was up to the ship's surgeon to ensure that his Irish charges did not suffer from discrimination at the hands of other emigrants or crew. Fortunately for them, Dr George Mitchell was an Irishman.

More than 50 unmarried women – from a range of backgrounds, but all representatives of the labouring poor – settled into their sleeping quarters. The Wade and Ball girls were amongst them, as was Irishwoman Catherine Maunsell. Catherine's brother, Patrick, found his lodgings in the bow of the ship, well away from the single women. His bunk was 21 inches wide: a fraction bigger than the allowance made for the women.

Joseph and Mary Ball lodged separately from their daughters in the married quarters, the location of which served as a buffer between the single males and single females. Timber bulkheads, louvred to permit air flow in conditions where every breath of ventilation was precious, separated the sections. Like other married couples, Joseph and Mary had 37 inches of shared space. They bunked in with other couples and families with children of 14 or younger. Infants slept in their parents' berths. The arrangement was not only uncomfortable but downright dangerous; it was not unknown for babies to be suffocated in their parents' bed at night.

Children were perhaps the greatest danger on board – to themselves and to others. Young children were prone to diseases like bronchitis, whooping cough, measles, diarrhoea and scarlet fever. They could even die from malnutrition if their seasickness was severe enough. Diarrhoea, wasting diseases and respiratory illnesses were the most frequent causes of deaths at sea; more than three quarters of deaths were amongst children under the age of six and almost half under one.

What was worse: once children contracted diseases, they

spread them. The younger the child, the greater the risk. This was the reason that the Colonial Land and Emigration Commission restricted the number of children per family under the assisted emigration system. From a health perspective, the number of children per family and the age of those children mattered more than the overall numbers and the size of the ship.

Nevertheless, the *Emigrant's* family quarters filled rapidly. Couples and families with young children streamed into their new lodgings, filling the dormitories with commotion and chatter. More than half of the passengers came as members of families: there were 74 children aged under 15, accompanied by their parents. Of these children, only 12 were infants of under two years of age: a small number that must have reassured the doctor. Boys and girls aged 15 or older who had embarked with their parents were regarded as adults and lodged in the quarters for single men or women.[24] For these families, the risks of the voyage were great but the hope of a better life for their children drove them on – though some would come to rue the decision.

THE BRIMBLE FAMILIES

The Brimble families were amongst those clamouring down through the hatchway, bearing their canvas bags and clutching the hands of their small children. The Brimbles comprised two families from Kingston Deverill in England's County Wiltshire. They came from a small village in a prosperous valley where farmers made a good living from crops, cattle, sheep and dairying.

But the Brimbles were not farmers, and their struggle was the struggle of so many of England's working classes. John Brimble was one of seven children, all boys. He was born into a labouring clan: a sprawling extended family that made up a large percentage of the village's population. John was a labourer-turned-gardener; he was a poor man with a wife and three children to support. One of his daughters, Elizabeth Emma, had died in infancy in 1841. His eldest son, Thomas, lay in the graveyard of St Mary's at Kingston. Thomas had died only the previous year at the age of 13; perhaps it was the tragedy of his death that had turned his parents' thoughts to starting life again in a new land. The healthy climate and promise of prosperity in Australia were tempting. At 42, John would soon be too old to secure an assisted passage to Australia. There was no time to waste.

Thus it was that John Brimble, his wife Elizabeth and their three remaining children – Lucy Jane, Alfred and Samuel – found themselves on board the *Emigrant*, bound for Moreton Bay. Lucy was 12 years old and her brothers Alfred and Samuel were seven and five.

John already had a connection with Australia, although it was a link he preferred to keep under his hat. One of the most important criteria for acceptance under the assisted emigration scheme was the applicant's good character. And while John had no blemish against his own name, he might have feared contamination by his connection with another. John's brother William had been in New South Wales for many years, having being transported as a convict in his youth.

William was three years older than his brother, and the disgrace of the family. At the age of 13 he had stolen a knife, bread and cheese from the home of his cousin (another John Brimble). This cousin, John, was outraged. He was newly married and his wife was pregnant; they were not a wealthy family and the loss was no trivial matter for them. John took the boy to court where, at the Wiltshire Quarter Session, he was found guilty and sentenced to a sound whipping.

Undeterred, William tried his hand at theft again 12 months later. On 24 May 1818, he broke into the home of a Mr William Dyer using 'force and arms'; he stole a purse of money from Dyer, a bag belonging to another and a purse, a tea caddy and £3 (about six weeks' pay for an agricultural labourer). The 14-year-old 'sheep boy' once again faced a judge and jury. They found him guilty of theft and sentenced him to hang, but later commuted the sentence to 14 years' transportation.

Young William languished for three years in a prison hulk in Portsmouth Harbour. It was not until 3 September 1821 that he departed, at last, for Port Jackson on board the *Mary II*. Before long he was assigned to a private settler as a farm labourer at Airds. His master was William Redfern, a prominent surgeon who had himself entered the colony as a convict. William should have counted his lucky stars; Redfern was a man of integrity and an advocate of emancipation, and would likely have been a fair master. But that wasn't William's style. In 1825 Redfern was horrified to find William, with another convict, 'committing a most violent and barbarous assault on the body of James Gallagher'.[25] The young man was tried at Bathurst, found guilty, punished with 100 lashes and sent to Port Macquarie on the *Amity*.

Subdued, William was later moved to to Richmond Vale, Wallis Plains, to work as a labourer. In 1832 he received his certificate of freedom. He went on to marry, produce 11 children, and settle at Brambles Green on the Myall River as a grazier.[26] In partnership with another man he purchased 80 acres of land. To his poor relations back in England it must have seemed astonishing, not to mention unjust, that their criminal kin had the means to acquire land of his own while they laboured at honest work with no hope of advancement!

By 1850, when his brother John sought to emigrate, William was settled in New South Wales and already had a multitude of children. Later in his life – long after the subject of this narrative was over – William's criminal nature would reassert itself. But that would all be in the future. The brothers William and John hardly knew each other; John had been only a child when William had been sentenced to transportation 32 years earlier. John could read and write but William was uneducated and may not have had the skills or inclination to correspond with the family he had left behind. Whether the brothers intended to reunite is unknown. It *is* clear that John was unwilling to broadcast his relationship with the former convict. On the official documents completed upon the ship's arrival, passengers were asked to declare any relatives in the colony. John made no mention of his brother.

He did, however, note that his cousin was a fellow passenger. In fact Andrew Brimble was the *son* of John's cousin, also named John: the very man who had taken young William to court for stealing his bread and cheese. But that incident was past history; it had taken place long before Andrew's birth and clearly had caused no lingering hostility between the families. Andrew was a young man: only 21 years of age. Like many in his family, he was a labourer. He travelled with his wife Louisa, a 20-year-old domestic servant, and their two-year-old daughter, Emily. Louisa was pregnant with their second child. The party was completed by Sophia Brimble: Andrew's 17-year-old sister, who had registered as John and Elizabeth Brimble's servant.

ON BOARD THE VESSEL

For three days, the *Emigrant* idled in the waters of Plymouth Sound as the passengers continued to come aboard. The weather continued to be cool and rainy, the sky a blanket of grey. The emigration commissioners inspected the vessel and pronounced its accommodation and provisions satisfactory. They had no way of knowing that in spite of Mrs Seaward's rigorous washing procedures, and in spite of Dr Mitchell's skilled inspections, there was at least one stowaway on board: an infected louse.

Blissfully ignorant of the danger, more passengers arrived in dribs and drabs to join the initial intake. It was the perfect time for them to explore the ship, to settle into their new home and learn its little quirks.

The toilets were a source of fascination: of wonder for some, horror for others. Most of the emigrants had never seen a water closet before. The water closet was a chute to the sea, covered by a flap for the safety of its users. The toilets were flushed directly into the sea with salt water – either from a bucket or from a tank that a roster of emigrants kept filled by manually operating a pump. These water closets would be used by the women and children; the men and the crew would relieve themselves from the 'heads' or lee side of the ship. The 'heads' was usually in the bow of the ship: a perilous position that the men were warned against using in rough weather.

The water closets were a tremendous novelty. It was a source of frustration to the emigration authorities that passengers frequently abused and damaged them. Some tossed their rubbish down the chutes, some failed to understand the correct use of the plugs, and others neglected to turn the water off and flooded the decks. It fell to the ladies of the EES/BLFES to instruct the passengers on the correct use of the facilities.

Dr Mitchell had reservations about the *Emigrant's* water closets. The entrance was via the berth deck[27] rather than via the upper deck, which would, in his opinion, limit ventilation.

Captain Kemp shared his concerns. There was nothing to be done, however; they would simply hope for good weather, which would allow the hatchways to remain open and fresh air to circulate as much as possible.

As more passengers filtered in to take up their berths, the immigrants began to learn the strict daily routines of shipboard life. Cleaning duties began on the day they embarked. They were given scrapers, brooms, dry sand and rubbing stones for scrubbing the decks, and they were taught the cleaning routines which would dominate their lives for the next three months.

They would also get to know their fellow-passengers. People whose paths might otherwise never have crossed were thrown together to live in close quarters. The *Emigrant's* Irish outnumbered the English by 159 to 113.[28] There were only two Scottish-born voyagers, one of whom was Mary Ball. The Catholic and Church of England churches had roughly equal numbers of representatives. There were ten Wesleyans, seven Baptists, seven Independents and four Presbyterians.

Thus the English Wade sisters found themselves rubbing shoulders with young Irish women like Catherine Maunsell and her compatriot, another Limerick girl named Mary Connor. Mary was a spirited young domestic servant of 20. A poor Roman Catholic, she was young but already demonstrating strength and courage. She had left her parents behind, but she was not alone. Her uncle, James Connor, a 29-year-old labourer of Tipperary, also boarded the *Emigrant* along with his wife (named Mary or Ann; sources differ) and infant son Michael. Another uncle and aunt had already settled in the colony, although they lived far from Moreton Bay in Campbelltown, New South Wales.

Young Mary was illiterate but astute and witty, competent and kind. Her good sense and compassion would be sorely needed over the coming months. But of the trials that lay ahead, Mary and her companions were as yet mercifully ignorant. Perhaps it was just as well.

A fresh wind gusted in from the west, brushing the clouds aside and plumping the *Emigrant's* newly unfurled sails into white pillows. The 'Blue Peter' – white rectangle within blue – fluttered from her foremast, announcing that she was ready to sail. Any visitors who remained on board were directed to leave. Imagine the sailors singing – *lend a hand, boys, lend a hand!* – as they hauled the anchor up to the ship's bow.

It was a cool spring day – an ideal time to set out – when the tug escorted the *Emigrant* to the mouth of the sound. One can picture the barque's deck cluttered with ropes and rigging, lifeboats, cargo and livestock, and the emigrants milling upon it, gazing back for a final glimpse of land; some singing, others praying; some watching in silent reflection. Perhaps the Brimble children ran excitedly about on the deck; perhaps Mary Connor watched them, dreaming of the children she might have one day in the new land; perhaps Elizabeth Wade clung to her mother's arm in fear.

Catherine and Patrick Maunsell, like all the Irish, had already farewelled their country, and most of the English had taken leave of their home towns – but for all the travellers, this was the final, irrevocable goodbye to their former lives; goodbye to all that was familiar. It was a momentous hour, and an emotional one. There may have been tears. For some, it was a thrilling moment, for others, full of trepidation. Who could tell what lay ahead?

As far as Dr Mitchell and Captain Kemp were concerned, it was business as usual. Each man was experienced in his role and well qualified to shoulder his responsibilities. The ship was sound and speedy and the sailing conditions favourable. No long-haul voyage was without risk or hardship, and yet both men had undertaken such journeys before; they had no reason to expect this one to present more dangers than the last.

The *Emigrant* was on her way, passing beyond the newly completed Breakwater, a massive strip of stone that curved around the Harbour's mouth and protected it from south-westerly gales; passing the lighthouse on the Breakwater's western end; a little further south, and she was in the open sea where the sharp triangle of Mewstone Island rose up to farewell her. Here the *Emigrant* shed her pilot and sailed on alone through the 'pathless deep'.

Part 2

The pathless deep

Sailors' Song on Heaving Anchor

LEND a hand, boys – lend a hand!
Our anchor we must weigh:
Come, lend a willing hand, boys –
The tide brooks no delay!
Pull readily, pull steadily,
Pull with a willing mind;
And raise a cheer for those most dear,
Whom we love and leave behind.
Pull away, boys – pull away!
The wind is fresh and fair.
Tho' we leave our native home, boys,
We find one everywhere.
Then, pull away, without delay,
With ready heart and hand!
Trust to His love, who sits above,
To guard both sea and land.
His voice is in the gale, boys;
His foot is on the deep;
His hand will guide the helm, boys;
His eye the night-watch keep.
Come – a long pull, a strong pull,
A pull all together!
Look to our Guide, whate'er betide,
Of calm or stormy weather.
And now, God save the Queen, boys!
God save our native land! And grant us soon again, boys!
To anchor on her strand. Then readily, and steadily,
Let's work with hand and heart,
Till we see once more our native shore,
And those from whom we part.[29]

Chapter 3

Australia bound

THE VOYAGE BEGINS

'Imagine a lofty barque, perhaps with all sail set and the sunlight and shadow playing over her fabric in delightful patterns of sheer loveliness.'[30]

The barque *Emigrant* sailed on southward beyond the protection of the sound and out to the open sea, guided by the Eddystone Lighthouse past the treacherous rocks of a hidden reef. She passed homeward-bound ships that, with shortening sails, glided northward into the sanctuary of Plymouth's harbour, their journeys all but over.

Before long, England slipped from view. There was nothing to see but sky and water. For many of the emigrants, this was their first encounter with the ocean, and for some it was a terrifying experience. '[I] was very much frightnde [sic],' wrote a young voyager in 1863, 'when I looked at the water and seen the sea so hight [sic] and it was very Dangerous.'[31]

The immensity of their undertaking would cause some, at this point, to quail, and be overcome with emotion. For the young unmarried women travelling alone, leaving behind a family and the only home they had ever known, venturing to a rugged land peopled by ex-convicts and Aboriginal people whose customs were so strange to them – a land of exotic marsupials and venomous snakes and screeching birds, of vast deserts and bush-land, of arid heat and flood – the future was a daunting prospect.

'Nearly all the single women sit down and have a cry the first thing,' wrote a passenger of the *Conway*, 'and I feel very much inclined to join them; but first ask myself what there is to cry about and as I cannot answer it to my own satisfaction, think it would be very foolish so [I] begin [sic] to put things in order in our berths.'[32]

For young ladies like Elizabeth Wade, the company of her mother and step-family was a blessing. Likewise, Mary Connor may have been comforted by the presence of her uncle and aunt on board and cheered by the prospect of reuniting with another uncle in Sydney; and Catherine Maunsell must have taken heart from the proximity of her brother.

Other brave young women who had embarked on the voyage alone must have trembled as they contemplated the future – women like Mary Anne Mahoney, a 19-year-old domestic servant from London, whose brother and sister had emigrated to Melbourne before her. For others, like Ellen Walsh, emigration was less of a gamble, for her home country offered so little hope. Ellen was a poor, illiterate, orphaned Irish Catholic who, at 30, might improve her dwindling chances of marriage by venturing to the male-dominated colony. And yet, leaving behind everything that was familiar was a terrifying thing.

Emigrants commonly settled their nerves by trying to create order in their living quarters. They didn't have much space, but what little they had would be turned into tiny nests of their own; they hung their canvas bags, stowed their few precious belongings, and settled in. The steerage quarters became a muddle of industry as emigrants slung their coats and hats upon pegs, arranged their foodstuffs on the shelves, and claimed their places at the long, wide central table – all in a dim half-light – as they tried to turn this strange, noisy, rocking cavern into a home.

But once the ship was out in the open sea, its motion would take a toll, and it was not long before seasickness would strike. Seasickness was not a trivial matter. It was ghastly and debilitating. Typically, it struck early in the voyage and it struck hard. Most passengers succumbed in varying degrees. Seasickness destroyed the appetite, sapped the energy and crushed the spirit; its effect was pure misery.

In steerage, the bunks were full of men, women and children gripped by nausea. Some were bedridden for days, unable to eat and vomiting up the little they did ingest. Imagine the stench in the closed confines of steerage. 'We had not been at sea one week,' wrote Herman Melville in his novel *Redburn*, 'when to hold your head down the fore hatchway was like holding it down a suddenly opened cesspool.'[33]

For women with young children, these days were hellish. The nausea was compounded by loneliness, homesickness, and the fear of the sea and its perils. Pregnant women suffered most of all. The dangers of prolonged seasickness to an expectant mother and her unborn child were grave; the stress, dehydration and malnutrition might have serious – even fatal – consequences.

Seasickness visited the passengers of the *Emigrant* as a matter of course. There wasn't much Dr Mitchell could do. If the vomiting was accompanied by nausea or diarrhoea, he might administer medicines, but for the nausea itself he could offer little relief. Lying down helped somewhat, as did eating, although the patients had no appetite. They would suffer in their berths until the nausea subsided and they found their 'sea legs'. As soon as they were able, Dr Mitchell would encourage them to venture onto the deck to take in the fresh air.

Thankfully, seasickness claimed no lives on the *Emigrant's* voyage. For most of the voyage the weather was fair and the passage smooth, and once the travellers were accustomed to the constant rolling of the ground beneath their feet, they found health and strength restored to them.

For the children, who were typically less prone to seasickness than their parents, it was an exciting time. Not only was the prospect of life in a new land an adventure, but the voyage itself presented novelties every day. There was plenty of fresh air – for all passengers were required to stay on deck during daylight hours – and there was leisure time: a new treat for many. For some of the poorer families, the food was more plentiful and nutritious than they had ever eaten at home. And there were other children to play with – children of all ages, from a range of backgrounds. From the Catholic Watersons to the Anglican Farmers, all played upon the same deck, sharing the same routines and rules, and marvelling together at the wonders of the sea.

THE WATERSON AND FARMER FAMILIES

The Watersons were from the inland county of Tipperary in Ireland's south. Henry was a 30-year-old labourer who was travelling with his 26-year-old wife, Mary, and their three children. Patrick was eight, Edward six, and Elizabeth two. Tipperary was one of the areas badly hit by the famine, and although Henry had some education, he had little hope of social advancement.

The problem of keeping his children fed and housed must have been a constant worry for him. He could not have known how dramatically his worries were about to increase.

The Farmer family came from a very different background, but given the closeness of their quarters and the commonality of their purpose, it is easy to imagine that the children of all the families, regardless of their histories, would have mingled. John Farmer was a 49-year-old farm labourer from the inland village of East Langton, Leicestershire, in England's midlands. His wife, Esther (or Hester) née Meadows, was 52; both were followers of the Church of England. They were travelling with their large brood of children. The eldest, Mary, was a 25-year-old domestic servant. The three older boys – Thomas, George and John – were all farm labourers. The younger three were also boys: Frederick (aged 11), Charles (ten) and Benjamin (seven).

John Farmer (senior) was, at 49, described by Captain Kemp as 'an aged married man'. He was resourceful, hardworking and adaptable, and his selflessness would later come to be greatly prized. John Farmer's age and large brood made him perhaps less typical of the assisted emigrants, but a man with his skills and disposition stood every chance of success in the colony. To survive and thrive, new settlers needed, above all, to be resilient. And through all the trials ahead, John Farmer would show that resilience was something he had in abundance.

THE DAILY ROUTINE

The first week passed uneventfully. Those passengers not laid up with seasickness fell into the routine of shipboard life, and in time the sufferers emerged one by one from the horrors of their berths to join them. The wind was mild which, while reducing the rolling motion of the ship, made for slow progress. But that was of little consequence to the passengers, to whom everything was novel.

Amongst other wonders, the constant noise took some by surprise: the cracking of the sails and the creaking of the timbers; the incessant shouting of the crew; the churning of the sea and the excited chattering of the children. The constant motion beneath their feet and the strange vastness of the ocean were unsettling.

But from the moment of embarkation, no time was wasted in establishing a daily routine. Each day was lived according to a strict schedule. All passengers – except those afflicted with seasickness – had to submit to the rules. Elizabeth Wade, Mary Connor, the Brimble families, the Farmers and the Watersons: all were bound to the same timetable.

Up at seven. Get dressed and roll up the bedding. If it was fine, they might drag their bedding up onto the upper deck to freshen it in the salty breeze. Then they would sweep between decks and beneath the bunks – removing the slats from the bottom berth – and scatter any dirt and debris overboard. At eight o'clock it was time for breakfast.

One of the mainstays of these routines was the 'mess' system. Just as in the Emigration Depot, the passengers were organised into messes of six to ten adults, with each mess being responsible for the cooking and cleaning for its section. Each mess consisted of people from similar backgrounds: single Englishwomen in one; Irish Catholic families in another. In this way, unofficial segregation was reinforced. It is likely that Elizabeth Wade was in a mess with her three stepsisters and two or three other young single Protestant Englishwomen. Family groups stuck together.

Each mess appointed a captain who supervised the cleaning and fetched the daily rations from the store, weighing and apportioning them according to strict guidelines. There was considerable responsibility in the role. If the captain should fall or drop the supplies as the ship lurched, there was no going back for more. The group would have to make do with spoiled food or miss out until the next meal.

With their rations, the groups would prepare their own puddings, and the mess captains would take them to the bakehouse in the common galley on deck to be cooked. The *Emigrant* carried a qualified cook – Henry Roberts – to prepare the passengers' food, helped by some of the male travellers. He was mercifully unaware that the journey ahead would be his last.

When the food was ready, the mess captains brought it back down from the bakehouse to the long table that divided the steerage compartment in half and set it down to eat. It was no easy task; the ship was in constant rocking motion, the ladders between decks were steep, and the lighting was subdued.

A mess captain of the *Conway* described her Sunday routine:

By the time I am dressed it is time to take the water keg on deck to get it filled with fresh water, then after that to take a can for the porridge for breakfast, then go to the store-room for the bread; after that we take the coffee pots to get them filled, and sit down for breakfast. After breakfast I have to make the plum pudding and take it to be baked, the materials for which is always given out on a Saturday afternoon as is also the pork which we have to put in a net and take to the cook as it lays in fresh water to soak till Sunday morning.[34]

Fresh water was a precious thing. By law, adults were allotted three quarts daily (about 3.4 litres). It didn't take long for the stored water to become smelly: as little as a week or two. Rainwater was always preferred. Rain brought on a flurry of excitement as emigrants scurried to collect runoff from sails and awnings in their mugs and bowls, for its freshness was prized. Later in the voyage, if rainwater was not available and the stored water had soured, the travellers would mix their water with wine or vinegar to disguise the smell.

Breakfast was over by nine o'clock. The mess captain took charge again, ensuring that the cleaning up was done – that scraps were thrown overboard, utensils were put away and the table and floor were cleaned. At one in the afternoon, the emigrants followed the same routine for dinner, and again at six for supper.

The food was basic but adequate. Elizabeth Wade gnawed upon a daily ration of 'ship's biscuit': a tough, long-lasting biscuit made from flour and water that would be soaked in water or stew before being eaten. The rest of the rations were doled out according to strict regulations. On Mondays, Wednesdays and Fridays, all adults received 6oz. (around 170g) pork, 6oz. flour and 3oz. oatmeal, ¼ pint (around 120ml) of peas, ½ oz. 'cocoa nibs', 4oz. sugar and 2oz. butter and 3 quarts of water. On Tuesdays and Thursdays, the pork was replaced with preserved meat and there was an additional treat of raisins and suet; instead of peas there were potatoes, and in place of cocoa and sugar there was tea. On weekends, Elizabeth and every other passenger dined on salted beef and rice. They received weekly allocations of salt, pepper, mixed pickles and mustard. Children received half rations, and infants under 12 months nothing but water. A half-pint of stout or porter was doled out to pregnant or nursing mothers daily. Alcohol was banned except for medicinal purposes.

THE MATRON AND HER CHARGES

The passengers were governed by a strict set of rules. Chief amongst all was the law preventing single women from mixing with the men. This rule was not negotiable. Tracts advising potential emigrants were full of exhortations to young women to maintain their 'purity of heart and conduct'. When a woman has lost her good name, they reasoned, she has lost her most valuable possession.

'The very appearance of evil,' insisted one such tract,

> will cause a maiden's virtue to be doubted. You cannot be too careful on board as to your conduct, your deportment, and your dress . . . Let nothing, then induce you to flirt with the crew, or passengers, or to go about the forecastle. Never be seen on deck in the morning before the decks are thoroughly washed and dry, which will not be much before breakfast. Rise early by all means; but spend the time in your own apartment, preparing yourselves, by reading and prayer, for the duties and temptations of the day. Never linger on deck in the evenings, after the order is given for you to go below. Dress neatly and modestly, and do not let the hot weather induce you to throw off your neckerchiefs, or expose your arms: attention to these points will guard you from improper remarks, and render you much more likely to marry well, than light, foolish conduct.[35]

Elizabeth Wade and her companions had a daunting set of standards to meet. They were warned not to gossip, not to be idle and not even to 'listen to an impure song or jest'. They must pray often and earnestly, and spend their time doing needlework and reading and writing. They had a duty not only to themselves but to their adopted country to be modest, diligent, obedient and godly.

As far as the young women were concerned, there might just as well have been no men on board, for all they saw of them. 'The highest crime a girl can commit is to be seen speaking to one of them,'[36] declared Fanny Davis in 1858, and her claim was no exaggeration. Transgressors could be – and were – punished.

But transgressions *were* made. On the voyage of the *Conway* a girl was ordered below for a whole week for speaking to a sailor; on the same voyage, a sailor was sent to work aloft all day for addressing a young woman. It was human nature to seek companionship and romance. The passengers of the *Emigrant* were just as inclined to take risks for the sake of love as any.

A young female passenger named Mary Ann Mahoney struck up an illicit friendship with the seaman James Hall. Mary Ann was 19, born in London in 1831. She was a small, compact woman with a round face and protruding lower lip; her straight brown hair was worn with a central part and tied back in a severe bun. Like most of her unmarried female companions, Mary Ann was a domestic servant. Her brother and sister had emigrated before her and settled in Melbourne; it may have been the young woman's intention to join them there.

James Hall was a 20-year-old sailor from Liverpool; a young man with curly dark hair, kindly eyes and a straight nose, who wore a beard and clean-shaven upper lip. Exactly when Mary Ann and James met is not recorded, and whether their shipboard liaison was noticed is likewise unknown. If it *was,* they would surely have been punished. Mary Ann's reputation would have been damaged and she might have found it hard to secure a job in the colony. And yet she was not the only young woman to form a relationship with a fellow-traveller.

One of the means of protecting the reputations of the female emigrants was the selection of a woman of 'good character' as chaperone: a ship's 'Matron'. A matron might receive a free passage for her efforts, or she might earn a gratuity of perhaps £5 on arrival if she had served satisfactorily. It was the matron's duty to 'obviate the evils consequent on the long period of undisciplined idleness during a four months' voyage, and to promote the moral and religious improvement of the emigrants, by providing them with suitable employment for the voyage, and by introducing an organised system of industrial classes on board.'[37] It was also her responsibility to report on the women's conduct for the benefit of their prospective employers in the colony. The matron would be Elizabeth Wade's and Catherine Maunsell's protector.

Matrons were usually middle-class single women or widows. Before departure, the proposed matron had to satisfy the chaplain that she met a strict set of criteria. She had to be 'physically robust and active, of a decided character and firm bearing, and of a high moral and religious tone of mind. She must also be of about the same rank in life as the young women among whom she is placed, yet sufficiently superior to them in education and acquirements to secure their respect.'[38]

Before the *Emigrant*'s departure, the ladies of the Emigrant Employment Society had selected Mary Burberow (or Barberrow) as matron. They were well pleased with their choice. Mrs Burberow was a 56-year-old Londoner who had been twice widowed. Born Mary Foster Hill, her first – brief – marriage was to William Hackett in 1818. Nine years later, she married widower William Burberow. When William died at the end of 1831, he was only 31 years of age; his grieving wife, Mary, was some six years older. William may have died never having met his daughter. Frances Jane Burberow was born sometime between April 1831 and April 1832. Now a young woman of only 18, she was accompanying her mother on the voyage to Australia.

Matron Burberow was poor but respectable. Life for a woman in her position was not easy and held little hope of improvement except through her daughter. Frances, on the other hand, had the possibility of a brighter future. If she worked hard and married well she had a chance of advancement and the means to support her aging mother. And while a person of Mrs Burberow's demographic was not the type of immigrant the colony sought, she was *exactly* the type required to chaperone the young ladies on the voyage.[39]

It was Matron Burberow's responsibility to see that her charges arrived at their destination with their reputations unblemished.

Above all, she was required to ensure there was no fraternising between the single women and men. But the matron's job was not easy. She was expected to supervise cleaning, food preparation and mealtimes, and to keep her charges occupied with useful activities such as needlework, embroidery and knitting. She might engage literate girls as 'Sub-Matrons' to read 'improving' texts to the others or to teach Scripture, which must be done daily. She was in charge of their instruction, entertainment and industry, and the guardian of their virtue. It fell to the matron to mediate quarrels and settle complaints; to protect her charges against the dangers and temptations of idleness, and to comfort, calm, encourage and reprimand when required. She had no respite; she was expected to remain vigilant at all times. Her work was seen by Christian organisations as 'of a missionary character', requiring both 'firmness and gentleness'. She was expected to inculcate 'pure and Christian feelings' in her charges and guide them in worship, teaching them by example the virtues of prayer, patience and self-denial.[40]

It was a demanding job, and some ships' matrons proved unequal to the task. Some were ignorant of basic hygiene practices. Some were bullies who abused their power, while others were poor disciplinarians. Some were drunks. There is no reason to believe that Matron Burberow didn't perform her duties capably or conscientiously. But matrons were no more immune to seasickness than any of their charges, and Matron Burberow was not in robust health. And with 50 young women to supervise – including her own daughter – it is reasonable to suspect that some minor misbehaviour escaped her notice.

Some matrons had dreadful journeys. They complained of the insolence, laziness, disobedience and dishonesty of the young women in their care. They had little sleep and faced opposition and resentment. The matron of the 1857 voyage of the *Fitzjames* was so appalled by the behaviour of her emigrant women that she wrote: 'I am ashamed to call myself a woman so depraved are many who are here'.[41]

There is no evidence that the women of the *Emigrant* caused Mrs Burberow any such strife. Petty squabbles they may well have had; perhaps Elizabeth was fretful, maybe her sister Emma reckless; and without doubt, Mary Ann Mahoney and others secretly defied the rule forbidding them to communicate with the men. But not a negative word has been recorded of any of the emigrants' behaviour during the voyage or quarantine. It appears they were a well-behaved lot.

Every night, the cooking fires that had been burning all day were put out, and the voyagers descended the ladder into the steerage quarters, where they picked their unsteady way through the shadows of beams and bolts, around chests and barrels and bags, and climbed onto tiny benches padded with mattresses of straw. By 10pm all were cocooned in their little berths, rocked to sleep by the motion of the ship. The darkness was incomplete; an oil lamp burned by each hatchway all through the night.

There were many perils, perhaps the most serious being the ever-present danger of fire. A fire on board would be disastrous. To guard against it, the married men were rostered on night watch, monitoring the hatchways, scuttles and ventilators. From 8pm to 8am they prowled, reporting every half hour to the officer on duty.

The girls, of course, did not do guard-duty, for to lurk around at night was, for them, unthinkable. Once the young women had descended between decks for the night, Matron Burberow locked the door to their quarters and secreted the key upon her person. There would be no sneaking out.

The noise and motion never stopped, not even at night. The girls lay in their berths while the vessel rocked and creaked 'like an old wicker cradle'.[42] The waves slapped against the ship's hull and the masts groaned above; the sails cracked and snapped, and their neighbours murmured and wept and snored.

The proximity of others at night was nothing new; these were the working poor who were used to cramped living conditions and sharing rooms – even beds – with others. And it was not long before they grew accustomed to the ship's motion and the noise and settled into their new lives.

Chapter 4

The surgeon-superintendent

DR GEORGE MITCHELL: THE SHIP'S PROTECTOR

There were good practical reasons for the strict routines of shipboard life. It was not all about Victorian etiquette. In the early
days of the century, emigrant vessels had been small and overcrowded. Avaricious captains would squeeze as many desperate
emigrants into their ships as possible. The only ventilation to the
steerage quarters, crammed with hundreds of poor souls, was the
hatchway, and in bad weather, there was none. But as people fled
the country in increasing numbers, and the rate of deaths from
starvation and disease at sea reached record figures, the government had to act.

Legislation to protect emigrants was enacted in Britain in 1803
and refined over the following decades. By 1850, the maximum
number of passengers that a ship could carry was regulated,
and ships were required to provide enough food and water for
their voyages. British maritime law made it compulsory for any
emigrant ship to carry a surgeon if it was bearing more than

50 passengers on a long-haul voyage through the tropics. Since the captain and surgeon were paid according to the number of living souls they delivered to their destination, they had incentive to keep their charges healthy.

Attending to the sick was only one of the surgeon's duties. More important was his role in *preventing* illness by maintaining hygiene on board. He had to see that passengers washed regularly, and that they kept the vessel clean, the decks scrubbed and deodorised, and below decks as well ventilated as possible, for 'bad air' was considered a source of disease. It was his job to ensure that all passengers received adequate and wholesome rations. He was expected to encourage exercise such as dancing on the deck, and monitor the children's attendance at school. He supervised the matron, checked the equipment for distilling seawater and fumigating, and occasionally gave lectures to remind the passengers of their duties.

The importance of discipline with respect to cleaning and sanitation cannot be over-emphasised. In a time when typhus, whooping cough, measles and scarlet fever were rife, untreatable, and often fatal, all measures of prevention were vital. The surgeon was authorised – and required – to ensure his charges adhered to the sanitation rules. His ability and willingness to exercise his authority could mean the difference between life and death. If a breakdown of discipline led to a high death rate, the surgeon-superintendent was held accountable.

The surgeon-superintendent's word was second only to the captain's. The surgeon administered punishments when passengers transgressed. For refusing to wash or for failing to follow the correct cleaning procedures, for appearing on deck at forbidden hours, or for committing violence or getting drunk, the surgeon might punish offenders by confining them to their quarters, withholding rations or even putting them in irons.

Often it was the surgeon's job to help the single women to find suitable employment on their arrival. In every way, he was their supervisor, their commander and their protector. His was a deeply demanding role, and for this reason, surgeons on these government ships bound for Australia were paid well.

In exercising his duty, Dr Mitchell would have enlisted the help of 'special constables' from amongst the married male volunteers. If they performed their duties well, they might be paid at the end of the voyage. These men would supervise the mess and cleaning rosters and the distribution of rations, and organise for the bedding to be brought on deck for a daily airing when the weather permitted. Sanitary constables disinfected and maintained the water closets and managed the water distilling apparatus. They supervised the washing of the coppers and the pumping of water into cisterns and tanks. They were guards for their little community; they helped the surgeon to maintain order and discipline.

That passengers would bathe regularly without encouragement could not be taken for granted. Most emigrants were satisfied with a saltwater sponge bath. When they reached warmer climes, if they were lucky, the crew might rig up a shower for the women, and the men might douse themselves with the fire hose.

Twice a week, Elizabeth Wade, her sisters and her fellow-passengers washed their clothing. They did not waste precious stored fresh water on laundry, but if they were able to collect rainwater by whatever means they had at hand, they might have the luxury of washing their clothes in it. At other times, they washed in saltwater, and soon their clothing became stiff and scratchy. 'We get all our things together and either dance on them under the pump or tow them overboard, then lay them on deck soak or scrub them with a brush, rinse and then hang them in the rigging,'[43] wrote an 1852 traveller on the *Blackwall*.

Passengers were strictly forbidden to hang their washing between decks, for medical practice at the time held it crucial to prevent dampness below.

The daily cleaning was a major operation. First, the men scrubbed the decks, the steerage quarters, the forecastle and the bulwarks with brooms and canvas. Then they wet, sanded and 'holystoned' the decks. The holystone was a large, soft stone that the men scraped backwards and forwards over the deck using long ropes at each end. Then they washed the sand overboard and swabbed the deck dry.

In steerage, the passengers scrubbed their berths with sand and holystones and sprinkled vinegar and disinfectants. Sanitary constables fumigated the steerage quarters with swinging stoves that burned tar, charcoal and other deodorants to 'sweeten the atmosphere'.

But in spite of the best efforts of Dr Mitchell and his helpers, and unknown to them, the lice that had secretly stowed away on the *Emigrant* refused to die.

It was usual for the surgeon to appoint hospital assistants. Dr Mitchell recruited the reliable Joseph William Ball, husband of Mary, father of Mary Ann, and stepfather of the Wade girls. Joseph was a conscientious assistant whose duties might have included anything from supervising cleaning routines to administering medicines. Dr Mitchell was a well-trained and experienced surgeon, but even in a ship free of disease, the job was too big for one man alone. In Joseph Ball, he found a willing and capable helper.

The pair would have been busy. Aside from the daily preventative routines, Dr Mitchell would have dealt with the various maladies and complaints of the passengers and crew: indigestion, injuries, constipation and seasickness. He would have dispensed medicines, given pre-natal care, treated sprains and bruises, and lanced boils. There was little time for rest. But George Mitchell's background had prepared him well for his duties.

EARLY LIFE

In the province of Ulster, just north of the modern-day border between the Republic of Ireland and Northern Ireland, lay the inland county of Armagh, with the town of Armagh at its centre. Five and a half miles to the south-east of the town lay the townland of Clady Beg. Travellers on the road from Armagh might pass down from the hilly country to the flats of Clady Beg and stop at the thriving post-town of Markethill, home to over a thousand inhabitants.[44] It was a lively place, with its own courthouse, police station, a bridewell,[45] and barracks for the militia. There were meeting-houses for the Presbyterians and the Wesleyans, a national school and a dispensary.

It may have been this dispensary that inspired the young George Mitchell to take an interest in medicine. For it was here in Markethill that George spent most of his childhood. Born in 1825, he was the eldest child of Alexander Mitchell and his wife Jane (née McMullan), whose families had farmed in the district for generations. Like most of their neighbours, the Mitchells were Presbyterians of Scottish heritage: 'Ulster Scots'.

George was probably born at the small farm at Ballylane, where his parents lived as newlyweds before they moved upmarket to their 40-acre freehold farm and house at Clady Beg. George Mitchell likely grew up in this home – a house with three chimneys, encircled by five trees – in the 'Scotch Quarter' of Clady Beg.

In Armagh, farmers grew crops of wheat, oats, potatoes and flax, tilling the land by hand with a spade. As was typical in

Ireland, property was in the hands of a few wealthy landlords and the farms were small. But in a country stricken by poverty, the people of Armagh fared better than most. Conditions were superior, on the whole, to those in the south; even the peasant classes enjoyed better housing, clothing and food.

The relative health and prosperity of the population was due largely to the linen industry. Linen from Ulster was amongst the finest in the world, for flax grew well on the shallow and boggy land of the north. And whereas the Industrial Revolution had bypassed much of 18th-century Ireland, the linen industry in the northeast had benefitted from adopting the new ways.

The Mitchells were flax farmers. Because the linen industry was a vital trade that received government support, flax growers were generally well-off compared with farmers of other crops. Young George would have enjoyed a relatively healthy lifestyle. He grew up in a wholesome rural environment, where linen bleachers took advantage of 'green lawns, clear streams, pure springs, and the open atmosphere'; where the 'towns are small and every hill and valley abounds with rural and comfortable habitations'.[46]

In fact, most tenant farmers in the north, like the Mitchells, enjoyed better social conditions and more rights than their southern counterparts. Northerners were entitled to sell their rights to occupy the land at prices that depended on the improvements they had made. This gave Ulster tenants more security and more incentive to improve their houses and land than farmers like the Maunsells, their countrymen in the south.

The Mitchells belonged to a fortunate class of tenant who held long-term leases on substantial property. Unlike many of their southern countrymen, who could be evicted at any time, their position was secure. And like most farmers in Armagh, they rented the land directly from their landlord; they had no greedy middleman to contend with as did many in the south. The Mitchells were tenants of Francis William Caulfeild, the second Earl of Charlemont. With many thousands of acres to his name, Charlemont was one of the biggest landowners in the county. He had hundreds of tenants and consequently a good deal of political clout. (There was no such thing as a secret ballot; the more tenants a landowner had, the more votes he could depend upon if he ran for Parliament).

As 19th-century Irish landlords go, Caulfeild seems to have been fair. His tenants were successful flax growers, due at least in part to his good management. His practice, so successful in Armagh, was held up as an example that other landowners throughout Ireland would do well to follow. Francis Caulfeild supported the introduction of modern farming equipment and practices such as better drainage, irrigation and rotation crops. Progressive landholders like him understood that what benefitted their tenant farmers benefitted them and their county.

By the time George Mitchell was born, however, recession had devastated the country and even the north-east had begun to struggle. In the wake of the Napoleonic Wars, agricultural prices across the land fell, wages followed suit, and the potato blight brought the country to its knees. The linen industry faltered and flax production declined.

The Mitchells, however, survived. They were wealthier than many of their countrymen. George's father, Alexander Mitchell, was a notable member of the Markethill Agricultural Society: a respected citizen. In the mid- to late-1840s he supplemented his income by serving as a Guardian of the Poor Law for the County of Armagh. The Irish Poor Law Act was an attempt to address the country's growing problems of poverty and unemployment. It divided the country into 130 unions, each with its own workhouse and each governed by a Board of Guardians. The County Guardians, or 'High Constables', administered the Poor Law, collected 'cess'[47] tax and oversaw medical relief in their districts. They were mostly gentry and aristocrats: people who wielded power in the community.

George Mitchell's father was not the only member of the family to be elected to such an important position; Alexander's brother David Mitchell was a 'Relieving Officer' for the Armagh Board. His role was to investigate the applicants for relief by examining their homes and state of health, their ability to work and their means, and reporting his impressions to the Board of Guardians. The board decided what form of relief to give, and to whom; it might grant admission to a workhouse, or food or medicine. The Mitchell family's involvement in the administration of financial and medical care for their fellows may well have fed young George's growing interest in medicine. The brothers' roles suggest that the Mitchells enjoyed a high status in their community.

When George was six, his sister Elizabeth was born. She was followed three years later by Mary, then William and Prudence.[48] Two more children would be born later, when George – by then an adult – had left the family home.

Flax farming was labour-intensive, and a typical farmer enlisted the help of his whole family in its cultivation: planting, harvesting by hand, and preparing the flax for spinning. Although George may have helped his father on the farm, his education was by no means neglected. His ambitions soon grew beyond the farming life, beyond Ulster, even beyond Ireland. George had decided to become a doctor.

The traditions of George's home county were shaped by quaint and colourful folklore. Rituals and chants were said to cure all manner of ailments. According to folklore, one could cure mumps by taking the sufferer to a drinking hole, leading him in silence with a pair of horses' winkers. There the patient should take three mouthfuls of water, saying to himself: 'in the Name of the Father and of the Son and of the Holy Ghost'. To cure toothache and a sore head, a tight band around the head and forehead was prescribed, along with the chant (repeated three times): 'As Peter sat on a marble stone Christ came by and said: *Peter, what ails thee? My dear Lord and Master my head and teeth doth ache. Arise, Peter, and in my name thy head and teeth shall ache no more*.'[49]

These traditional 'cures', however, had long been making way for the more modern and sophisticated practice of medicine. The world was on the brink of major breakthroughs: the introduction of microscopes leading to the discovery of microorganisms; experiments in the use of ether and chloroform facilitating surgery, and a better understanding of hygiene and sanitation slowly improving public health. Vaccination against smallpox had been introduced in 1796, the stethoscope invented in 1816, and the first successful transfusion of human blood performed in 1818. It was a time of scientific advancement. A time during which superstition was gradually being replaced by science.

But medical knowledge still had far to go; in the dispensary of Markethill and in the infirmary and fever hospital at Armagh, doctors still applied leeches and enemas and dispensed emetics to remove evil 'humours' in the hope of a cure. Antibiotics were a long way off, as were X-rays; germ theory; vaccines for tetanus, diphtheria, tuberculosis and whooping cough; and the identification of vitamins and development of reliable birth control.

And although it was a time of poverty, political and religious unrest in Ireland, and although hunger and disease ravaged the country, it was an exciting time for medical science. But a career in medicine carried risk. Doctors' duties in rural Ireland during times of famine were harrowing, for they witnessed daily the grotesque poverty, malnutrition, squalor and suffering of their countrymen. The mortality rate amongst medical men was high.

It took ambition to leave the home and the region in which George's family had farmed for generations to embark on the journey to becoming a doctor. But it also took a sense of civic duty, compassion and courage. An adventurous spirit – a spirit of youthful optimism – was essential. George was 16 or 17 when he left home to study medicine. He moved forty miles away to Belfast, where he enrolled in the Medical School at the Royal Belfast Academical Institution. It was 1842. It was a decision that would change George's life forever.

BELFAST

Belfast was a rapidly growing town: an industrial hub, sustained by ship building and linen manufacture. Most of its citizens were, like George, Presbyterian of Scottish descent. They were businessmen – tradesmen, professionals, clergy, successful farmers.

The Belfast Medical School was new and dynamic, having opened only seven years before George enrolled. It belonged to the Royal Belfast Academical Institution (known as 'Inst'), which was partly a non-denominational boys' school and partly a further education and university college.

Inst had grown from the desire of the ambitious and wealthy Presbyterian men of Belfast to give their sons a better station in life. It was a preparatory college: a school that did not issue certificates of its own but prepared its students to sit for their final examinations in one of the recognised licensing bodies.

The school provided an ideal opportunity for young George Mitchell. As a Presbyterian, he was barred from Catholic colleges, and Dublin – where he might have been admitted to the university – was a long way from home for a young man. Ulster Presbyterians were wary of Dublin. The city was morally suspect. In his address at the 1814 opening of Inst, Dr William Drennan declared that 'The Academical Institution will prevent the hard and disgraceful necessity . . . of [parents] sending their children to seek in other countries, with much risk to their health and morals, for that instruction . . . which might be equally well attained at home'.[50]

George made his way from Markethill to the medical school, where he took lessons in anatomy and surgery. With anaesthesia yet to be developed, surgery was a brutal business. George would have learned how to amputate limbs, to open abscesses, to remove tumours or other diseased tissue, to repair hare-lips, to remove stones from the urinary tract, and to excise discs of bone from the skull. George did his practical training at the Belfast Fever Hospital and General Dispensary, with which Inst had a joint teaching and staffing arrangement. Here he gained a real taste of life as a doctor.

George arrived at Belfast's medical school towards the end of its brief heyday. He was one of about 80 students to enjoy the school's glowing reputation. He had not been there long, however, before the cracks started to appear: financial pressures and religious disagreements dogged the establishment. Of greater concern for medical students, the supply of cadavers dwindled.

It was time for George to move on.

Dublin was far away: 80 miles or so from George's family. And it was big – at least three times the size of Belfast. For George Mitchell, son of a Markethill flax farmer, moving on to the University of Dublin was a huge step. But by 1843, George was mature enough and ambitious enough to spread his wings.

DUBLIN

The School of Medicine at the University of Dublin is better known as Trinity College. It is the oldest medical school in Ireland; when George began his studies there, it had already been operating for more than 200 years.

Dublin itself was past its prime: crowded and poverty-stricken. But while the city of Dublin deteriorated, the university did not. Its stately granite buildings and beautiful parklands were much admired and its reputation as a place of learning held fast. 'Beautiful as it all is, perhaps most beautiful when the moonlight veils the stern edges of the granite and lends a touch of softness to the massive columns.'[51]

Medicine had been taught at the university for centuries. Even in George's day, however, only a small percentage of doctors in the United Kingdom had university degrees, most received their education through apprenticeships or on-the-job training in hospitals.[52] The social status of doctors was not especially high; a university education was considered unnecessary by many. This attitude, however, was changing.

George studied in a time of rapid advancement of medical knowledge. It was an exciting time to be in such a field. At Trinity, internationally acclaimed doctors were transforming the teaching of medicine: people like Robert Graves (whose teaching methods were groundbreaking) and William Stokes (who was renowned for his studies of cardiac and pulmonary diseases and his pioneering use of the stethoscope).

In Belfast, George had been surrounded by fellow-Presbyterians. It was a different story in Dublin, where Protestants were in the minority. At university, however, George still had an advantage over his Catholic peers. Although some laws that discriminated against Catholics had been repealed in the previous century, Protestants still had the upper hand. In George's day, students of any religion could get degrees at Trinity, but scholarships and Fellowships were granted only to Protestants.

At Trinity, George studied anatomy, surgery, midwifery and practical midwifery, learning skills that would serve him well in his later career as surgeon on an emigrant ship. He also attended public science lectures and studied Latin – for at Trinity, all medical examinations were oral and conducted in Latin.

But although he was receiving tuition from Robert Harrison – one of surgery's most internationally renowned doctors – George was unable to earn a degree in surgery at Trinity. The university conferred degrees in medicine only.

This was not enough for the ambitious young Irishman. He had set his sights higher. So it was that in 1844, George Mitchell would make the journey across the Irish Sea to the University of Edinburgh to continue his studies, returning to the land of his ancestors, but leaving his homeland forever.

EDINBURGH

South College Street ran parallel to the University of Edinburgh. It was a busy cobbled street, the southern side of which was lined with tall, grey slabs of tenement buildings. It was here, in an apartment in the five-storey building at number ten, that George took lodgings with a widow named Mary Mitchell. The street door opened into a long dark corridor that led to a stone spiral staircase up to his apartment. It was not lavish accommodation by any means. But George's home was handy to the college in which his lectures were held (now known as 'Old College'); just a short walk eastward to South Bridge, a turn to the left, and there stood the imposing building of the College on his left.

George's teachers were some of the top men in their fields. In his first year at Edinburgh, George studied theory of medicine, chemistry, natural history, clinical surgery and practical anatomy. His chemistry lecturer was Dr William Gregory, who had been responsible for a major scientific discovery: morphia. It was Dr William Gregory who made a breakthrough that would open the way to the wider use of morphia for pain relief; in 1831, he found a cheap way to isolate and purify morphia using only water. The hypodermic needle was yet to be invented; when it was – in 1850, the year that this narrative begins – the medical use of morphine would become commonplace.

Perhaps the most distinguished doctor to teach George in his first year at Edinburgh was Dr James Syme. He has been described as one of Scotland's finest surgeons; according to one of his students, 'no greater teacher of surgery ever lived'.[53] A highly intelligent man with a magnetic but quarrelsome temperament, Dr Syme was known as the 'Napoleon of Surgery' – perhaps a reference to his surgical skill, or perhaps to his cantankerous nature.

In 1844, 19-year-old George Mitchell's lecturer James Syme was the Chair of Clinical Surgery, and as brilliant and innovative a teacher as he was a surgeon. His method of teaching was to bring his patients in person before the students to demonstrate his process of diagnosis.

Twice a week, George would have clamoured to attend Syme's lectures at the hospital. It was Syme's practice to drive to the hospital in a grand yellow chariot pulled by two big horses; then he would move up to his room and, surrounded by a select group of assistants, friends and practitioners hoping to arrange a consultation, he would examine each new case brought to him. Before the admiring eyes of George and his peers he would make a diagnosis, which to them 'seemed magical and intuitional, with certainly the minimum of examination or discussion'.[54]

Then from the waiting patients, cases were selected for the following day's lecture or operation. A student who attended the school around nine years after George Mitchell described Syme's lectures thus:

> ... a tremendous rush of feet would be heard of the students racing to get the nearest seats in the large operating theatre where the lecture was given ...
>
> He comes in, sits down with a little, a very little, bob of a bow, rubs his trouser legs with both hands open, and signs for the first case. The four dressers on duty, and in aprons, march in (if possible in step), carrying a rude wicker basket, in which, covered by a rough red blanket, the patient peers up at the great amphitheatre crammed with faces. A brief description, possibly the case had been described at a former lecture, and then the little, neat, round-shouldered, dapper man takes his knife and begins ...[55]

Syme was the surgeon of the Royal Infirmary, a new surgical hospital complete with operating theatre a short walk from George's home. It was here that George Mitchell received his practical hospital experience, which was part of his training for two years.

Dr Joseph Bell, a student of medicine some ten years after George, was scathing about the nursing care that patients received at the Infirmary – and in hospitals in general. 'Without apparent exaggeration,' he wrote, 'it is almost impossible to convey to this generation the depths of disgraceful ignorance and neglect in which nursing lay in hospitals in 1854.'[56] Florence Nightingale was yet to revolutionise the nursing profession – indeed, to turn it *into* a profession – and nursing care was, in Joseph Bell's opinion 'wholly inefficient, and, in the light of this day, simply disgraceful'. In 1854, the infirmary's experienced and kindly staff nurses were aided by night nurses, 'poor old useless drudges, half-charwoman, half-field worker, rarely keeping their places for any length of time, absolutely ignorant, almost invariably drunken, sometimes deaf, occasionally fatuous'. Their working hours were long and thankless, and their skills were negligible, and the result was a high risk of post-operative complications.

'Just imagine what chance a tracheotomy case would have under such conditions of nursing,' Joseph Bell wrote, 'unless the students volunteered.' After a big operation, the house surgeon relied upon students like George to work unpaid night shifts.

George's training at Edinburgh continued into 1845 and 1846. He studied 'Practice of Medicine' under Dr William Pulteney Alison, whose specialty was the fevers that had ravaged Edinburgh in the early 1800s. He was known for his efforts to improve social conditions for the poor Scots; his work in Edinburgh had given him first-hand experience of the dreadful living conditions of his patients. Understanding that poverty was a major cause of fever epidemics, he campaigned successfully for better relief for the poor. Young George Mitchell, as Dr Alison's student during these years, had ample exposure to Alison's wisdom, benevolence and extensive knowledge of physiology.

Under Dr Robert Christison,[57] George studied 'Materia Medica' (medicine). Christison was a celebrated toxicologist with an intimate knowledge of poisons. As medical adviser to the Crown, he assisted in most of the important legal cases for decades. He was also an ardent campaigner against the idea of women studying medicine, believing that women – who lacked, in his opinion, the intellectual capacity of men – were intended to be mothers and housekeepers, and exhorting them to 'become midwives, not doctors'.[58]

During George's second year at university, he studied 'Medical Jurisprudence' and botany under the tutelage of the top men in their fields. Of all George's eminent lecturers, however, it was perhaps William Henderson whose teaching would become, for George, the most pertinent. Dr Henderson's expertise was in a field in which George Mitchell was fated to gain grim first-hand experience: typhus.

William Henderson was physician to the fever wards and a pathologist at the Royal Infirmary. In 1841, he became one of the first to use the microscope in the study of pneumonia, when he described its effects on the lung. As an advocate of homeopathy, Henderson was a controversial figure in the medical world. It was said that his lectures were 'good, even eloquent; but they utterly failed to impress his hearers. He had no strong views to express, no clear and decided opinions of his own to teach.'[59]

In 1845–46 Henderson was George Mitchell's pathology lecturer. Henderson's recent studies into disease were highly pertinent at a time when Edinburgh was being ravaged by fever. 'Fevers' had long caused immeasurable suffering especially in the poorer, crowded, unsanitary parts of Scotland's cities. An epidemic had swept through the country from 1842 to 1844; the number of cases in 1843 was calculated at 9000 in Edinburgh alone.[60] The cause of infectious diseases was still unknown, and a distinction between different types of 'fever' was yet to be made. The name 'fever' was applied to a range of illnesses. Some diseases were named according to the conditions of their origin; typhus was known as 'gaol fever' when it appeared in a crowded prison, 'camp fever' during times of war or 'ship fever' when it occurred at sea.

In the early 1840s, Edinburgh physicians studying fevers began to recognise that they were dealing with three distinct diseases: typhus, typhoid and relapsing fever. It was Dr William Henderson who, in 1843, became the first person to differentiate between typhus and 'epidemic fever'. He asserted that the diseases were caused by different 'poisons', while acknowledging that medical science was yet to discover the nature of those poisons.

George had the best of teachers, but medical science had a long way to go. Louis Pasteur was yet to suggest that micro-organisms might cause disease; the experimental method of scientific study was still to be proposed; and Joseph Lister had not yet demonstrated that disinfection reduced post-operative complications. These advances would be made within the next few decades, along with the discovery of the microorganisms that cause tuberculosis, cholera and diphtheria, and the development of a vaccine against rabies.

Perhaps the most revolutionary development, however, was already brewing: modern anaesthesia. The effects of nitrous oxide had been studied as far back as the 18th century, but its use in surgery was yet to be explored. In 1846 – only months after George graduated – the first use of general anaesthetic in surgery was reported. From that time on, the use of anaesthesia was expanded and refined, opening the way to the development of ever more sophisticated surgery.

It was a thrilling time to be a student of medicine. In Edinburgh, George was in the heart of the action – the centre of new discoveries, of new procedures and new ways of thinking.

George was a solid but unremarkable student. In mid-1846 he sat for his first set of examinations. On 24 April, he completed a Latin test, which he passed with a grade of 'S.B.' (satisfactory to good). Although most of the medical exams were no longer conducted in Latin in Edinburgh, students were expected to be well 'acquainted' with the language. On Tuesday 5 May 1846, George sat for written exams in anatomy, chemistry, physiology and natural history, passing all with a 'satisfactory to good' result.

He also passed his oral examinations. George was assessed on a breathtaking range of details in anatomy, chemistry, physiology, and natural history, and was awarded a grade of 'satisfactory to good' for all. Then on 13 July, he submitted to – and passed – another round of oral assessment. It included a botany examination and a further chemistry examination, more physiology, and natural history.

George sat for another – and somewhat less satisfactory – major round of examinations three days later. In *Materia Medica*, his efforts were 'good', and in medical jurisprudence and midwifery 'sufficient'. His 'insufficient' grades in surgery, practical physic, prescriptions and pathology were improved by an oral examination a week later. He also had to re-sit a written test on prescriptions, passing the second time around. He passed his oral examination in midwifery and his written examination in surgery – with an admonishment for his spelling.

In 1846, George completed a thesis on tetanus. After four years of gruelling study, he qualified at last as a doctor. He paid the hefty sum of £25 (about the annual wage of a labourer) and earned the right to add the letters M.D. after his name. He was 21 years old: the minimum age at which a student could graduate as a doctor from Edinburgh.

Meanwhile, back in George's home village of Clady Beg in Armagh, life went on. George's brother, Alexander, had been born on 20 July 1843, when George was studying in Ireland. George may have never met this brother nor, almost certainly, his youngest sibling, Rachael. While George was immersed in his studies in Edinburgh, Rachael was born in Armagh, and baptised in the Tullyallen Presbyterian Church in 1845.

THE WORKING SURGEON

Upon his graduation, George took up work at sea. Perhaps he hoped from the start to become a well-paid surgeon-superintendent of an emigrant ship, or perhaps he simply sought adventure.

The British East India Company had existed in various incarnations since 1600, having been formed to share the benefits of the East Indian spice trade. It began as a trading body but later became involved in politics. By the middle of the 19th century, the East India Company was an important instrument of British imperialism in India. It had its own private armies to protect its interests, and through this military power it came to rule large areas of India. Its troops numbered in the hundreds of thousands.

The British East India Company engaged George Mitchell to give medical care to the troops during their conveyance to India. The company only employed surgeons who had obtained diplomas from the College of Surgeons in London, Edinburgh, Dublin or Glasgow. Preference was given to British residents of India and men with experience at sea. Given that George had no maritime experience, it is likely that his position was a junior one. He was, however, engaged for a few years in the service of the company, where he gained experience that would serve him well in his future career.[61]

Then late in 1848, according to Captain Kemp, George took up a position as assistant surgeon at the London Fever Hospital at St Pancras.[62]

The Fever Hospital was a busy place, in 1847 admitting over 1360 patients. Only servants and the 'decent poor' were patients here, paupers being sent to the workhouses and the wealthy being nursed in their homes. The hospital had been attached to the Smallpox Hospital until 1848, when it was rebuilt in Liverpool Road, Islington. The imposing, modern building opened in 1849 despite the locals' fears and protests about locating the 'deadly pest-house' in their neighbourhood. It may have been here, in the brand-new hospital, that George served as assistant surgeon.

The Fever Hospital served the whole of London and at times had trouble meeting the demand. If George was indeed employed at the Fever Hospital, he would have gained a wealth of experience. Typhus, scarlet fever and diphtheria were his daily fare. Here he would have put to good use all the wisdom he had acquired from doctors Alison, Christison and Henderson. The job would have been ideal training for George's next role as surgeon-superintendent on an emigrant ship. But nothing could truly prepare him for what lay ahead.

FIRST VOYAGE AS A SURGEON-SUPERINTENDENT

On 9 November 1848, a ship named the *Osprey* sailed from Deptford to Plymouth. There it picked up more passengers and left for Australia. On board the ship as surgeon-superintendent was Dr George Mitchell. While Dr Mitchell had gained experience of sea voyages during his years with the British East India Company, this was his first engagement with an emigrant ship. For a young, single man, it was a good career move that would pay well. He would start on a pay rate of ten shillings for every passenger who survived the voyage, and the rate would be higher on his third and subsequent voyages.

Dr Mitchell had 313 emigrants under his care. The *Osprey*'s captain was Andrew Petrie Honeyman who, like many of his passengers, was a Scot. It was a well-run ship; a 'noble vessel' much praised for the 'admirable arrangements and extreme cleanliness on board her'.[63]

The voyage was difficult. Foul weather tossed the vessel about mercilessly for the first third of the voyage, and dysentery broke out in the latter part. Despite the diligence of the captain and his surgeon-superintendent, ten passengers died.

'With regard to the voyage,' wrote one of the emigrants,

> I do not mind it at all, but the living is dreadful; this ought to be known. The meat was very bad; we were dieted according to the scale, with rice and peas, and only a ½ lb of flour for each adult, and 2 oz for children. I believe nine-tenths of the sickness was caused by the diet. I would seriously advise all who think of coming, to bring all the flour they can with them, also some onions, apples, suet, and a little brandy, this being useful for the sickness.[64]

When the *Osprey* arrived in Geelong on 21 March 1849, 13 patients remained under Dr Mitchell's care; one of these was a young woman who, having survived the rigours of the long voyage, died on board in Geelong Harbour three days after giving birth.[65]

The journalist who reported the ship's arrival hastened to assure readers that 'no contagious malady has ever made its appearance amongst them'.[66] The illnesses that had prevailed during the voyage and claimed ten lives were dismissed as 'trifling'. The authorities and members of the Immigration Board at Geelong inspected the ship and gave Dr Mitchell a certificate strongly recommending him for further employment.[67] The emigrants were released, and Dr Mitchell sailed with the *Osprey* back to England via Melbourne and Lima.

He was not long back in Britain when tragedy struck the Mitchell family. On 5 April 1850, George's father passed away. The *Armagh Guardian* mourned the loss of Alexander Mitchell who was 'for many years High Constable of this County'.[68]

As the eldest son, George was duty-bound to support his family. George's mother, Jane, remained on the land at Clady Beg. She now had a large family to care for alone; her daughter Elizabeth had just married and Mary was approaching adulthood, but at least four others were still children. George had stronger incentive than ever to earn a good income; one day he might want a wife and family of his own, but in the meantime, he was responsible for his mother and young siblings. His successful superintendence of the *Osprey* made him an excellent candidate for the role of surgeon-superintendent on further emigrant ships. George Mitchell and his widowed mother must have rejoiced at the good fortune that had given him this promising start on such a lucrative career.

As George boarded the *Emigrant* to take on the medical care of its passengers, he must have felt that he was well on the way to an exciting and successful life at sea.

Chapter 5

The long journey

April – August 1850

PASSING THE TIME

The *Emigrant*'s passengers were working-class people; they were used to keeping busy. Leisure time was a treat that few of them had previously experienced. But now, despite the rigid routines of cooking, cleaning and washing, the passengers found themselves for once enjoying the delicious luxury of free time.

How did they fill it? For health reasons, Dr Mitchell insisted they stay out in the open air as much as possible. They read and walked about the deck. Some penned letters home and others wrote journals.[69] Patrick Maunsell may have joined the other men as they fished and learned what skills they could from the sailors. They watched the strange wonders and changing shapes of the sea; they marvelled at the exotic fishes that surrounded the vessel. They told stories; they may have held debates or lectures; they might have played cricket or held concerts.

They chatted and learned each other's foibles, although they had been warned against the evils of gossip. 'I would entreat you to cultivate kindly feelings towards one another,' the tracts advised. 'There will be different dispositions among you, as in a family; but learn to bear and forbear; let there be no party feelings, no envyings, no jealousies.'[70]

The Wade girls, Catherine Maunsell and Mary Connor would have joined the other women on deck with their knitting, sewing and embroidering. They may have taken turns at reading Scripture aloud to each other. They played word games, sang and kept each other's spirits up by speculating about their future.

On Sundays, weather permitting, they attended church services on the poop deck. The passengers turned up after breakfast, around 10 or 11am, as fresh and clean as they could make themselves. Government-sponsored ships were required to provide regular Church of England services, but passengers weren't obliged to attend. Since the *Emigrant* carried neither a clergyman nor an official schoolmaster, Dr Mitchell (or perhaps Captain Kemp) would have read the services. He would have distributed Bibles, prayer books and hymn books that kept the passengers occupied until dinner time. In the afternoon, they passed the time by reading and singing.

Some – particularly Christian groups championing emigration – saw such voyages as opportunities for passengers to 'improve' themselves. They urged young people to use their leisure time to become more familiar with the Bible and develop their general knowledge. Those who could read and write were encouraged to tutor the illiterate.

Young children attended school. Dr Mitchell may have appointed a teacher from amongst the passengers. Normally the surgeon-superintendent chose a sober, educated man to be schoolmaster, who might in turn appoint helpers. The *Emigrant* carried one passenger who gave her occupation as 'governess': Fanny Burberow, the 18-year-old daughter of the matron. Fanny's name – like her mother's – was missing from the embarkation list of assisted migrants. It is possible that Fanny either paid her way or worked for her passage by employing her teaching skills. If the latter were true, she would have worked hard for her dues.

There were more than 60 children between the ages of two and 14 on board, a good many of whom would have attended the school. The two older Waterson children, eight-year-old Patrick and six-year-old Edward, would have taken their place in the 'schoolroom' along with the other young folk like Lucy and Alfred Brimble, and possibly even five-year-old Samuel Brimble. The youngest Waterson, two-year-old Elizabeth, was, of course, too young for school; she may have played upon the deck with the other toddlers or perched on her mother's lap as the women talked and knitted and sewed. The pregnant Louisa Brimble might have joined them with her two-year-old daughter.

School classes were held daily in the open air. Attendance was typically good, and prevented only by illness. For many children, this would be their best chance to receive regular instruction. Patrick Waterson, for instance, at eight, was still unable to read or write; these classes may have been his introduction to formal schooling. At home, parents needed their children's help on the farm; out here on the ocean, the demands on their time were fewer. School, for once, was accessible and an attractive alternative to spending long days in idleness.

Lessons began with reading, writing and arithmetic and may have gone on to include history and geography. Classes ran in the morning until the midday meal, and then resumed in the afternoon. Most likely, the same teacher would conduct Sunday School classes as well. In the evenings, classes may have been held for the young adults.

When the chores were done, and the meals were eaten, and

schooling and Divine Services were over, and fishing and needle-work and writing had worn thin, another pastime filled the long days: conversation. The travellers whiled away the hours on deck exchanging stories about their future home: Australia.

Amongst emigrants, their future home was a favourite topic of conversation. There was a never-ending supply of rumour. What was this wild and strange land really like? Tales of vast spaces, glorious sunshine, strange flowers and exotic fruits, bizarre animals, abundant work and easy riches were bandied about. There was fear, excitement and speculation. What would the future hold? Would the riches and good health they had been promised truly be theirs for the taking?

They expected to find good work easily. With employers so desperate for help, it was widely believed that Australian masters treated their workers more kindly than the British did, for fear of losing them. 'Mistresses are not so sassay [sic],' wrote a satisfied young woman of her situation, 'they are glad to get any person to work for them.'[71] These newcomers expected better wages and easier work than the poorly paid drudgery they had left behind. And they expected their wages to stretch further; they had been told that food – especially meat – was cheap. They expected to live well.

Emigration propaganda extolled the virtues of Australia's climate. Less damp and frigid than the United Kingdom, but lacking the enervating heat and humidity of Africa and the West Indies, Australia's climate was said to be beneficial to the health. 'No climate can be more salubrious than that of New South Wales,' wrote an emigrant in 1852. 'It is the climate for invalids. The air is bracing, pure, and balmy. The atmosphere, owing to its great capacity for absorbing moisture, is generally dry.'[72] Some reached absurdity in the excess of their praise.

The salubrity of Australia is proverbial. Of a community of 1200 persons, only five or six have been known to be sick at a time; and at some of the military stations seven years have elapsed without the loss of a man. Old people arrived in the colony from Europe have suddenly found themselves restored to much of the hilarity of youth; and I have seen several persons upwards of 100 years of age.[73]

Dubious claims such as 'such is the general healthiness of the people, that medical practitioners frequently complain that this climate affords but few chances for the exercise of their vocation . . .' might have been tempting to believe, however unlikely they were to be true.

Australia was pastoral country in which there was money to be made. Its steppes and plains were ideal for sheep farming, and its abundant mineral resources promised a prosperous future in the mining industry. In Moreton Bay, agriculture was starting to thrive. The land yielded generous crops of corn, potatoes, onions and tobacco. The opportunities seemed endless to the young men eager to make their fortunes. Perhaps they exchanged ideas and advice, or shared tips gleaned from relatives who had written home of their farming successes.

The flora and fauna of Australia were curiosities. 'Australia,' a correspondent marvelled,

is the land of contrarieties. It is the land of which it is extremely difficult to convey to a stranger an adequate idea. Everything here is different from what it is with you. We have summer when you have winter; we have day when you have night; we have our longest day when you have your shortest day; at noon we look north for the sun; we have our feet pressing hard nearly opposite to your feet. But these are not the only respects in which we differ from you: Nature, out of sheer spite to England, seems to have taken a delight in producing a complete dis-similarity between us; take the following examples: —Our swans are black, our eagles are white, our valleys are cold, our mountain tops are warm, our north winds are hot, our south winds are cold, our eastwinds are healthy, our cherries grow with the stone outside, our bees are without any sting . . . our birds without music, many of our flowers without any smell, most of our trees without shade, our population without any poor, our cuckoo coos only in the night, while our owl screeches or hoots only in the day-time, our moles lay eggs, and one of our birds (the Melliphaga) has a broom in his mouth instead of a tongue.[74]

But while some wrote of the differences between Australia and the United Kingdom, others were eager to reassure emigrants of the similarities. 'The towns look very like English ones, the English Language being spoken and the great bulk of the people being British it does not strike one much as a foreign country, and the less so as the Government is also British.'[75] Australia was just like Britain . . . but better.

Of the Indigenous people, outrageous tales were told. Propagandists hastened to reassure emigrants that the Aboriginal peoples of Australia were 'completely subdued' and 'seldom give us any trouble'. *The Emigrants' Penny Magazine* gave cruel descriptions of Australia's original inhabitants and informed its readers that the 'Austral Negro is a melancholy and pitiable specimen of humanity, and appears to occupy the lowest place in the scale of created beings, while the Caucasian family maintains its position at the top'. Nevertheless, the tract reported that these people were 'comparatively harmless, but manifest an extreme disinclination to adopt the usages of civilised life,' and lamented that 'the hope of rendering them useful as servants, or as labourers in cultivating the soil, is extremely small'.[76]

The stories of Australia were overwhelmingly positive. But they were tempered by words of warning. In a colony peopled largely by ex-convicts and adventurous young men, vice was a constant temptation – the two commonest evils being 'drunkenness and avarice'. A good income was so easy to come by through farming and stock work that education was a low priority, and society was unsophisticated as a result. And the disproportion of the sexes was 'another obstacle to the moral improvement of this colony'. Emigrants were cautioned to work hard, stay sober and pray. And all would be well. In short, as a satisfied settler wrote: 'In so limited a work as this, it is impossible to enumerate all the advantages which Australia holds out to intending emigrants.'[77]

23 APRIL – NEW LIFE

The *Emigrant* had been at sea for less than a week when the passengers celebrated a joyful event: the birth of a child. Anne Salisbury (or Sallisbury, née Mudford) was a 34-year-old native of County Somerset, England. She and her farm-labourer husband, Isaac, already had five children.

On 23 April, Anne gave birth to a healthy son. Seafarers were a superstitious lot; they saw the birth of a child on board as a harbinger of good luck and a high wind. Emigration authorities thought otherwise.

The risks to a voyager in a state of advanced pregnancy were serious. Pregnancy made women more susceptible to seasickness, often with dire consequences. It could trigger premature labour, for instance. Or a seriously reduced ability, in the mother's weakened state, to withstand the trials of labour. And if she and the infant survived the trauma of the birth, there was still the problem of breastfeeding; a wretched seasick mother might find herself unable to produce milk, and the feeble baby unable to suckle.

This would be disastrous, for a good substitute for mothers' milk was simply not available. A baby born on board would struggle to subsist on provisions from the surgeon's store: soft starchy foods such as rice, sago, semolina and preserved milk. For a baby born on board, the chances of survival were slim: less than half of that of an infant born prior to embarkation.

For this reason, any woman in late pregnancy was advised to wait until after the birth to sail. But the Passenger Act stopped short of *preventing* pregnant women from embarking. Many women ignored the advice and chose to travel despite advanced pregnancy – and not without some justification. This was an age when the rate of infant mortality was high anyway; 24.7 percent of children in the United Kingdom died before their fifth birthday. At sea or on land, the risks were great. Besides, on a government-sponsored emigrant ship a pregnant woman could enjoy the services of a qualified doctor *and* the opportunity to rest: both luxuries she could never have afforded at home.

At least six couples on the *Emigrant* had decided to take the gamble. The young Brimble couple, Andrew and Louisa, were expecting their second child, and the Halletts of County Somerset were expecting their sixth. William and Amelia Canning, a young couple from Bath, awaited the birth of their first. William, a draper, was 24 years old; his wife 23. They were two of only six Baptists on board. Then there were the Meara and Lipscombe families. Like the Salisburys who had just welcomed a baby, the Mearas were older parents – 38 and 32 – with a family already.

Timothy and Mary Meara were Irish Catholics from County Tipperary with two sons: 13-year-old James and ten-year-old John. The Lipscombes, on the other hand, were new to parenthood. Henry Lipscombe was a 22-year-old brickmaker from Surrey whose new wife Elizabeth was expecting their first baby.

For the Salisburys, the gamble appeared to be paying off. Their baby boy was born alive and well. His mother, Anne, was allowed to rest (as much as the sea and the cramped quarters would permit) and was attended by Dr Mitchell. Her diet was supplemented with stout or port wine – half a pint daily – which was considered essential for the health of a nursing mother and her baby.

While the sailors might have delighted in the good fortune that the birth portended, Mary and Joseph Ball and the other passengers in the married quarters had less reason to rejoice; they would now have to contend with the sounds and smells of yet another baby in their cramped lodgings. And the stink was appalling.

Nappies were in short supply. Emigrant mothers of infants were advised to bring large numbers of nappies – enough to last the voyage – made up from old linen, and to discard them overboard immediately after use. For steerage passengers, however, luggage restrictions made this advice impossible to follow.

In practice, Anne Salisbury *might* have been lucky enough to supplement her supply of nappies with linen from the surgeon's store. In any case, with the child's birth taking place so early in the voyage, there was a real danger of running out of nappies during the long months at sea. Anne would have changed them as seldom as possible. Like many mothers of infants at sea, she may also have refrained from tossing the used nappies overboard as advised, and chosen to stash them by the family's berth until washing day instead. With washing set for two days each week, the used nappies had plenty of time to infuse the already foetid air with their stench.

THE HALLETT FAMILY

Another family expecting a new arrival during the journey was the Halletts. The Halletts of County Somerset were a large family; they had five children already and were now expecting a sixth. Charles, a labourer, was 41, and his wife Hannah 43. They came from the village of Middle Chinnock, in the valley nestled between hills to the north and south, and the Broad River to the west. With a population of just under 600, Middle Chinnock was farming country. The flax and hemp industries were important to the village and, like many of his neighbours, Charles had spent some of his working life as a bleacher.[78]

The Halletts' eldest son, James, at 15 was registered separately on the passenger list as a single adult male. He had three younger brothers: Charles (aged 13), Henry (11), and George (four), and a seven-year-old sister, Ann (or Anne). One can only imagine what a struggle life must have been for the family in England, with Charles on a labourer's wage and so many mouths to feed. He might have earned only 10 shillings a week, and would have had to part with one or two of those shillings to pay the rent. A pound of butter would have cost him another shilling. While the older children had clearly had some schooling – they were able to read and write – James, at 15, was already expected to bring in a wage. If he had remained in England, he might well have entered the linen trade, an important industry in the district. If the children became weavers, as many in their district did, chances were they would develop lung diseases and die prematurely.

Despite Hannah's advanced pregnancy, this chance to emigrate must have seemed like a godsend. Certainly, the potential returns were great – as long as no ill-luck came their way. In their case, the advantages appeared to outweigh the risks by a long shot. Tragically, they lacked the benefit of hindsight.

2 MAY – THE FIRST DEATH

The days passed. A routine was well established; apart from a little seasickness, nothing untoward had happened. Then on 2 May, a baby who had been suffering from diarrhoea took a turn for the worse. By nightfall, little William Frith was dead. The second son of William and Emma Frith of Swineshead, Lincolnshire, was only eight months old.

For the family, the death was heartbreaking. No doubt for their fellow-passengers – especially those with small children – it was also a sobering reminder of their own vulnerability. Hannah Hallett may have held her little ones closer that night. But in their experience, infant deaths had always been sadly common, both on land and at sea. William's death was distressing but not a cause for alarm.

The baby had to be buried as soon as possible; at sea, funerals were not delayed.

Out of respect for the grieving family, Captain Kemp undoubtedly cancelled entertainments and music for the day. The Union Jack was flown at half-mast, and ship's bell tolled. The passengers gathered upon the deck. The men removed their hats and milled upon the deck, the poop, or even climbed the rigging to hear the burial service. As there was no clergyman on board, Dr Mitchell or Captain Kemp read the service.

William's tiny body had been sewn up in canvas with weights at his feet. The sailors put the little bundle onto a plank and carried it to the lee side of the ship, where they balanced it momentarily upon the bulwark. When the time came to commit the body to the deep, the captain gave the order to stop the ship. Then the sailors tipped up the board, and the bundle slid down it and fell with a splash into the ocean.

And then the mourners sang:

Funeral Hymn For a Christian at Sea
We therefore commit his body to the deep.
—Burial Service at Sea.

Why should we shrink, dear friends, to lay
Our brother in the wave?
The body can alone decay;
'Tis not the Spirit's grave.

Safe anchored from the storm of life,
Beneath the Saviour's Cross,
He feels no more the tempest's strife,
Heeds not the wild wave's toss.

Dear brother, though we now resign
Thy body to the deep,
No stone to mark the holy shrine,
No yew-tree o'er it sweep;

Thy memory still we shall retain,
Thy early loss deplore;
And strive that blissful land to gain,
Where thou art gone before.

Then, fare thee well!—we may not stay
O'er thy salt tomb to mourn;
Our ship is on her watery way,
To reach her distant bourne.
But though in that far land *we* sleep,
Within the church-yard gloom,
And *thou*, beneath the heaving deep,
Art laid in ocean tomb;

At the last day of solemn dread,
When all yield back their trust,
The sea gives up his living dead,
And earth her breathing dust;
Brother beloved! We then shall meet:
Again the theme prolong
Of Jesus' praise, in accents sweet,
And everlasting song.[79]

3–12 MAY – HEADING FOR THE TROPICS

The *Emigrant* carried on southward. As William Frith's little body drifted to rest on the ocean bed, the travellers resumed their daily routine. It was important not to dwell too long on what might have been.

They had been warned to prepare for extremes of climate, for on this voyage they would be both crossing the equator and nearing Antarctica. The temperature rose as they sailed past the island of Madeira. The tiny Portuguese-owned island lay off the western coast of Morocco and was a favourite stopover for vessels needing to re-stock with water. The vast mountains of the island rose steeply from the ocean, their vibrant colours impressing all passers-by with their majesty.

The *Emigrant* did not stop in Madeira but sailed gaily by. No doubt the passengers gathered on deck to enjoy their first sight of land in almost three weeks. And what a marvellous sight it was. 'The view of Madeira is exceedingly fine & romantic,' wrote one traveller, thrilling at the island's 'lofty cloud capp'd peaks,'[80] rugged cliffs and woods, and its rich blues and purples that mirrored the brilliance of the sea, presenting a sight that was breathtaking in its vividness and beauty.

The mountains of Madeira were not the only marvel on offer. In this part of the voyage the sparkling seas teemed with life; all manner of exotic creatures frolicked in the waves and filled the emigrants with wonder.

How the children must have delighted in the novelties of the sea. Dolphins leapt about the bows, and shoals of flying fish sprang from the sea upon 'wings quite transparent like gauze,'[81] their silvery bodies glistening with sunlight. The Hallett children may well have rushed to the sides of the vessel to watch their marvellous flight, while the seagulls shrieked and swooped, and the glittering fish, in their eagerness to escape, leapt upon the deck. Teenager James Hallett may have helped his younger siblings Anne, Charles, Henry and four-year-old George to chase and grasp the flying fish as they flapped and slithered. The flesh of the fish might later be served at their table, while their wings could be dried on cardboard to be kept as a souvenir or sent to friends back home.[82] With their mother Hannah about to bring yet another child into the family, to the Hallett children the world must have seemed a magical place.

At this latitude, the trade wind blew in from the north-east, and life on board was full of wonders. The men tried their hands at fishing, while Elizabeth Wade and the other ladies busied themselves with their sewing and crocheting under the shade of the awning that the crew had raised upon the poop. The weather was warm and full of promise.

Before long, the island of Tenerife came into view, its towering peak visible from a great distance across the ever-changing colours of the lively sea.

Now and then they may have encountered other ships. This was always a cause for excitement. In spite of the many chores and other occupations in which the passengers engaged, the endless routines and hours of idleness quickly became monotonous. But when another vessel came within sight, what a commotion! The crew would hoist their ensigns and send up skyrockets to prevent a collision. All passengers would crowd upon the deck to catch a glimpse. Perhaps the vessels would sail close enough to each other so that the voyagers could wish each other well. If they came across a ship that was 'homeward' bound – to the United Kingdom – they might even have the opportunity to send letters back to loved ones. They would scramble to fetch writing materials and envelopes, and dash off frenzied letters to be passed in a bag over to the north-bound vessel. And with mixed feelings they would farewell the ship again.

They sailed on towards the equator. The heat began to oppress. Elizabeth Wade, Catherine Maunsell and the other women dared not bare their arms or shoulders lest they compromise their reputations. Their flannel undergarments and ankle-length skirts, fitted bodices and high necklines became almost unbearable.

It was so hot and airless in steerage that the women dreaded descending at night; they stayed as long as possible upon the deck, savouring the breeze and admiring the stars that seemed so much larger than the stars in England. It was so hot that they put bed time off until the latest possible hour; and then some would lie sleeplessly tossing in their bunks, their clothes drenched with sweat, while others gave up and lay down upon the timber floor. It was so hot that in the mornings they rose early, eager to escape the foul air that was like a warm soup of body odour and toilet vapours, and clamoured up through the hatches to the fresh air on deck.

The men suffered less; at night they were allowed on deck, and when the heat became too much to bear, they would bathe and sometimes even sleep naked under the stars. Like the women, they tried to keep busy, but the manner of their industry was different. The men helped with the daily running of the ship, assisting the crew with the adjustments to sails and operating the pumps to keep water from the hold.

Here in the tropics, some captains were unlucky enough to experience the 'doldrums', when the wind withheld its breath and day after day passed with no relief from the sweltering heat. Discomfort, frustration and boredom would shorten tempers and trigger arguments. This Torrid Zone was one of the more dangerous sections of the voyage, where even healthy children were most susceptible to fevers and infections. But it seemed as though the passengers of the *Emigrant* would be lucky; the wind kept up and bore them on steadily through the iridescent tropical sea.

12 MAY: ILLNESS STRIKES

On 12 May[83] the *Emigrant* glided past the Cape Verde Islands. It was then that the contagion that had been up to this point dormant in steerage emerged.

Catherine Maunsell, the 22-year-old servant girl from Mountshannon, sister of fellow-traveller Patrick, began feeling unwell. If the course of her disease was typical, it can be supposed that Catherine could not eat; she was nauseated and prostrated with fatigue. Her head became heavy and her limbs ached. Despite the rapidly increasing warmth that drew the other women to the breezy shade of the awning, Catherine shivered. And when she was not shivering, she was sweating with the effects of a fever.

Dr Mitchell examined the girl and removed her from the steerage quarters to the female 'hospital' compartment of the ship. There were separate hospitals for men and women, located fore and aft. In the hospital, Catherine had a little more privacy and comfort and the chance to rest and recuperate. Dr Mitchell would be in regular attendance and give her the best treatment that medical science had to offer. But, with all the wisdom of his experience and training, her symptoms must have horrified him.

Over the next few days, Catherine's temperature rose. She became flushed and her eyes grew bleary. A pale rosy rash blossomed upon her chest and spread to the rest of her body, darkening to a dull red as it took over every inch but the palms of her hands and the soles of her feet. The rash confirmed Dr Mitchell's dreadful diagnosis: *Typhus*.

SHIP FEVER

Typhus is a potentially deadly disease caused by infection with one or more *rickettsial* bacteria. Spread by infected lice, it is one of the most devastating diseases in human history. It causes fever, cough, a rash, delirium and, in many cases, death. Severe outbreaks ravaged the populations of France and Ireland during the Napoleonic Wars and the Irish Potato Famine. It caused millions of deaths during the First World War and was epidemic in the refugee camps and Nazi concentration camps of the second. In modern times, its grip upon humanity has weakened but the disease has not yet been eradicated. In the 19th century, typhus – especially amongst the poorer folk – was rife.

In 1850, the cause was unknown. Theories about its origin and method of transmission abounded. It was widely (and wrongly) believed that typhus could be directly transmitted from one individual to another. (Typhus is not directly contagious but rather the disease is spread by the infected lice moving from victim to victim.) In the middle of the 19th-century doctors proposed that a 'peculiar change in the blood' was responsible for a victim's suffering. 'This change in the blood,' wrote Magnus Huss, M.D.,

> is caused by the introduction into the system of some foreign matter, sometimes a miasm, sometimes a contagion, sometimes a decided poison (putrid water, putrid food). It is this foreign matter, introduced by means of the respiratory or digestive act (by the reception into the stomach of putrid water or food), that alters the blood in its chemical composition and vital power.[84]

There was no shortage of agents to blame for its cause. 'Poor living, a confined, stagnant atmosphere, grief, and other depressing passions of the mind, sedentary living, intemperance, excessive indulgence in the use of intoxicating liquors, profuse evacuations, and exposure to cold, united with moisture'[85] were all held responsible.

While physicians disagreed in their theories as to the cause of the illness, they were unanimous on one point: typhus thrived in crowded, filthy places. Typhus was – and is – a 'disease of poverty, deprivation and misery' and 'its subjects the houseless poor and the ill-befriended emigrant'.[86]

It proliferated in gaols and amongst the weary, malnourished troops during times of war. It loved the crowded tenements of London and the damp, squalid hovels of the poor Irish. It thrived in the close, airless confines of the steerage quarters on an emigrant ship.

The organism that causes typhus was not identified until 1916. It is now known that the bacterium *Rickettsia typhi* is usually transmitted to humans through the bites of infected fleas and lice. When a louse sucks the blood of a person with typhus, the *Rickettsia* enters its gut. When its host gets too hot from fever or dies, the louse crawls from the body to find a new host. It might also reach its new host when the doctor or other carer removes the clothing from an infected person and scatters the vermin about. The louse then bites its next victim and excretes the *Rickettsiae* in its faeces. The new host scratches the itchy lesion and inadvertently rubs the louse's infected faeces into the wound. In this way, the disease enters the new host's bloodstream.

Typhus should not be confused with the disease *typhoid*. By the mid-19th century, medical science had already made this distinction. Their symptoms are similar, but their causes and methods of transmission are not. While typhus is carried by infected lice or fleas, typhoid is caused by consuming food or water contaminated with the bacterium *Salmonella typhi*. Both diseases can be fatal.

Even in 1850, when the cause of typhus was unknown, physicians understood that its spread could be minimised by proper sanitation and ventilation. But lice are hardy creatures. And although the emigrants' clothing and bodies had been washed and scrubbed at the Emigration Depot, infected vermin had managed to hitch a ride on one or other of them. And the crowded, airless hull of the barque provided a perfect environment for it to flourish.

During the preceding decades, typhus had taken a terrible toll on travellers in emigrant ships. During the mass exodus of poor Irish to Canada and America in 1847–1848, it had killed an estimated 20,000. It was Captain Kemp's proud claim that he had only lost one passenger during that ghastly epidemic.

Likewise, Dr George Mitchell was only too familiar with the disease. He had worked at the London Fever Hospital, where hundreds of cases of typhus were treated every year. George knew what typhus could do. And he knew that the confinements of a ship amplified the danger. His dismay can be imagined.

And lacking the vital knowledge about typhus' cause, the doctor was powerless to prevent its spread. Despite his best efforts, over the next few days, three more young women began complaining of illness. They would have suffered nausea and headache, chills and fever, abdominal pain and backache, vomiting and diarrhoea. The light hurt their eyes and a cough troubled them; their skin became hot and dry; they were thirsty; they were felled by headaches and joint and muscle pain, and sank into confusion and delirium. And then the rosy rash appeared upon their chests.

One of the women who fell ill was Mary Meara (or O'Meara), the 32-year-old mother of three. Mary was the wife of Timothy Meara, a farm labourer from Ireland's County Tipperary. Their sons, James and John, aged 13 and ten, had embarked with them, and an infant daughter, Mary, appears to have been born on the voyage.[87]

George Mitchell spared no effort to save the women.

These days, typhus can be cured with antibiotics. In 1850, medical science recommended myriad treatments. None of them was effective. Dr Mitchell would have employed the most popular methods of the time, which included purging of the bowels or bloodletting, either by opening a blood vessel or applying leeches.

In an attempt to reduce fevers, he would have sponged the patients' bodies with water and vinegar. Administration of wine and other 'stimulants' was a commonly accepted practice.

It was generally agreed in the medical profession that the first matters to attend to in cases of typhus were ventilation and fumigation. The environment in steerage, of course, precluded the former. Undoubtedly Dr Mitchell redoubled all efforts to fumigate the ship. He may have administered emetics, designed to 'clear' the stomach and 'relax' the skin, in the early stages. Patients were to be kept quiet and free from mental exertion. Dr Mitchell may have dispensed various tonics: muriatic acid or a chamomile infusion, draughts of quinine or laudanum, opium, sweet-wort, yeast, or even cayenne pepper. To relieve cold extremities, he might have applied hot water bottles or mustard poultices. If the sufferer had diarrhoea, Dr Mitchell might have made her a pill of the compound powder of ipecacuan.

The patients were encouraged to eat, but not to excess. Dr Mitchell had no access to the fresh fruit and starchy vegetables that were recommended; instead he may have resorted to arrowroot, sago and bread. Meat was avoided. Patients were allowed to drink freely to quench their thirst.[88]

But treatments were ineffectual. No matter how earnestly Patrick Maunsell may have prayed for his sister's health, or how anxiously Mary Meara's family waited for news, Dr Mitchell had no cure to offer them. Some sufferers lived and some died; medical intervention did little to alter the disease's course.

MID-MAY

An outbreak of disease was alarming, but it was no reason to abandon the carefully planned routines of shipboard life.

If anything, routines would help to soothe and reassure, to bolster the spirits. And now, with the spectre of disease lurking, procedures that maintained hygiene were more important than ever.

About four weeks into a typical voyage, the emigrants' belongings were stiff and threadbare, and it was time to bring the spare luggage up from the hold. It was time to put aside their well-worn garments – which must, despite all precautions, have been starting to smell bad – and don some fresh, clean clothing. Blessed relief! This was a welcome distraction from both the tedious routine of shipboard life and the scare of fever.

Bringing up the boxes was no simple matter. The crew had to wait for fine weather so they could open the hatchways and get access to the hold. Grasping lanterns, they and a group of male passengers descended into the bowels of the ship to retrieve some 200 boxes and drag them up onto the deck.

From the moment the boxes emerged, the passengers were upon them 'all in a bustle', seeking the luggage labelled with their names, seizing the items with glee. 'Nobody can form any idea of the bustle and confusion there is on these days,' wrote Fanny Davis on the 1858 voyage of the *Conway*. This was an opportunity to put away the worn and dirty clothes and bring out new finery, to brush out clean dresses and bonnets and start afresh.

Some may have been dismayed to discover their clothing spoiled. People who had foolishly stashed jam or other foodstuffs with their other belongings may have found their clothing stained by leakage. Whether the news was happy or sad, the business occupied them all, providing a welcome break from monotony and fear.

Unfortunately, the respite was brief, for typhus was gathering strength.

LATE MAY

Over the days that followed, Catherine Maunsell's fever peaked and waned. It began to appear as if she might recover. Two of the other young women followed suit, their recovery a few steps behind Catherine's. Poor Mary Meara, however, sank further. Weakened by childbirth, her symptoms deepened. Her breathing would have slowed and thickened as her lungs filled with fluid and, exhausted, her mind gave in to delirium. Then she slipped into unconsciousness.

Within days, death visited the *Emigrant* for a second time. But, shockingly, this death was not Mary Meara's and it was not caused by typhus.

Sometime in the preceding weeks – mid-May – Hannah Hallett of County Somerset had given birth to her sixth child: a son. The joy that this baby's birth had brought was sadly short-lived. On 24 May, his mother Hannah died suddenly of 'apoplexy'. She left behind a stunned and grieving husband and six children. The eldest, James, was 15, and the youngest only a week or two. Without a mother to feed him, the infant's chances of survival were slim. And if he *did* survive, his future looked bleak. Hannah's husband Charles, now a widower, faced almost impossible decisions: who would care for the little ones while he worked? How would he earn enough to feed, clothe and house them all, teach them and protect them from harm? James was almost an adult and could bring in an income, and Charles junior, at 13, would soon be old enough to work as well – but Henry, Anne and George, at 11, seven and four, would need more attention than a man of his generation could easily give them. They had no relatives in the colony, no one to share the load. How Charles must have despaired. How his children must have wept.

Once more the passengers gathered upon the deck and

climbed the rigging to witness the committal of the deceased; once more the bell tolled, the surgeon (or the captain) read the burial service and the emigrants sang a farewell hymn. The crew tipped Hannah's body, sewn into canvas and weighted with metal, feet-first into the glittering sea.

On the day after Hannah Hallett's death – 25 May – Mary Meara passed away. Her funeral must have been a grim occasion. The third death in a little over three weeks, and the first from the dreaded disease that still lurked in the female hospital beds. Deaths at sea were not unusual. Life in Victorian times under any conditions was a precarious thing. But when death struck repeatedly, and when it lay in wait so stealthily on board the vessel in which the community was captive, it was deeply disturbing. And although these people of the Victorian era were familiar with death, burials at sea were foreign to them. The burial followed the death so quickly – sometimes within hours – that those left behind had barely the time to say farewell; moreover, there was no coffin and no grave to mark the place where the deceased lay. These funerals were bewildering and heartbreaking.

After living in such close quarters for the past weeks, the other families must have mourned Mary Meara's passing as if she was one of their own. The Watersons in particular, fellow-Irish from the same county in similar circumstances, must have felt her loss keenly. Typically after a death at sea, the passengers would take up a collection to give the family left behind. It may have helped, but it did nothing to dispel the shadow of death that followed them across the ocean.

✳

Two days later, the *Emigrant* crossed the equator, or the 'line', as it was better known by seafaring types. Despite the heat, this was a part of the passage that normally held many attractions for travellers. 'Now in the evening,' wrote Fanny Davis in 1858, 'we amuse ourselves watching the sky . . . the sky tonight is perfectly beautiful, it looks like a large flock of sheep lying down. They call it the shepherd and his flock. The moon shines brilliantly – how we do enjoy the evenings'.[89] The birds were exotic and beautiful, the flying fish magical, the sunsets 'brilliant'.

At night, the people would gather upon deck to watch the moon rise and to marvel at the heavens. A milestone had been reached, and it was marked by a change in the night sky. No longer did the 'Great Bear' and Orion's Belt shine down upon them, but new and wonderful constellations like the Southern Cross. Elizabeth Wade might well have looked upon the night sky with excitement and fear, as its strangeness reminded her of her rapidly changing circumstances.

Crossing the 'line' was usually an occasion for a traditional ritual. A sailor dressed as King Neptune would 'enter' the ship and demand that certain members of the crew or passengers be lathered, shaved, and then plunged into a bath. It was a playful occasion: a celebration and a welcome break from routine. It was the marking of a turning point – a historic moment.

But the *Emigrant* sailed across the line carrying the mark of death. Three people had died so far, including one who had perished from a disease that still lingered on board. With Mary Meara so recently deceased, it is hard to imagine the crew indulging in these frivolous games. More likely that, out of respect, they guided the vessel quietly, without fanfare, into the southern hemisphere.

The barque made good progress. Likewise, the patients remaining in the female hospital were coming along nicely; their fevers had broken and they showed every appearance of making a full recovery. A few more cases of fever were reported, but they were mild, and Dr Mitchell was able to guide their sufferers towards speedy recovery. The exhausted young doctor was elated. It seemed that the worst was over. One death from typhus was tragic, but if the toll could be limited to one, then the voyage could be considered a success. The oppressive heat of the tropics would soon be behind them; the hospitals would be 'clean' once more, and the emigrants could look forward again to their new lives in the antipodes. Dr Mitchell's relief was profound.

But it was also premature.

3 JUNE – 2 JULY

Catherine Slattery was the infant daughter of Edmund (or Edward) and Alice (Alley). Like the Mearas and the Watersons, the Slatterys were Roman Catholics from County Tipperary. They had boarded the *Emigrant* with two children, but they would disembark with only one: their five-year-old son, Thomas. Little Catherine fell victim to the dreadful malady that claimed the lives of so many Victorian infants: diarrhoea. She slipped away on 3 June and, to the mournful strains of the passengers' farewells, she was tipped into the ocean to join William Frith, Hannah Hallett and Mary Meara.

The diminished Slattery family would later have a brief and unpleasant stay in Brisbane – a stay that was cut short by altercations with a bullying and lecherous employer. They would settle in Sydney, where Edward would take up work as a policeman. He would die in 1860, leaving Alice with four small children. Young Thomas would grow up to work as a solicitor and serve for 15 years in the Legislative Assembly, but his colourful and controversial nature and legal transgressions would bring his career to an ignominious end.

But the Slattery family's future, of course, was unknown on that sad day when they left their baby behind on the ocean bed. The barque sailed on, bearing its cargo of still-hopeful emigrants ever closer to their new lives.

On 8 June, Elizabeth Wade celebrated her nineteenth birthday. On some voyages, the captain might allocate extra provisions on special occasions like Christmas or birthdays. But Elizabeth was a poor, young, steerage passenger – a nobody. And following so close on the heels of the deaths of four of her fellows, a lavish celebration would have been out of the question. If the anniversary was marked at all, it was likely in a subdued manner.

Two weeks after the passing of little Catherine Slattery, death claimed yet another infant. On 18 June, the deceased Hannah Hallett's new baby boy died, also from diarrhoea. With no mother to feed him, the odds had been against his survival right from the start. The little boy was only a month old. His widowed father, Charles, perhaps afraid to hope that his son might survive to adulthood, had not named him.

On the day before the baby's death, another passenger fell ill. Poor Matron Burberow – Mary – had been 'brought very low from nervous debility', and no wonder; she had had to endure seasickness and adjust to the dreadful conditions of the steerage quarters; she had witnessed five deaths, and she had lived in fear of the deadly disease that lurked behind every bulkhead, under every mattress, upon the deck, in the breath of every passenger. And on top of this, she held a position of heavy responsibility. It was *her* job to ensure that the young single women – all 50 or so of them – reached Moreton Bay with their health and reputations intact.

A fever found its way to poor Mrs Burberow. For a few days she burned with it until, on 19 June, she breathed her last.

Dr Mitchell attended her and declared the cause of her death to be 'decay of nature'. Mary Burberow was 56 years old. Her 18-year-old daughter, Fanny, would have to make her own way in her new home.

She wouldn't make a success of it. After suffering a bout of typhus, Fanny would recover and arrive in Brisbane alone with no friends or relatives in the colony. She would take up residence in Ipswich and, on 20 July 1852, marry Joseph Longman.[90] The marriage would be disastrous; within just four months Fanny would desert her husband. The indignant Joseph would publicly declare that Fanny had left him 'without any just cause',[91] and that he would not be answerable for any debts that she incurred. Fanny's fate thereafter is unknown. It is likely that she left the district. She may have changed her name or married again.

Six deaths. One older woman, three infants and two young women, both of whom had recently given birth. And the threat of typhus still lay hidden in every corner.

Death was not unexpected on a voyage of this length, and typically, after a funeral, the emigrants would try to put grief behind them. They would return to the shipboard routines and focus on the future which, after all, still promised glorious things – for most. But every death was a blow, and each body consigned to the deep took with it some of the hope that the ship had carried from Plymouth. Gloom began to settle and fear to grow.

With the matron now resting on the ocean floor, the reputation of the Wade girls and other young ladies was in grave danger. Matron's death caused consternation amongst the unmarried women. It was the kindly Mrs Kemp who took the girls under her wing. She 'paid every attention to the emigrants, particularly the young females and children,' wrote emigrant Jane T. Cullen. 'When the matron died she came down to us and saw that we were all well, and attended to the rules of the ship.' The captain's wisdom and compassion were also appreciated by the stricken emigrants. 'Certainly government could not have sent us under a better or more humane person than Mr Kempe [sic]. We were most fortunate to have Mrs Kempe on board; and I must say that my sisters and I would have felt the loss of a kind father and mother were it not for Mr and Mrs Kempe.'[92]

The ship carried on southward. As she put some distance between herself and the equator, temperatures began to fall, and Captain Kemp and Dr Mitchell hoped that the change might bring better fortune. If only the toll would stop at six . . .

The *Emigrant* sailed on past the southernmost point of Africa. 'The Cape of Good Hope' it was called, and how Captain Kemp must have prayed that hope would indeed find them there. But the emigrants continued to fall ill.

They veered east around the cape, heading into the Southern Ocean. 'The voyager to Australia looks forward to his arrival off this cape with peculiar interest,' wrote one diarist, 'for to him it is a kind of half-way house, and as soon as it is passed, and the vessel's bows directed eastward, every degree tells rapidly towards shortening the voyage.' [93]

Here more wonders of nature were to be seen; cape pigeons flocked about the ship, and large black cape hens, whose heads and beaks and webbed feet resembled ducks', flew and swam around the vessel. The majestic albatross was commonly seen in these parts. It was a favoured pastime of the men to 'fish' for the great birds by fastening meat to a hook and attaching it to a piece of wood, which they floated over the stern. When the albatross tried to swallow the bait, the men would haul it onto the deck amid much merriment. It was here also that travellers might catch a glimpse of the whales, their spouts blowing triumphantly a mile from the ship, and then their great forms shimmering close by. For people like Henry and Mary Waterson and their three children, who came from landlocked Tipperary and might never have seen the sea before, these sights must have seemed truly miraculous.

But Dr Mitchell and Joseph Ball had no time to admire these wonders; they were kept busy day and night, attending to the sick who were filling the hospital beds at an alarming rate. To make matters worse, this was typically another difficult phase of the voyage, when the wind picked up and the sea churned; the ship would roll with the waves and her sails would crack, her masts groan and her sides creak. Cold weather was approaching. The surgeon dreaded the increased susceptibility to disease that could be expected as the ship progressed through the freezing temperatures of the Southern Ocean. But Mrs Kemp did not give up hope. 'Our hospitals now began to look fearful, although we were in hopes that the cold weather would put a stop to its progress,' she wrote.[94]

Dr Mitchell continued to bleed his patients, to purge their bowels, to sponge them with vinegar and water, and to dole out wine. What was more, there was still discipline to uphold and now, more than ever, it was vital to keep the ship clean. Someone had to ensure that the decks were scrubbed and the bedding washed and aired. These responsibilities fell to Dr Mitchell, and yet his attention was demanded in the hospitals. He was desperate for help.

This was when Joseph Ball, stepfather to the Wade girls and the surgeon's assistant, came into his own. Joseph was of great help and comfort to Dr Mitchell, struggling through the ordeal 'in a most wonderful manner'.[95]

Perhaps Joseph passed a basin to the surgeon as he bled his patients, or doused the sufferers with vinegar to soothe their fevers, or held cups of wine to their lips, washed their gangrenous wounds, or turned them over in their beds to relieve their pressure sores. Perhaps he gave them opiates for their pain or held a bowl before them while they vomited.

There was too much work for two men. John Farmer, a 49-year-old farm labourer from East Langton and father of seven, needed no prompting to help. Captain Kemp marvelled at the untiring labours of this 'aged married man', wondering at how he bore the fatigue. George Heuston, a 26-year-old labourer from Dr Mitchell's home county of Armagh, also willingly gave his help to the sick and dying in hospital.

But these men were in the minority. The other passengers were terrified. They wanted nothing more than to keep as far as possible from the sick. It was a torment to be confined on a ship with this terrible and mysterious disease amongst them and no prospect of escape. Dr Mitchell struggled to find anyone to help him, despite employing the 'utmost persuasion'.

A few *were* persuaded: Ann Campbell, Ann Ford (or Forde) and Charlotte Hardwidge attended the sick, and several of the men gave a hand in the hospital. Patrick Maunsell, the bright and industrious 23-year-old labourer from Mountshannon, was also eager to assist. His younger sister Catherine, who had been the first to fall ill, was by now recovering.

The surgeon and his helpers struggled on, and the dread amongst the passengers continued to mount. But the worst was yet to come.

3–22 JULY

On 3 July, typhus claimed another victim. Ann Cunningham was the next to fall. She was a single woman: a Roman Catholic from

Westmeath, Ireland. Her 33-year-old brother, Peter (an illiterate farm labourer), was also on board. The brother and sister, whose parents were both deceased, had been hoping for a new life in the colony where their cousin had settled in Sydney before them.

Ann's death opened the floodgates.

Mary Waterson, the 26-six-year-old Irish mother of three, developed symptoms of a violent cold. Her malaise and cough rapidly worsened. Soon poor Mary was showing worrying signs: headache, joint and muscle pains, fatigue, fever ... and the dreaded rash. How fearfully her husband Henry and his three children must have watched as Mary slipped into delirium. Patrick was only eight years old; his brother, Edward, was six, and little Elizabeth only two. How anxiously they must have prayed for their mother's recovery.

Mary died on 10 July. Another canvas-shrouded body slid along the plank and splashed into the sea. The seventh death.

Over the following days, two more fell ill with the 'violent cold' that had afflicted poor Mary. The first was James Chapple, a 31-year-old labourer and one of the few Wesleyans on board. James and his wife, Julia, hailed from Ermington, Devonshire, and had brought three young children on the voyage: six-year-old Thomas, four-year-old James, and baby Robert. By the time that he developed full-blown typhus and died,[96] Ann Gleeson had also caught the same 'violent cold'.

Ann was 29 and a mother of two. Her husband, Thomas, was an Irish Catholic farm labourer of Newmarket, County Clare. Their two daughters were only aged seven and four. As with Mary Waterson and James Chapple, Ann's 'cold' turned out to be something far more sinister: typhus. Ann died on 22 July.

Now there were ten dead. Four children had been left motherless and one without a father.

The months at sea moulded the body of passengers into a community. For weeks on end they had shared each other's hopes and fears. Friendships had been formed; even illicit romances were in the making. Living as they did in such close quarters, they had no privacy and few secrets. Each death was a blow, not just to the immediate families of the deceased, but to the community. And each death posed the question: who would be next?

24 JULY – 5 AUGUST: BASS STRAIT

The *Emigrant* sailed on eastward across the Southern Ocean, making her way towards the southwestern tip of Australia. It was mid-winter by the time the *Emigrant* crossed the Southern Ocean, and the extreme heat of only a few weeks ago was replaced by bitter cold. During this part of the voyage, it was not unusual to sail through rain, fog, sleet, hail and snow.

A few weeks earlier, as they had crossed the equator, descending the ladder into steerage had felt like sinking into Hell; now, the compartment was a refuge from the icy winds on deck. 'Now is the time we begin to enjoy our bed as it is the only place we can keep warm,' wrote Fanny Davis of the *Conway*.[97]

Even in bed it was hard to get warm, despite the stoves that hung from the beams and gave off smoky odours. The passengers' fingers and toes swelled and ached with chilblains. 'The wind cuts down our hatchway and nearly blows the hair off our heads and we are obliged to sit with a thick shawl on and even then we cannot keep a spark of warmth in us,' Fanny Davis continued.

They were entering the last leg of the journey. Three months had passed at sea, and, with luck, only a few weeks remained. This was a time when passengers began to look forward to their arrival, to make plans, to prepare for the 'New World'. The crew scraped the masts and cleared the deck; the passengers sorted their meagre belongings and talked hopefully about their futures. Would they secure employment? Would they find husbands? Would they make their fortunes?

On this voyage, even more than on most, land was eagerly anticipated. To be away from the confines of the ship, where lethal gases lurked so ominously! To be in the fresh mild air of Australia; to escape from the ghastly contagion!

The emigrants kept their eyes on the horizon. Even the Waterson and Hallett children, so recently bereaved, must have searched for signs of land with renewed hope. Even now, though motherless, they must have longed for the reassurance that their journey so far had not been in vain. The coastline shimmered in and out of view, and land birds flew onto the rigging. All eyes sought out the signs: the birds, the changing patterns of the waves, the seaweed in the foam. 'At length the cry of "Land!" is heard, and echoed throughout the ship.'[98]

The barque continued eastward, cutting across from one endpoint of the arc formed by the Great Australian Bight to the other. On the ninety-eighth day at sea, the *Emigrant* entered Bass Strait. It was at this time, when Dr Mitchell and his helpers were wretched with exhaustion, and looking forward so desperately to the end that seemed so close at hand, that the dreadful disease unleashed its full fury.

They entered Bass Strait on 24 July. The wind became 'light and foul' and the ship's progress slackened. More passengers complained of headaches and nausea; fevers plagued them; rashes erupted and delirium prevailed.

Both male and female hospitals filled up with dozens of the sick, and still more succumbed. Poor Dr Mitchell was at his wits' end. He extended the hospitals, taking over some of the steerage bunks for use by the stricken. Joseph Ball, John Farmer and George Heuston worked by his side day and night to give relief to the sick. Others lent a hand: John Shears, George Willis, James Buckley, John Williams and John Clarke Foote.

They sailed on through Bass Strait then turned northward to follow the east coast of Australia up towards Moreton Bay, hampered all the way by light and variable winds. But while the ship's progress flagged, death gained speed.

On 26 July, Ann Charlton passed away. She was a 20-year-old single domestic servant from Leicestershire. On the same day, George Hayward died. Two days later, young Sophia Brimble was the next to fall. She was only 17 years old, one of the large Brimble clan who had embarked together: sister of Andrew and servant to her father's cousin, John. The next day – 29 July – Ann[99] Connor died. Ann was the 25-year-old wife of James Connor, a Wesleyan gardener from Tipperary, whose niece (Mary Connor) was also on board. Ann left behind an infant son. The bodies of the dead were consigned, one after the other, to the deep.

It was not only the passengers who suffered. It was probably during this period, when typhus raged through the vessel like a hurricane, that Mrs Kemp fell ill. 'When the fever was very bad . . . she came among us until she caught the contagion, and was very ill for some time,'[100] wrote emigrant Jane T. Cullen. On so small a ship and so long a voyage, many of the passengers would have become personally known to Captain Kemp, and their deaths must have grieved him. But now even his own wife was ill and his young daughter at risk. The disaster of typhus had become personal to him.

And then the fever attacked the crew. James Lancaster was a supernumerary seaman: a seaman engaged temporarily, rather than as a contracted sailor. As the *Emigrant* sailed up along Australia's east coast, Lancaster fell prey to the disease.

Lancaster was one of around 40 crew.[101] The life of a sailor was neither easy nor well-paid. Seamen signed up for a return voyage (for up to two years), and penalties for deserting were harsh. During their time of service, no alcohol was allowed, and the crew were required to sign an agreement to 'conduct themselves in an orderly, faithful, honest, careful and sober manner, and to be at all times diligent in their respective duties and stations'.[102] Wages ranged from the healthy sum of £5 50s per calendar month for the first mate right down to a meagre ten pence per month for midshipmen. Most of the seamen were paid about £2 per month – about the equivalent of a farm labourer's pay.

No officers or seamen received wages until their discharge, and their pay could be docked for any infringements of the rules: absence from the ship at port without permission, neglect of duty, wilful or neglectful damage, loss or embezzlement of any articles belonging to the ship, or incompetence. For refusing to join the ship after signing the agreement, or being absent without leave, a man could face up to 30 days' imprisonment. The work was hard and dangerous. Seamen worked long hours without respite, regardless of weather conditions. Accidents such as falls from the rigging were not uncommon. Seamen received similar rations to the emigrants, and were, like the emigrants, susceptible to disease.

It was not surprising that the fever found its way to James Lancaster, given the close confines of the ship. The male passengers were often in the company of the sailors; male migrants were expected to help with the running of the ship. And although friendships between the crew and *female* passengers were strictly forbidden, bonds invariably formed between the crew and the male migrants. The sailors regaled the men with seafaring stories and tales of Australia; they taught them how to fish and to navigate and to identify the strange birds, the sea creatures and the stars.

When passengers died, the crew mourned as well. And when the supernumerary seaman James Lancaster died on 31 July, no doubt the passengers grieved. His death was the fifteenth since the voyage had begun.

The next to die was Catherine[103] Loder, who was only 15 when she embarked on the voyage with her sisters and brother-in-law. Her sister, Martha Loder, was an 18-year-old domestic servant from Salisbury, Wiltshire. The two single girls were accompanied by their older sister, Maria Trowbridge, and Maria's 30-year-old farm labourer husband, Josiah. The women had left living parents behind in Salisbury to seek better lives in Australia. Catherine died on 3 August at the age of 16. As her sisters joined the miserable gathering of mourners on deck, they may already have had an inkling of more suffering to come: Catherine's married sister, Maria, was soon to feel the effects of the fever herself.

THE BLOXAMS

Fanny Bloxam was the mother of three children: John (aged 14), 12-year-old Anne, and ten-year-old Thomas. Fanny, like her husband Thomas, was from County Galway. Thomas senior was an illiterate weaver in the flax-growing parish of Inniscealtra (Inishcaltra or Inis Cealtra), who had been struggling to support his family on an acre of land. His parish had been hit hard by the famine. Between 1841 and 1851, starvation and emigration had reduced its population from 2510 to 1457.

Like many in their parish, the Bloxams were Protestants. Their home was the village of Mountshannon (not to be confused with the Mountshannon in Limerick County, which was the home of the Maunsells). The Bloxams depended on the linen industry which, by 1850, was struggling. Thomas would have worked long hours and been poorly paid. Conditions in the factories were damp, noisy and hot, and mortality rates were high.

According to emigration records, the Bloxam's oldest child John, at 14, was already a farm labourer. No doubt witnessing the endless drudgery of his father's life would have been great incentive for him to reach for something better. John's life would hold many trials, beginning with a poverty-stricken childhood. In his next stage – his adolescence – he would have to contend with bereavement.

John's mother, Fanny Bloxam, died from typhus on 5 August – only three days before the *Emigrant* reached Moreton Bay. Her children would have to grow up fast. They would endure struggle and heartache and at least one of them would end up no better off than he'd been at the start.

Fanny's death was the last on the open sea. But the worst was not yet over. In fact, the carnage had only just begun.

GEORGE MITCHELL

It was towards the end of the voyage that George Mitchell began feeling unwell.

Although he did not know the cause of the disease, George knew that it thrived in airless, confined places; he knew that cleanliness and ventilation were of paramount importance. He was diligent in his precautions. But George had been toiling day and night without respite for over two months, exposing himself daily to the deadly pathogen. It was almost inevitable that, weakened by fatigue, he would eventually succumb.

As land shimmered into view and the end of the hellish journey drew nearer, malaise and fever took hold of George Mitchell, and he recognised with horror the headache, the dread of the light, the aching limbs, and the rosy rash upon his chest. And as the *Emigrant* sailed into Moreton Bay, fever overwhelmed him.

8–13 AUGUST: MORETON BAY IN SIGHT

On 8 August the sea was slate blue with white-capped wavelets stirred by a salty winter wind. Low-slung islands littered the bay: scrubby, wind-swept strips of land ringed with mudflats and mangroves. As they neared land, the deep blue of the sea lightened to a cheerful green, and land birds circled the ship.

Captain Wickham, police magistrate of Moreton Bay, was expecting them. He had arranged for a pilot to board the *Emigrant* and guide her safely into the bay. The ship anchored north of the 'Ship Patch' off Moreton Island, in clear view of the mainland and the scattered islands. 'I was never more astonished in my life at the singular sight of the country, or Moreton Island, which lay near us,' wrote a new arrival in 1864. 'Sand, chalk stretches and gum trees met the eye. Everywhere the land itself seemed like so many gigantic molehills.'[104]

Moreton Bay had no official health officer. Wickham appointed Brisbane doctor, David Keith Ballow, to act in the role and on 10 August,[105] the surgeon proceeded with the customs officer to Moreton Bay as directed, where he boarded the waiting vessel. What he observed was grim. Dr Ballow found the surgeon-superintendent, George Mitchell, in the throes of disease, although lucid enough – at this stage – to give a verbal report to the health officer. Dr Mitchell told him that he had attended to 64 cases of typhus since the voyage had begun.

Dr Mitchell related to Dr Ballow the dreadful story of the voyage: how the fever had first stricken the ship months earlier and gained in virulence as the vessel passed the Cape of Good Hope. In Dr Mitchell's hospital beds there were still 15 passengers under treatment and 12 more who were convalescent.

Amongst the sick was one of Dr Mitchell's most faithful helpers: Joseph William Ball. Joseph had acted as the surgeon's assistant throughout the terrible voyage, working day and night by his side. Now Joseph was beginning to show signs of the fever himself. This was an alarming development for his daughter, Mary Ann, and for his wife and three stepdaughters. If Joseph were to die, poor Elizabeth Wade would have lost three fathers in her mere 19 years of life. Even more alarming for the girl was her mother's state of health. Mary Ball had been stricken alongside her husband and was laid up in the hospital. Elizabeth was exhausted, miserable and afraid.

On 8 August, as the *Emigrant* had sailed into Moreton Bay, Euphemia Furphy had joined the list of deceased. Euphemia, at 67, was the eldest of the migrants. She was a widow who, like Dr Mitchell, hailed from Ireland's County Armagh. Euphemia's husband had died some 15 years previously and she was travelling to Australia with three of her adult children: John, Jane and Elizabeth. John Furphy was 23 years old and accompanied by his wife, Matilda; his sisters were unmarried dressmakers.

To uproot oneself from home, endure a long and arduous voyage and start a new life on the other side of the world in a nascent colony, one had to be optimistic and brave. To attempt it at the age of 67 – a considerable age for a woman in Victorian times – was remarkable. Mrs Furphy must have been brave and robust and devoted to her family. Her eldest son, Samuel, had immigrated to the colony ten years earlier. He had settled in the Port Philip district (later Victoria) and was raising a brood of children, one of whom – born only the previous year – was named Euphemia after his mother.

Samuel's son Joseph Furphy would gain celebrity in 1903 as the author of the classic Australian novel *Such is life*, which he would write under the nom de plume 'Tom Collins'. Joseph Furphy had been a farmer-turned-bullocky before he turned his hand to writing. His novel, which he described as 'offensively Australian', concerns the lives of bullock drivers, squatters and itinerant travellers during the 1880s.

Joseph's brother, John, would become a household name for quite a different reason. John was a blacksmith made famous for his invention of a water cart that consisted of a large cylindrical iron tank mounted on a horse-drawn timber frame on wheels. The carts were used by farmers to carry water, but became more popular during the First World War when they were put to use by the Australian Army. With the name 'Furphy' painted on the tank, the carts became known as 'furphies'. It is said that during the war, soldiers would gather around these water carts to gossip and tell tales, and that as a result they became associated with the spreading of rumours. This may have been the origin of the Australian slang word 'furphy', meaning a tall tale that is being represented as fact: a widely believed but untrue rumour.

Sadly, Euphemia (senior) would neither live to meet these grandsons nor to hear of the success that they went on to make of their lives. After enduring the three-month-long voyage, she died and was buried at sea. Having waited ten years to reunite with her son, she perished within sight of his adopted land, but without ever having setting foot upon it.

But perhaps the most terrible death yet occurred on the day that Dr Ballow boarded the ship.

Mary Waterson had died back on 10 July, as the *Emigrant* had moved from the heat of the tropics to cooler climes, dashing the surgeon's hopes that a cool change would check the progress of the disease. Since that day, her husband, Henry, had fallen ill. How fearfully his three young children must have watched as the fever took hold of their father and he vomited and shivered and burned his way into a fatal coma. Exactly one month after Mary's death – on 10 August – Henry joined his wife on the ocean bed.

The Waterson children – Patrick, Edward, and two-year-old Elizabeth – were now orphaned. They had no family in the new colony; they were illiterate, penniless, and completely alone. No doubt they grieved for their departed parents, but it is perhaps a blessing that they were too young to be aware of the extent of the misery that lay ahead.

They were not the only children whose futures looked bleak. Hannah Hallett had passed away in late May, stricken by 'apoplexy' after giving birth. Her death had been the second fatality of the voyage; her infant son's the fifth. Since Hannah's death, her widower Charles had been left to care for the remaining five children alone. And as the waters of Moreton Bay buffeted the *Emigrant*'s sides, Charles languished in a hospital bed. Seeing the Waterson children orphaned, how anxiously the Hallett children must have prayed for their father's recovery.

Having made his inspection, Dr Ballow directed the pilot to lead the vessel to the quarantine station and await further orders. The doctor allowed the mail – once it had been fumigated – to be transferred to the postmaster in Brisbane, and from there into the hands of Brisbane's citizens who waited hungrily for news from 'home'. The *Emigrant*'s cargo was transferred to the *Aurora* and shipped upriver to the mainland settlement: 100 casks of bottled beer and cider, a 'garden engine' and many cases of other goods bound for the businesses of Moreton Bay. Dr Ballow ordered the pilot to allow *no one* to come on board or leave the vessel. Then he advised Captain Kemp to await further instructions from the police magistrate.

Dr Ballow submitted his report to police magistrate Captain Wickham, who, without hesitation, supported his order to divert the vessel to the quarantine station at Dunwich. For the travellers, this was a terrible blow, but by no means an unexpected one. They were anxious to begin their new lives in the colony. Their ties with the old country had been severed and the future was uncertain. A hundred days at sea and who knew how many more in the limbo of quarantine?

Those passengers who were not prostrated with fever looked eagerly to land. They were tired of the confinement and the strict rules, of the dull routine and the chores. They were sick and weary and fearful. They had had their fill of the sea and the constant presence of the Grim Reaper. To be relegated to quarantine was something of an anticlimax, but it was a necessary evil. And although the island that awaited them was not their final destination, what excitement there must have been at the prospect of standing on land again at last.

Undoubtedly there was joy, and the thrill of novelty after weeks of unchanging routine. Yet as they watched land approaching, all on board must have paused to reflect upon the wretchedness of the past few months and consider their past optimism in a new light. 'When I last had the pleasure of seeing you,' Sarah Kemp would later write to the British Ladies Female Emigration Society, 'I little thought we were about to proceed on so disastrous a voyage.'[106]

And so with a mixture of joy and sadness, the bereaved prepared to greet their new lives without their loved ones.

The two Brimble families had made it so far with all young children's and parents' lives intact but not without loss. Though they mourned the death of Andrew's 17-year-old sister at sea, they still had every chance of building a better life in Australia. Andrew's wife Louisa prepared to give birth to their second child just as the prospect of arriving on land grew real; how impatiently they must have looked forward to both events. Perhaps John and Elizabeth Brimble, gazing upon the bright coastline, began making plans for Lucy, Alfred and Samuel. Amongst the emigrants, the fear of the dreadful disease and the lives it might yet claim remained, but this fear was outstripped by hope, for who could doubt that, once free of the confinements of the ship, the fever would finally be beaten?

On 12 August, the pilot guided the vessel back southward across Moreton Bay, into the passage between Stradbroke Island and the mainland. The wind was strong and 'contrary', forcing Captain Kemp to manoeuvre the *Emigrant* slowly across the churning waters of the bay. Across the foam-flecked waves she struggled, finally coming to a halt the following day a few miles west of a stone convict-built causeway that stretched its finger out across the mudflats from Stradbroke Island. To the north was tiny Peel Island with its long arc of sand; beyond, the dunes of Moreton Island. To the west, the shallow mouth of the Brisbane River, tantalising in its nearness.

The quarantine station lay in wait at Dunwich, at the end of the causeway upon Stradbroke Island. But the bay was too shallow for a nearer approach and the weather too violent to consider ferrying the emigrants to the causeway. Captain Kemp guided the barque as close as he dared, dropped anchor, and waited.

Part 3

A better country

Untitled poem from
Moreton Bay Free Press, 20 Dec 1853

Stay! For thou treadest on a sacred spot!
Stranger! Tread lightly, this is hallowed ground!
Beneath doth lie the dust, perchance forgot,
Of those who sought – and seeking, here have found
If not a home, at least repose so sound,
That nought can now disturb them till the day
When Michael's trump shall loudly peal around,
Awaking all that sleep, where'er they lay,
To meet their God upon the Judgement Day!

Sad is the story written here around,
Well may it cause the sympathising tear;
For those, who in this spot a grave have found,
Left 'home, sweet home!' and all most lov'd and dear,
To seek (what there, perchance denied them) here
Their daily bread, and yet, whilst on the way,
Malignant fever blighted their career;
And bravely though they fought it many a day,
Pale Azrael's dart had sped – he marked them for his prey!

But yet they lived the 'promised land' to reach,
And hope revived, no doubt, in many a breast,
Delusive as the *mirage* travellers teach,
On Reggio's sea is clearly seen impress'd-
Fata Morgana; but, to tell the rest,
They died, the table says, in quarantine-
A fate most wretched, even at the best-
Unsolac'd by their kindred's love I ween,
Which cannot be replaced, in such an hour 'tis seen.

They died! These are their lowly graves!
Far from the land where first their breath they drew,
Just as they reached the goal across the waves,

And almost grasped the prize they had in view.
They sought a home – a 'better country' true,
'Tis hoped they found; let's join in the prayer,
And pity's tear drop o'er the gallant few,
Or turn away, one should not tarry there
Who cannot breathe a simple, silent prayer.[107]

Chapter 6

Land: the prize 'almost grasped'

BRISBANE

Brisbane in 1850 was a fledgling town, no longer quite the wild convict outpost it had been but not yet the modern society it would soon become.

While several nations of First Peoples had occupied Moreton Bay and surrounding areas for tens of thousands of years, white settlement only began in late 1823, when Lieutenant John Oxley sailed north to seek a new place to send New South Wales' recidivist convicts. He made his way to Redcliffe (or Red Cliff) and discovered there the wide and winding waterway that would later be named the Brisbane River. He was aided in this discovery by a group of Sydney timber-getters who had been shipwrecked in Moreton Bay. The Indigenous people of the central and southern parts of Moreton Bay – the Quandamooka – had cared for the stranded men, giving them food and shelter and guiding them to the mainland. When John Oxley arrived on the scene, he was surprised to discover these white men there before him. With their guidance, he was able to explore upriver.

The following year, the first batch of convicts arrived in the brig *Amity* at the new settlement at Redcliffe. But before long the area proved unsuitable and it was decided that the penal settlement should be moved up the river. The site selected was tentatively known as 'Edenglassie' until, after a visit from Governor Brisbane, a new name for the town was chosen in his honour. The local Indigenous people knew it as Mianjin (or Meanjin). The entire region, from the Caboolture River in the north to the Logan in the south, bordered by the Great Dividing Range in the west and the ocean in the east, was known by the white settlers as Moreton Bay.

In those early days, ships entered Moreton Bay through the South Passage between Stradbroke and Moreton Islands (the route was changed to the northern entrance after shipwrecks of the 1840s). After the passage had been surveyed in 1825, a depot and pilot station were set up at the northern end of the island to facilitate shipping. The point, called 'Pulan' by the Quandamooka people, was named 'Amity Point' by the Europeans, after the ship that had brought the first convicts to these northern shores. The island, previously known as 'Minjerribah', was named 'Stradbroke Island' by Governor Darling.

Darling had been unimpressed with Brisbane as a site for the penal settlement and sought alternatives. Commandant Captain Logan put Stradbroke Island forward as a possible site. Under Captain Patrick Logan, the third commandant of Brisbane, Brisbane was a brutal place. He was notorious for the harshness of his punishments and the freedom with which he dispensed them. But it was during his term that Brisbane's earliest substantial buildings were erected and the district's geology and botany were explored.

Instead of moving the whole settlement from Brisbane as Logan had suggested, the governor ordered the establishment of a small convict outstation on the island. Logan set up a military post and stores depot at Dunwich (then called 'Goompi' by the Quandamooka people or 'Green Point' by the Europeans), where stores for the penal settlement could be loaded and unloaded. A sandbar at the mouth of the river prevented larger ships from sailing directly into Brisbane Town, but a depot at Dunwich would allow them to deliver their cargo quickly to smaller vessels for transfer to Brisbane. The convicts built a stone causeway out from Dunwich for this purpose.

In 1830, the brutal regime of Captain Logan came to an end with his murder. The following year, his replacement Captain Clunie proposed the closure of the Dunwich settlement. The government agreed; the settlement closed and in its place a timber depot was established.

By this time, Brisbane Town had grown. In 1830, the white population of Moreton Bay consisted of 1000 convicts and 100 soldiers. But by the 1830s, public opposition to transportation of convicts to New South Wales was mounting. Free settlers resented both the competition for labour and the uncivilised ways that convicts brought with them. In 1837, Governor Bourke proposed the closure of the Moreton Bay penal settlement. Over the following years this idea gained traction, and the prison began to empty. All female convicts had been removed by the middle of 1839. Then in February 1842, the New South Wales *Government Gazette* proclaimed that the penal settlement at Moreton Bay was no more.

Up to this point, the settlement had been exclusively for convicts, their keepers and their guards' families. But when the penal settlement shut down, Brisbane Town and its surrounds were declared open to free settlement. The town was surveyed, the first land sales were held, and pioneering types began flooding in. Businesses were established and homes were built; a ferry service began and elections were held. Steamships started conveying passengers from Sydney, and other vessels began plying the river route between Brisbane and Ipswich. For the white settlers, it was an exciting time of real growth and development. In 1843, Captain John Clements Wickham was appointed police magistrate and, as such, became the senior government official in charge of the town.

Initially, relationships between the Indigenous people and some of the white settlers – particularly the German missionaries who settled in Brisbane's north – had been mostly cordial. But the original inhabitants had no desire to see their way of life destroyed and little interest in adopting the newcomers' customs or religion. Misunderstanding, resentment and conflict inevitably arose. Tensions escalated when the region was thrown open to free settlement and increasing numbers of European farmers moved in to claim parcels of land.

By 1850, European settlement was firmly established in Moreton Bay. The white settlers had effectively quelled Aboriginal resistance and taken the land as their own.

But Brisbane was still very much a frontier town.

By 1846, 960 non-Indigenous people lived in Brisbane Town. Almost two thirds of them were males, and a quarter of those men had convict pasts. In the Moreton Bay region – which included Ipswich – non-Indigenous residents numbered almost 1600. It was a young population. In Moreton Bay, there were six medical practitioners, one clerk and only 26 'other educated persons'. The rest were shepherds, labourers and mechanics, stockmen and domestic servants.[108]

The population had not grown since 1830; on the contrary, it had shrunk since the height of the convict era. In the years following the penal establishment's closure, Brisbane was still a rough place. In a town where men outnumbered women so greatly, drunkenness and vice were rampant.

The free settlement of Brisbane grew slowly but steadily. Trade and commerce developed, and solid buildings of brick and stone began to appear.

But the growth wasn't happening fast enough for the enterprising men of Brisbane. They were frustrated by the slowness of its development. With convicts no longer available, a labour shortage inhibited progress. Brisbane desperately needed young healthy men to provide labour, and young healthy women to keep the men in check. It needed couples to reproduce and populate the town. To alleviate this problem the colonial government turned to assisted immigration.

The first government-assisted ship to sail directly into Moreton Bay from the United Kingdom was the *Artemisia*. She left Plymouth in August 1848 and arrived in December the same year, bringing 240 much-needed immigrants to Brisbane.

This was the start of the influx. But it wasn't enough. The Rev. John Dunmore Lang was a Sydney Presbyterian clergyman who, having visited Brisbane in 1845, saw its potential. But he was disturbed by its low moral standards. Lang was an advocate for free settlement who had opposed transportation, and in Moreton Bay he saw an opportunity. He proposed a scheme to the government, by which reputable free settlers might receive a free grant of land in Australia if they paid for their own passage. Despite opposition from both the government and the squatters, Lang went ahead and chartered ships to bring his settlers to Moreton Bay.

The first of Lang's ships, the *Fortitude*, sailed into Brisbane in January 1849, only a month after the government ship *Artemisia*. The *Chaseley* and the *Lima* arrived later the same year. But Lang's plan had not been formally communicated to Captain Wickham, the police magistrate, and the *Fortitude*'s arrival threw the officials of Brisbane into a spin. They had received no notice of such an influx of immigrants and had insufficient accommodation for them. Worse, the government refused to recognise the land grants that Lang had promised the newcomers. Wickham was not allowed to house the immigrants on Crown land, nor supply them with government rations.

In 1848 and 1849, there were almost 1000 new arrivals in Moreton Bay. Wickham took it upon himself to organise a temporary village in Yorke's Hollow, where the new arrivals built their own accommodation. The district would soon become known as 'Fortitude Valley', after the ship that had delivered them there. Since Brisbane was unprepared for such a sudden population boom, the influx was alarming and controversial, but the furore soon settled as the immigrants found employment and set about building their homes.

Enough of the new arrivals stayed in Brisbane to change the nature of the town. These were respectable free settlers: mostly Scottish Protestants, educated and sober. Trade blossomed and new buildings sprang up.

During the voyage of the *Fortitude*, a passenger had died from typhus. The same illness killed a second victim whilst the vessel idled in Moreton Bay, and the passengers were taken to quarantine at Moreton Island. This sudden boom in immigration made the need for a quarantine station urgent.

Consequently, in *The Moreton Bay Courier* of 29 July 1850, the following declaration appeared:

Now, I, the Governor aforesaid, with the advice of the
Executive Council, do, by this my proclamation, declare and
order that the northern portion of Stradbroke Island, within
or near the harbour or roadstead of Moreton Bay . . . shall
be a station and place for the performance of Quarantine,
according to the several provisions of the said recited Act,
and subject to the several rules, regulations, and restrictions
contained therein.[109]

STRADBROKE ISLAND

North Stradbroke Island, at 275.2km² today, is one of the world's
largest sand islands. It lies in Moreton Bay, about 15 miles as the
crow flies from the mouth of the Brisbane River. In 1850, North
and South Stradbroke were still one long island, the land mass
having not yet broken into two. The original settlements were
on what is now known as North Stradbroke Island, or 'Straddie'.
It is a beautiful island, teeming with wildlife: echidnas, koalas
and waterbirds. The blue waters around it are alive with turtles,
dugongs, dolphins and rays. The eastern (ocean) side is edged
with long white beaches, towering dunes and swamps, while the
bay side is known for its mangroves and wetlands. A string of
ancient inland lakes provides an endless supply of fresh water.

Minjerribah (North Stradbroke Island) has been a home to the
Nunukul and Goenpul people for at least 21,000 years: the Nunukul
in the north, and the Goenpul in the south. The Aboriginal people
knew Moreton Bay as 'Quandamooka'. There had been contact
between the Quandamooka people and Europeans since 1799,
when Matthew Flinders had entered the bay. The first significant
interaction had come in 1823, when the local Indigenous people
had cared for the shipwrecked timber-getters who later surprised

John Oxley with their presence in the area. The Quandamooka people's hospitality had been repaid by white occupation of their land, as the newcomers built their pilot station at Amity Point and the depot at Dunwich.

By the time Moreton Bay's convict era ended in 1842, the convict outstation at Dunwich had been long abandoned. The settlement had included a convict-built stone causeway, barracks for prisoners and the military, and a store. In 1843, four Passionist priests set up a Catholic mission for the Indigenous People at Dunwich. They had hoped to use the abandoned buildings but found them in a derelict state. Faced with a range of insurmountable obstacles, the mission failed and closed in 1847.

The government buildings at Dunwich lay more or less unused over the next few years. During this time, the derelict structures fell further into disrepair. Timber rotted and stones crumbled, and nature started intruding once more into the settlement. The original owners must have begun to hope that their home might be returned to them. Such was the state of the island when the government declared it as a quarantine station, less than a month before the *Emigrant* sailed into Moreton Bay.

13 AUGUST: AT ANCHOR

For the weary travellers, 13 August was an eventful day.

One of the events was joyful news: a burst of sunlight through dark and gloomy clouds. On board the *Emigrant*, while it rocked at anchor in Moreton Bay not far from the quarantine station at Dunwich, Louisa Brimble gave birth to a healthy son. The boy was Louisa and Andrew's second child and first son. They named him William. For the Brimble family, his birth must have seemed a happy portent. They had endured months of discomfort and dread, suffered the loss of life (Andrew's sister, Sophia's) and now at last, with land and the end of the ordeal in sight, their forbearance had been rewarded with new life. They were young and had only to bear a few more weeks in the limbo of quarantine before they could embark on a bright and prosperous future.

As it turns out, celebration was justified; the baby would be one of the few born at sea to survive to adulthood. That is not to say that the Brimble family's suffering was over. Far from it.

The Brimbles' rejoicing was, in any case, necessarily subdued, for on the very day of the baby's birth, death struck again. Daniel Gorman, a 39-year-old labourer from Tipperary, was the last to die on board. He left behind a wife, Mary (née Ryan) and four children. Mary Gorman could read but not write, and bringing up four children in this new land without a husband was going to be a struggle. Her eldest child, Patrick, was 13, the youngest, Thomas, only seven.

Mary's grief and dread as she watched her husband slip into the coma from which he would never recover can only be imagined. How would she cope? It must have seemed to Mary that her best option would be to marry again. In fact, she *would* marry again, not long after her arrival in the colony, and settle in Brisbane. But misfortune had not finished with Mary, whose daughter and daughter-in-law would one day predecease her. Mary's eldest child, Patrick, who was 13 at the time of the family's emigration, would marry at 21. Tragically, the negligence of an attending midwife would result in the death of his young wife in childbirth. Mary's daughter, also named Mary, would also suffer and die young.

But all of this lay ahead of the Gorman family as they watched their husband and father's canvas-shrouded body splashing into the white-capped waters of Moreton Bay. Daniel's death was the twentieth since the departure of the *Emigrant*, but it was not to be the last. No more bodies would be consigned to the deep. Hereafter, the dead would be buried on land.

The third milestone of 13 August was the worsening of Dr Mitchell's condition.

George Mitchell was a young man – only 25 – but the months of unremitting toil at sea had sapped his strength. He had witnessed the deaths of men and women, young and old, and he knew that typhus did not discriminate. Now he began to consider his own mortality. His thoughts turned to his family back in Ireland. The fate of his widowed mother and younger siblings – at least one of whom George had likely never met – weighed upon his mind.

George summoned Captain Kemp and asked him to witness his will. George dictated, and the captain wrote:

> To the owners of ship as per order given Capt Kemp the sum of thirty pounds. The remainder to be forwarded to my mother (if alive) Mrs Jane Mitchell, relict of the late Alex^r Mitchell Clady Beg Market Hill County Armagh Ireland, and if my mother not alive to be divided amongst my sisters.

George then took the pen and shakily signed 'Geo Mitchell M.D., Surgeon superintendent of the ship "Emigrant".[110]

QUARANTINE STATION

While the *Emigrant* lingered in Moreton Bay, Captain John Clements Wickham, police magistrate, prepared to transfer her passengers to the quarantine ground. Having received Dr Ballow's grim report, Wickham wrote to the colonial secretary confirming that he had placed the ship under quarantine.

'I shall proceed tomorrow morning to the quarantine station for the purpose of making such arrangements as our scanty means will admit of, for the accommodation of the sick on shore,' he wrote, adding that 'the sooner they are removed from the ship the better.'[111]

Captain Wickham had grave concerns, however, about the accommodation at Dunwich. The remaining old government buildings were, he feared, 'in too dilapidated a state to afford any shelter to the sick'. In the government stores he had only 12 small tents, each large enough to contain three iron bedsteads, to offer as housing for more than 250 people. The tents were not in the best condition. To supplement the accommodation, he proposed to requisition sails and awnings from the ship, promising that the government would compensate the shipowner for any damage.

Wickham appointed the customs officer, George Watson, to superintend the quarantine station. Watson would be responsible for communications with the mainland, for keeping the station stocked with provisions, and for the day-to-day running and security of the station. Security was a serious matter; it was vital that those in quarantine had no uncontrolled contact with outsiders. Captain Wickham had particular concerns about the Indigenous inhabitants of Stradbroke Island. It was necessary, he wrote, to prevent them having any contact with the quarantine station for fear that 'they might be induced, from curiosity, to go amongst the immigrants, and be the means of spreading sickness through the district.'

To this end, he engaged four pensioner guards recently arrived on the ship *Bangalore*. The *Bangalore* had brought around 400 souls – two-thirds of them convicts – to Moreton Bay from Plymouth in April 1850. She was the last ship to transport convicts directly to the east coast of Australia. Many of the free men on board were military pensioners acting as convict guards, who had brought their wives and children with the intention of settling in Moreton Bay. These men would be put to work at Dunwich.

Wickham already suspected that the immigrants might face a 'considerable time' in quarantine. It would be necessary to establish communications between Dunwich and the mainland, and to ensure a regular supply of fresh food, medicines, bedding and other provisions. He chartered the ketch *Aurora* for this purpose.

Having prepared as best he could for the arrival of the immigrants, Captain Wickham made sure that he was at Dunwich ready to settle them into their crude accommodation.

CAPTAIN WICKHAM

Captain John Clements Wickham had been police magistrate at Moreton Bay since January 1843. By 1850 he was 52 years old, a married man with two young sons and a daughter. Born in the port town of Leith, Scotland, Wickham had been a seafarer for most of his youth. The son of a naval man, Wickham had joined the navy as a midshipman at only 14. As a young man he had served in a number of survey expeditions with the British Navy including a mission to chart the coasts of Peru, Chile and Patagonia.

In 1831, he was appointed the second in command on the famous round-the-world voyage of the *Beagle*, a voyage he shared with the controversial naturalist Charles Darwin. Six years later, Wickham was promoted to commander of the ship, and set out on an expedition to survey the coast of Australia. Before he could complete his mission, Wickham fell ill. His poor health forced him to retire from the navy and return to England. But having spent some time in Port Jackson – and possibly having already fallen in love with his future bride – Wickham was drawn back to New South Wales. He returned at the end of 1841 and married the following year.

When Brisbane Town was declared open to free settlers, Captain Wickham became its first police magistrate and, as such, held the most senior government position in the town. The police magistrate was generally regarded as a just and wise administrator. He had begun his career in a town that was rough and relatively lawless, and had overseen a period of major development. According to his obituary, under Wickham's leadership,

A marked change soon became apparent; courts of petty session, courts of request, and other necessary details were brought into successful operation by the Police Magistrate, and the then embryo city became a model of good order, and the abode of a thriving and industrious community of free settlers.[112]

Wickham was an industrious man who took his responsibilities seriously. By 1850, he had served at Moreton Bay for seven years and knew its inhabitants well. The *Emigrant* was the fifth immigrant vessel to have arrived in the last couple of years, and Wickham understood the need to follow strict procedures. The plight of her passengers was worrying, but he had no reason to be unduly alarmed. Wickham expected that, once they were in quarantine, things would improve.

14 AUGUST: DISEMBARKING

On 14 August, the immigrants prepared to disembark. Captain Wickham was already at Dunwich, having selected the sites he deemed most suitable for the 'different classes' of persons to

settle. To his dismay, he had found the crumbling old government buildings to be every bit as dilapidated as he had feared they
might be. They had been uninhabited for some time and would
provide little shelter from the weather.

Wickham asked Captain Kemp to supply spare sails and
awnings for temporary accommodation until huts could be built,
and Kemp readily agreed. Wickham promised the immigrants
that more tents would be available soon; although there were only
a few in the Brisbane store, he had ordered more from Sydney. The
men discussed arrangements for getting the immigrants ashore,
and Kemp agreed to come with them to supervise the erection of
the tents.

In the first batch of immigrants to be brought ashore there were
59 young men, 27 married men and women, and 13 children:
99 in all. Elizabeth Wade, with growing dread and despair, waited
on board with her stepsisters. Her mother and stepfather still
languished in the ship's hospital. As the young women marked
time, the first batch of immigrants climbed down from the barque
onto a smaller vessel that would ferry them across to Dunwich.
The boat edged up to the stone jetty and the crew hitched it to the
post on the end of the causeway. The passengers clamoured from
the vessel onto the jetty.

For the first time in more than a hundred days, the ground
beneath them was solid and still. If they paused to take in the
view – as surely they must have – they might well have been
overwhelmed by the island's strangeness and beauty.

The causeway took them to the southern end of a small bay
that arced around to their left, with its tiny beach white, flat and
pristine, and the shallows lying serenely upon it like blue-green
glass. Further along lay mudflats studded with the sturdy upright
prongs of mangroves. Black and white pied cormorants dotted

the bay; squat, long-beaked pelicans sailed by and common silver gulls flitted here and there on the briny air.

Eastward, the land continued flat from the beach to the grasslands where, to the left of the track that led inland from the causeway, sat a cluster of buildings. A large square construction with a peaked roof and surrounding fence, that had once been a store, and behind it, a smaller building, squat and symmetrical and book-ended by a pair of chimneys, greeted them. The buildings were neglected and decaying. This was to be home until the doctor could say with confidence that the fever had been defeated.

Behind the tiny settlement, the land sloped up ever so gently, following a gradual rise to a distant ridge that was dense with dark, stringy vegetation, on the eastern side of the island. Here on the lee of the ridge they were sheltered from the worst of the August winds, but it was a strange and wild scene, alive with exotic birds and marsupials and reptiles the likes of which they had never imagined.

In this outlandish place, barely separated from the damp and biting winter weather by ramshackle walls and flimsy tents, they were to make themselves a home. Exactly how long they would be exiled on this tiny island, it was impossible to know.

More disturbing than the problem of the accommodation, however, was the condition of the surgeon. Poor George Mitchell's health had deteriorated and he was quite unable to attend to his patients. And alarmingly, the number of sick was rising hourly. In the hospital beds on board, nineteen – mostly men – lay suffering. The widower Charles Hallett was still amongst them.

Captain Wickham returned to Brisbane that evening on the harbour master's boat, promising to find another doctor to take over Dr Mitchell's duties. This would not prove an easy task. The medical men of Moreton Bay were understandably reluctant to take on such an arduous and risky commission. At first Captain Wickham's pleas for help were unanswered. At last, one man put himself forward: Dr Patrick Walsh Mallon. Wickham gratefully accepted Dr Mallon's offer and dispatched him to the quarantine station that very night on the harbour master's boat.

DR PATRICK WALSH MALLON

It may have been a comfort to Dr Mitchell that the surgeon who came to his aid was a fellow Ulster man. Despite their differences in age and religion, the two surgeons had much in common. Patrick Walsh Mallon's native place, Ireland's county of Tyrone, bordered on George Mitchell's home county of Armagh. Tyrone, like Armagh, was in the heart of flax-growing land, and Patrick's father, like George's, was involved in the main industry of the counties: the linen trade.

George Mitchell's father was a grower, but Patrick Mallon's was a merchant. Arthur Mallon and his wife Jane (née Walsh) welcomed their son Patrick into the world in 1806 or 1807. They lived in Dungannon, a market and post-town ten miles northwest of Armagh. Patrick grew up in a town that was orderly and attractive: a town of industry and agriculture, prosperous thanks to its bleach-greens, distillery, colliery, iron-works and flour mills.

Patrick Mallon's family, unlike the Mitchells, were Roman Catholics. In Tyrone, Catholics were a disadvantaged minority, but those involved in the linen trade fared better than others. Merchants in particular were relatively well-to-do members of the middle class, and Patrick's parents were wealthy enough to educate their son.

Like George Mitchell, Patrick Walsh Mallon trained in Edinburgh. A Christopher W. Mallon of County Tyrone, who studied medicine at Edinburgh at around the same time, might have been a younger brother. The Mallons were from an earlier generation of medical students than George Mitchell's. Theirs was a time when medical practices were still based more on superstition and tradition than science. Training facilities were diverse and poorly regulated. University training was optional; one could become a doctor simply through an apprenticeship.

In the days of Mallon's training, doctors still believed in the healing powers of such 'cures' as mercury and arsenic, 'changes of air', leeches, purging and prayer. But progress was under way, particularly in the study of anatomy.

Patrick Mallon began his studies in 1825 at the University of Edinburgh but continued them at the Royal College of Physicians. The latter institution awarded him a Licentiate of Midwifery. As a student, he was president of the junior Medical Society and Member Extraordinary of the Anatomical Society of Edinburgh. He went on to study anatomy, surgery and pharmacy at Edinburgh's Royal College of Surgeons, and was awarded his Licentiate from that institution in March 1828.

That year was a notorious time in the study of anatomy at Edinburgh. It was a time when the medical world was beginning to realise that surgery should be guided by a thorough knowledge of anatomy and physiology. Edinburgh led the world in anatomical research. In the academic year of 1827–1828 – the year that Dr Mallon graduated from the Royal College of Surgeons – Robert Knox was conservator of the College Museum and head of the College's Anatomy School. It is likely that Dr Mallon attended his extremely popular extramural anatomy class. Knox's colourful lecturing style and his guarantee that his students would witness full dissections made him world-famous and highly respected as an anatomist and lecturer.

But the scarcity of bodies available for dissection was a constant and worsening problem. According to the Murder Act of 1752, only the corpses of executed murderers could be used for dissection. But as the demand for scientific knowledge grew, so did the need for cadavers. At the same time that the medical schools of Scotland were expanding, the supply of cadavers was drying up. In the early 19th century, anatomists pressured the government to let them use the corpses of paupers from workhouses for dissection. Unsurprisingly, there were objections on religious and ethical grounds.

But meanwhile, the medical school was receiving bodies from grave-robbers. These body-snatchers or 'resurrection men' would dig up freshly buried bodies from their graves in the middle of the night and sell them for large sums. Then in 1827, an Irishman named William Hare found one of the lodgers in his boarding house dead and realised he could profit from the man's misfortune. He and his friend and lodger William Burke decided to sell the body to Dr Knox for £7 10s.

This generous sum gave Burke and Hare the idea for further business transactions. Two months later, a lodger at Hare's establishment came down with a fever. Concerned that the fever might spread or at least frighten off other tenants, and with an eye to a profit, Burke and Hare murdered her and sold the body to Knox. This was the first of 16 murders the pair committed in order to sell the bodies to the medical school. Their first victims were Hare's tenants, but the killers later moved on to prostitutes and random strangers on the streets. The pair used a particular method of suffocation that later became known as 'Burking': they would get the victims drunk and then suffocate them by compressing the chest until they stopped breathing.

The scandal was revealed in 1831 when Hare's suspicious

lodgers discovered a body under Burke's bed. The murderous pair was arrested and tried. For agreeing to testify against Burke, William Hare was granted immunity, while Burke was found guilty and sentenced to death. He was hanged in Edinburgh on 28 January 1829, and his body was dissected at Edinburgh Medical College. A pocket-book made out of his skin is still displayed at the college museum.

Robert Knox never faced trial for there was no evidence that he knew about the murders. But for Dr Mallon and his peers, the revelation that the bodies they had dissected in anatomy classes had been, at best, stolen from their graves – or, at worst, the victims of murder – must have been horrifying. The case led to the passing of the Anatomy Act 1832, which allowed medical practitioners, students and teachers to dissect the bodies of the poor who had died 'unclaimed' in hospitals, workhouses and prisons – thereby ending the illegal trade in corpses.

By the time the Act was passed, however, Dr Mallon was finished with his studies. And shortly after his graduation, he left the United Kingdom to settle in Australia.

He arrived in 1830, and by 1834 had settled in the Green Hills area of Maitland. Why he chose Maitland is uncertain; he may have had family in the district.

In 1836, Dr Mallon married Catherine Ann Irwin (or Irvine), the daughter of the Royal Navy Lieutenant Samuel Graves and Hester Graves (née Gore). Like Patrick, Catherine was from Ireland's county Tyrone and had been not long in the colony. The pair may have known each other before emigrating.

Although Patrick had been raised a Catholic, his bride had not, and the pair was married by special licence in the Church of England in Maitland. Patrick was a man of intriguing contrasts. A devout Catholic who married an Anglican; and a proud

Irishman who signed his name – along with scores of other residents of Maitland – to a letter expressing congratulations, affection and loyalty to Queen Victoria upon her accession to the throne.[113]

The Mallons settled in Maitland, where Catherine's immediate family lived, and Patrick went about establishing his practice and acquiring property. He bought land on the west bank of the Hunter River and established a home that he called 'Ranfurly Terrace', undoubtedly as a reminder of the grand Ranfurly estate in his native Dungannon. At first, things went well. The Mallons acquired a couple of convict servants and increased their land holdings. Patrick had high standards of behaviour, both for himself and his hired help. He had a social conscience but was not above employing convict workers, nor enforcing discipline.

The doctor was an emotional and strong-minded man whose outspokenness sometimes landed him in hot water. In mid-1838 he became involved in an extraordinary chain of events that began at the Langs' estate of Dunmore on the Paterson River. Dunmore House was the family home of Andrew Lang, brother of the Rev. John Dunmore Lang, the clergyman who pioneered the Bounty system for assisting immigration of selected settlers in NSW and later had such an influence on immigration into Moreton Bay. The Langs accommodated many newly arrived immigrants at Dunmore House while they looked for work and got settled in the colony.

In 1838, one of these immigrants – a Scottish woman by the name of McSwaine – died in childbirth at Dunmore. After the poor woman had been buried, Dr Mallon raised suspicions that unskilled treatment by her attending surgeon, Mr Lewis, was to blame for her death. To the horror of the dead woman's relatives, whose feelings were 'dreadfully harrassed by the proceedings,'[114]

Mrs McSwaine's body was exhumed and put through a post-mortem examination. An inquest was held at Dunmore and, after much deliberation, the jury decided that Mr Lewis was blameless; Mrs McSwaine's death had been a 'visitation of God'.

Dr Mallon wasn't satisfied. Determined to instigate a further inquiry into Mr Lewis's conduct, he set off from Morpeth for Sydney in the company of John Dunmore Lang himself. The men embarked on the Hunter River steamer, *King William*, on what was to be a perilous voyage. The vessel had been originally built as a river boat and was no match for the rough seas that she encountered on the stormy voyage. After the steamer left Newcastle, a stiff wind blew up and shunted her off-course; with struggling engines, leaking boilers and choked pumps battling against high seas, and with her life-boat torn adrift, she was lucky to make it safely into Port Stephens.

It appears that nothing came of Dr Mallon's pursuit of Mr Lewis, despite the rumour that he was prepared to put up £400 of his own money to see the matter properly investigated.[115] The *Sydney Gazette and New South Wales Advertiser* reported the incident, implying that Dr Mallon was a meddler motivated by professional jealousy. When Dr Mallon took 'most dreadful offence' at their report, the newspaper affected wounded surprise. Although religion had nothing to do with the case, the reporter hastened to describe Dr Mallon as 'A Roman Catholic surgeon'[116], demonstrating the unease simmering between Catholics and Protestants in the district at the time.

(Dr Mallon was not the only local surgeon to entertain doubts about Mr Lewis's treatment, and he may have had valid reason for his concerns. Although Dr Henry George Lewis was known as an 'old and respected surgeon',[117] no evidence that he was qualified or registered to practice has yet come to light.[118])

Battered and fatigued, Dr Mallon returned to Maitland vowing that he would repeat his pursuit of justice in Sydney at the first opportunity. Nothing more was reported about the case, however; perhaps, grateful to have come through the ordeal at sea alive, Dr Mallon put the matter behind him.

In June 1839, he entered into partnership with Dr Joshua Dowe, and the two men announced plans to open a small hospital in Maitland. Their plans came to nothing. Maitland may not have been large enough to support two hospitals; another private hospital with its own dispensary was already operating under the management of a qualified surgeon and apothecary.

By this time, Dr Mallon was qualified as a medical witness and was called upon to give evidence in court at intervals over the following years. He was active in the community, both in his professional and religious life, and he was generous in sharing his skills. He was fond of public speaking and delivered well-attended lectures throughout his professional life.

Although the doctor's religious attitudes were ecumenical, he was committed to his Catholic roots. In 1840, Dr Mallon was the Honorary Secretary of the Central Committee of the Auxiliary Catholic Institute of Hunter River, whose purpose was the 'propagation of the Faith'.[119] In November of that year, he attended a special meeting of the committee, which was called after Dungog's Police Magistrate Thomas Cook posted a notice to the courthouse door stating that 'none but Protestants need apply' for the position of constable. Thomas Cook had also published an inflammatory letter in the *Herald*, suggesting that the Catholic Rev. Mr. Mahony had 'tampered with the constables, and encouraged them to a dereliction of duty'. [120]

The magistrate's order sparked understandable outrage in the Catholic community. The Catholic Institute agreed that 'the

Catholics of the said district are bereft of legal protection in the enjoyment of their property, personal safely, and liberty', and called further meetings to deal with the grievances.

The Sydney Gazette and New South Wales Advertiser's vicious and patronising response to these published grievances gives us an idea of the bigotry and snobbery that prevailed in the community at the time. The *Gazette*'s reporter was scathing about the members of the institute, asserting that 'with the exception of Mr. Patrick Walsh Mallon, who is a medical practitioner, there is not one among the number above the rank of petty shopkeepers'.

He sprang to the police magistrate's defence, claiming that 'Mr. Cook came to the very natural conclusion, that a Popish constable would pay a stricter attention to the commands of his ghostly adviser, than to those of the civil magistrate (because the Church of Rome holds that the spiritual authority is above civil authority).' Not content with merely defending the police magistrate, the reporter even questioned the right of the Catholic Institute to exist at all. He concluded that 'We tell our brother Protestants that the establishment of the "Catholic Institute" so called, has treason for its aim, and blood for its end.'

In March the following year, Dr Mallon announced his plans to return to Ireland. He advertised a sale by auction of his property which, by this time, was considerable. His rent roll, the advertisement announced, was upwards of £500 per annum and properties included Ranfurly Terrace and his other residences – 13 in all – at Port and West Maitland. There were several 'brick built and beautifully finished' tenanted cottages, a brick surgeon's residence let at £60 per annum, and seven slabbed houses.

Dr Mallon's plans to return 'home', however, came to nothing. He remained in Maitland and continued to accumulate property.

In September 1841, he resumed practice in the Medical Hall at High Street, West Maitland.

But the following year, after a decade of success in the colony, Mallon's good fortune started to desert him. When a shoemaker named John Redman complained of pain in his chest, Dr Mallon was summoned to treat him. He proceeded to bleed the patient, who promptly died during the operation. A post-mortem examination concluded that he had died of natural causes. Dr Mallon was not to blame for the death, but the business was an unsettling one.

Meantime, the doctor's finances had begun to suffer. During the land boom and economic prosperity of the 1830s, he had invested heavily in property. But from the beginning of the 1840s, to his dismay, land values began to fall. Drought had made investment in stock and land less attractive, and the price of Australian wool, wheat and livestock dropped as a result of the downturn in the British economy. Wages fell and unemployment grew. This period of economic depression was disastrous for Patrick Mallon.

By the middle of 1842 he needed to liquidate some of his assets. He advertised for the sale of the unexpired lease of the Apothecaries' Hall in Maitland, along with its stock of drugs, bottles and fixtures and the good will of the business. The property was going cheap and on liberal terms but *not*, Mallon warned, for less than £100 cash.

Until 1843, he kept his head above water. And he had not yet felt the pinch enough to abandon his philanthropic ways.

On 1 January 1843, the Maitland Benevolent Society opened its doors. Its objects were 'to afford an asylum to the sick and destitute, and to dispense medicine gratis to the poor'.[121] The asylum was funded by subscription and run by a sub-committee that included Dr Patrick Mallon, who provided his services for free.

By this time, Dr Mallon was interested in not only professional and religious matters, but in politics as well. He joined a committee in support of Major D'Arcy Wentworth in his bid for election for the Northumberland boroughs of East Maitland, West Maitland, and Newcastle. Major Wentworth was the son of Irish-born D'Arcy Wentworth, the late principal surgeon at the Sydney Hospital. He was also the brother of well-known explorer, journalist and politician William Charles Wentworth.

Both brothers were conservatives who supported the abolition of transportation. While electioneering, the Anglican Major Wentworth expressed his views that all people should be free to hold their own religious beliefs, and that all classes should have access to education[122] – views that won the hearty approval of Dr Mallon. Both brothers stood for election in 1843 – Major D'Arcy for the Northumberland boroughs and William for Sydney – and both were victorious. D'Arcy Wentworth's career as member of the NSW Legislative Council was brief and lacklustre; he was forced to resign due to incompetence after two years, while his brother went on to have a long and stellar political career.

On the night of the election victory, a delighted Dr Mallon lit candles in the windows of his home to celebrate the victory. For Patrick Mallon, 1843 was a year of highs and lows. 1843 saw the birth of his first child: a son, whom he named Arthur Wentworth Mallon; Arthur for his father and Wentworth for the politician (and, possibly, friend) that he so admired. Patrick's joy, however, was dampened by the persistent worsening of his financial state.

By March, he was forced to announce his insolvency. He was still trying to sell his lease of the Apothecaries' Hall, but was no longer in a position to bargain. 'In the insolvent estate of P.W. Mallon, surgeon,' he advertised with growing desperation. 'To surgeons, druggists etc. FOR SALE, the interest in the Lease of Apothecaries' Hall, West Maitland, with the Fixtures, Shop Fittings, and a small stock of Drugs.'[123]

His financial strife deepened. Soon he was also trying to offload his Ranfurly Terrace properties, each of which consisted of four rooms, a detached kitchen, stable, and enclosed yard, as well as several small tenements, 'at a trifling rent'.[124]

It was not an ideal time to be adding to his little family, but another child was on the way nevertheless. Discouraged but not beaten, Patrick Mallon moved his family and his practice to Sydney. Before long, his suffering would increase beyond measure.

In late May of 1845, Patrick's wife gave birth to a daughter, whom the couple named Catherine Mary. Two days later, Catherine Ann, the 'beloved wife of P.W. Mallon, Esq., M.D. of Clarence St, Sydney, aged 31 years', whose 'many amiable qualities and virtues had justly endeared her'[125] to her sorrowing husband and friends, passed away. For a man with professional qualifications in midwifery, his inability to see his wife safely through the ordeal of childbirth must have been a torment.

Sorrowing though he was, Patrick Mallon was not one to give in to despair. He carried on working with 'great skill'[126] and engaging with the community. Despite his financial embarrassment, he continued to donate funds to the Catholic Church. Proud of his Irish roots, he chaired the preliminary committee meeting of 'Irishmen and the friends of Ireland', established to arrange a national festival on Saint Patrick's Day, 'with the view of cherishing a love of Green Erin, and of promoting, a cordial and patriotic unanimity, of feeling among all classes of Irishmen and their descendants in Australia'.[127]

But trouble continued to dog him. In late 1847, Mallon moved to a new residence in Elizabeth Street. Only days later, he was robbed; a prowler entered through the parlour window and made off with a work box, a lady's gold watch and chain, some lady's jewellery, and a Catholic prayer book. The items had likely been the property of Patrick's late wife, and their loss must have hurt.

It is not clear what arrangements Patrick made for the care of his children during these years. Arthur was only two when his mother died, leaving Patrick with a toddler and a helpless newborn daughter. A widower would not be expected, in those times, to bring up his motherless children; a man with Dr Mallon's professional commitments even less so. It is likely that his late wife's relations stepped in to take charge of the children; little Catherine in particular would have needed more care than her father could provide. But their father maintained a relationship with his children throughout their lives.

In the short term, he was very much present in young Arthur's life. In 1848 father and son took a trip to New Zealand together, returning many months later via Hong Kong. The journey might have been a farewell tour. Less than two months later – on 3 April, 1849 – Dr Mallon embarked alone on the *Champion* and sailed from Sydney to his new home in Moreton Bay.

Dr Mallon threw himself into the community with his usual gusto. Within weeks of his arrival, he had been engaged as Medical Attendant for the Strangers Home Lodge of the Independent Order of Odd Fellows, Manchester Unity. The Independent Order of Odd Fellows was an international organisation devoted to philanthropy. Emerging in a time when neither government welfare nor social security existed, the purpose of its lodges was to provide aid to its members when they were in need due to sickness, injury or bereavement. Given Dr Mallon's religious tolerance and humanitarian bent, his involvement with this organisation, which was (and is) not affiliated with any religion or political party, was characteristic.

As far as medical practice was concerned, Patrick Mallon hit the ground running. One of his earliest cases was a murder. The body of a missing man named John Leonard was found horribly mutilated – his skull fractured, his throat cut, his abdomen and legs stabbed. The man last seen in his company, Owen Molloy, was found in possession of the victim's coat, scarf and dog, and was charged with his murder. Dr Mallon examined the body and at the inquest testified that the head wounds had caused the victim's death, and that the serrated wounds on the body, inflicted after death, may have been made by a tomahawk found amongst the accused's belongings. Molloy was committed to stand trial.

Although Captain Wickham had the authority to try minor cases in Moreton Bay, there was no Supreme Court in the district; Molloy's trial was held in Sydney. So on 16 August, Dr Mallon boarded the *Eagle* and arrived back in Sydney three days later, where he delivered a witness statement in court. The evidence against Molloy was damning, and he was convicted and sentenced to hang. Dr Mallon lingered in Sydney a few days; perhaps he took the opportunity to reunite with his children. Then on 6 September he set off again for Moreton Bay, arriving four days later on the *Eagle*. On 18 September, the murderer was led, weeping and praying, to the gallows at Darlinghurst Gaol and delivered, deeply repentant, to his death.

Meanwhile Dr Mallon showed every intention of settling in Moreton Bay. He bought 36 perches (around 910m^2) of land in Brisbane. His duties took him as far west as Drayton in the Darling Downs. But professionally, the road for Dr Mallon was not to be an easy one.

In the latter part of 1849, Dr Mallon had attended an innkeeper in Drayton. The journey had been long and the patient's illness extended; Dr Mallon had remained at the inn for 19 or 20 days. Upon the patient's recovery, the doctor had given him a bill for £40 19s for medical attendance, and added £12 for the expenses of his journey. The patient disputed the charge and refused to pay. This must have been maddening for Mallon, who was still trying to get back on his feet financially. The matter would eventually go to court, but it would not be settled for some time yet.

And only months after his involvement with the murder case, Mallon came once again before the courts – this time not as a witness, but as a defendant.

It was another petty squabble over money. In early 1850, Dr Mallon had been called to attend upon a man who subsequently died. There was a dispute over the payment, the deceased's friend claiming that Dr Mallon had charged more than the agreed amount. The court found in favour of the complainant and ordered the doctor to repay the balance. The dispute seems to have resulted from poor communication and was perhaps aggravated by the strain of Dr Mallon's tight finances.

In January 1850, Dr Mallon was elected to the Committee of Moreton Bay Hospital. When the committee met in January 1850 to report upon operations and finances and elect its members, it could not have foreseen the disruption that lay ahead. For Dr Mallon, 1850 would be a terrible year.

15–17 AUGUST: IN THE HOSPITAL

Dr Mallon crossed the wintry waters of Moreton Bay after dark on 14 August. He was not to know how long he would be confined to the island, but he knew that his stay was not likely to be brief. He settled into his accommodation as best he could and rested up for the night. It was the last peace he would have for a long time.

On the *Emigrant*, which bobbed at anchor in the harbour, Elizabeth Wade and the other remaining travellers waited for their turn to disembark. Twenty patients lay in the hospital, including Mary and Joseph Ball. Charles Hallett's illness was in the early inflammatory stage, and kind young Mary Connor had taken his motherless children under her wing, along with the Waterson orphans. By now another seaman, by the name of Ward, had fallen ill. Three patients were reported to be in the 'inflammatory' stage, and one worsening. Six were described as 'recovering' or 'convalescent', although one of these – James Bugsby (Buckby or Buckley) was 'sore from lying'. Ann Lyon, a 30-year-old single domestic servant, was hospitalised with 'nervousness and weakness'. Only one patient was in a state that was not pathological: Louisa Brimble, who was recovering from childbirth.

Dr Mitchell was still gravely ill.

Since the first signs of his fever, Robert Chapple had been by the doctor's side. Robert was a 19-year-old unmarried labourer from Ashcott, Somersetshire. He was one of the few Baptists on board; a literate young man who had left two living parents behind to try his luck in Australia. He would later be commended for his devotion and constant attendance on Dr Mitchell.

When Dr Mallon arose on the morning of 15 August, he took up duties at once.

By 17 August, he had arranged for the rest of the immigrants to be brought to land. What a relief it must have been, after so many days bobbing idly upon the bay, in clear sight of land, to set foot finally upon that stone causeway, to trudge with unsteady legs up the slight incline to the tents and rough cabins that would be their home. But if they had hoped that being free of the confines of the ship – in the fresh air and on solid ground – would enable them to defeat the disease, their hopes were soon to be dashed.

The illness did not die away; on the contrary, it gained momentum and attacked with renewed ferocity. For one in particular, those ruined hopes would prove too much to bear.

Within only three days after the first landing, Dr Mallon found himself reporting unhappily that 89 immigrants were in various stages of disease. Forty-nine were seriously ill and 40 convalescent. And the rate of illness continued to rise.

21 AUGUST: BUILDING A COMMUNITY

The little island community got to work. Captain Kemp supervised the stripping of the timber fittings from the ship: bulkheads and bunks were removed and ferried across to Dunwich. The bay rang out with the rasping of saws and the pounding of hammers as the men fashioned the timber into huts for their accommodation. The majority of the men were labourers, and this was work they took in their stride.

One of these men was David Hobbs. He was a carpenter by trade; an earnest 23-year-old Church of England man from Birmingham. Hobbs was of medium height and build, with a dark complexion and grey eyes. He worked hard, day and night, erecting and repairing the buildings.

With so many sick, there was much to do. Dr Mallon could not possibly attend to 89 patients alone; as well as the building, there was food to prepare, clothes and bedding to wash, and stores to be rationed. A whole village had to be established in an instant; a village in which one half of the community was helpless and the other half under threat of contagion.

And then another blow fell.

Within days of his arrival, Dr Mallon began feeling unwell. With alarm, he recognised signs: the malaise, the aches and pains, the nausea and the dreaded fever. There was no help at hand; with poor George Mitchell still prostrated, Patrick Mallon was the only medical man on the island who was not completely incapacitated. There was no alternative; he had to keep working until relief arrived.

He didn't have long to wait. On 21 August, Captain Wickham sailed across the bay with Health Officer Dr Ballow to check up on the little community. They found it in a state of deep distress. The hospitals were overflowing, Dr Mitchell was on his death bed and Dr Mallon was struggling to keep going. Mallon told the men that he was 'unequal' to the task of tending the sick and begged for relief.

Wickham and Ballow agreed to find another doctor to replace him. But they could not leave the island in so desperate a state, even for a day. They set about organising the community. Dr Ballow appointed hospital attendants: John Clarke Foote, John Shears, George Willis (or Wells), James Buckley, John Williams; and nurses: Ann Campbell, Ann Ford (or Forde) and Charlotte Hardwidge. Robert Chapple continued devoting his care to Dr Mitchell.

Disheartened as they were, Wickham and Ballow assured Dr Mallon that medical aid would soon be on its way. Then they set off again at about midday and made haste back to Brisbane to solicit that help.

THE SAD DESTINY OF ELIZABETH WADE
In the meantime, for one young woman, the suffering had become too much to bear.

For Elizabeth Wade, just turned 19, there was no end in sight – no hope. The darkness was overwhelming. Her mother sweated and shivered in her hospital bed, and her stepfather lay dying in his. Elizabeth had already suffered enough in her short life. Taken from her natural father as a baby, she had been brought up by her first stepfather, but was still a young girl when she lost him. Her younger brother and sister had died in infancy. Now it looked as if she was about to lose not only her second stepfather but also her mother – the only constant in her life, the only blood relative known to her.

Her life had become a nightmare. Her hopes of a bright future in a new colony had crumbled. The voyage had been an ordeal more horrifying than she could ever have imagined, and now, just when it had seemed that the worst might soon be over, fate was offering her a glimpse of a lonely future without her mother.

For days – perhaps weeks – Elizabeth had been caring for her sick mother. She was tired, fearful and despondent. And worse: she was beginning to feel ill.

A few hours after Captain Wickham and Dr Ballow departed on the customs boat to Brisbane, Elizabeth took a loaf of bread and a bottle of water to the hospital for her mother. When she reached the door of the hospital, she changed her mind. She placed the food and drink at the door and turned away. Twenty minutes later, ambling outdoors, she came across Mary Ann Mahoney.

The two young women had much in common; they were the same age, both domestic servants from London, both literate and Protestant. During the months of close confinement in the ship, they must have got to know each other well – perhaps even become friends. Mary Ann, by this time, had troubles of her own. The sailor with whom she had fallen in love was quarantined separately on the barque anchored in Moreton Bay. If there was no further appearance of disease on board, the ship would sail within weeks. She might never see James Hall again.

Mary Ann noticed that Elizabeth was melancholy. She remarked upon it, and Elizabeth confided that she was not well – that she was 'very dull and low spirited'.

At three o'clock, it all became too much. Elizabeth crossed the wharf and wandered down to the beach. Out in the bay, two seamen on the ketch *Aurora* were going about their business. From the *Aurora*, William Smith saw Elizabeth reach the sand and break into a run. Believing that she was intending to bathe, he thought nothing of it.

Elizabeth jogged across the beach to the water's edge, heavy skirts clutching at her ankles. George Jefferson, seaman of the *Aurora*, saw her determined strides and called out in alarm.

Elizabeth ignored him. She may have been too intent on her mission to hear his cries. She charged into the chilly water without pause. Jefferson and Smith watched helplessly as she lurched further into the bay. When the water reached her knees, Elizabeth lay face down in the sea.

At once the two seamen raised the alarm and turned their vessel to shore. *A woman is drowning*, the men screamed from the ketch to the startled immigrants on the island.

On the land, Mary Ann Mahoney and a small group of horrified immigrants cried out and rushed to the beach. James Foote – a 22-year-old farm labourer from Frampton – was by the bay with several others when he heard the alarm from the *Aurora*. He looked about for the cause and saw a young woman lying prone in the shallows. He ran across the beach and into the bay. Elizabeth was lying inert in less than two feet of water.

James lifted her limp body up out of the sea; behind him, his brother John Clarke Foote, John Shears and John Tolman waded out carrying the base of an iron bedstead. Between them, they dragged Elizabeth's sagging body onto the bedstead and carried it out of the water. In the tiny community, word of the drowning spread like a fever, and within an instant, the news had reached Dr Mallon.

The doctor was unwell but, as there was no alternative, he was carrying out his duties as usual. He hurried to the beach, where he found the young men emerging from the sea with the body of Elizabeth Wade dripping from the bedstead in their grasp. *Bring her to the store*, he instructed them, and followed the men up to the little settlement, the body bouncing on its platform between them as they jogged up to the stores.

James Brennan (or 'Braman' or 'Beannan'), who had been acting as a hospital assistant to Dr Mallon, was immediately on hand to help out. James was a 28-year-old Irish Presbyterian, a labourer whose cousins had preceded him to the colony of New South Wales. Dr Mallon and his assistant set about trying to revive the young woman.

They worked on her for two hours.

Dr Mallon did not specify the methods he used to try to revive Elizabeth Wade. Medical science was in a period of indecision about the best way to resuscitate a drowning victim. Until 1829, the preferred method had been to inflate the lungs with a set of bellows. This procedure fell out of favour when it was found that it could cause lung damage and death. Doctors experimented over the next century with various other methods using mechanical devices and tubes, but it is unlikely that Dr Mallon had access to any of these devices. He was working under primitive conditions with limited equipment.

Most likely he would have used one of the many methods of manual or postural ventilation that were in experimental stages at the time. Dr Mallon may have placed Elizabeth gently in the prone position, with one wrist under her forehead. He may have waited for any fluid to drain out and for her tongue to drop forward and leave the airway clear. He would have waited and watched, hoping that she would resume breathing on her own. When she didn't, Dr Mallon would have tried to 'excite' breathing. This might have been done by turning Elizabeth onto her side, exciting her nostrils with snuff, or tickling her throat with a feather. He may have rubbed her face to warm it, before splashing it with cold water.

When this failed, his next attempt may have been to 'imitate' breathing. He may have placed Elizabeth face up on a bed and applied gentle pressure alternately to her chest and abdomen, hoping to reproduce respiration by expelling and drawing in air in turn.

Or he might have rolled the girl onto her face, raising her chest with a folded blanket beneath it, using the weight of her body and the pressure of his hands upwards on her chest to expel the air from her lungs. Then he may have rolled her onto her side, relieving the pressure on her chest in an attempt to draw the air back in, rocking her gently to and fro, sometimes to one side and sometimes to the other.

At the same time, with James Brennan's help, Dr Mallon would have tried to keep Elizabeth's blood circulating. They would have kept her warm by swathing her in flannels and applying heated cloths to her torso and legs. They may have rubbed her limbs, using their hands, handkerchiefs and warm soft flannels, pressing always upwards in an attempt to push her blood through her veins towards her heart. They may even have tipped a teaspoonful of aromatic spirit of ammonia into her nostrils, or stroked the inside of her nose with a feather dipped in ammonia. Dr Mallon may have injected her with a stimulant: a pint of water mixed with a tablespoon of ground mustard and a teaspoonful of cayenne pepper. He may even have applied a mustard poultice to her anus, or injected a solution of ammonia, wine, camphor or brandy into her rectum.

In the end, their efforts came to nothing. By the time the sun sank into the mainland across the bay, the pair had to admit defeat; poor Elizabeth's life could not be restored.

Next day, George Watson, the customs official who had been charged with superintending the quarantine station, gathered a melancholy group of witnesses together. Dr Mallon and his helper James Brennan; James Foote and Mary Ann Mahoney; the two seamen from the *Aurora,* William Smith and George Jefferson all gave their accounts of the drowning. A panel of twelve men – a makeshift 'jury' – after considering the evidence, concluded unanimously that the young woman had committed suicide 'whilst labouring under temporary insanity brought on by excessive fatigue in attending her sick parents'. The men signed their names to the verdict; they were: John Farmer, Henry Lipscombe, Francis Lyon, William Smith, Josiah Trowbridge, William Short, Thomas Gleeson, Thomas Perkins, James Foote and Thomas Hastings – and Henry Wallace and Andrew Brimble, who signed with the illiterate's cross.

Once the inquiry was over, there was another grim task to be done: Elizabeth's burial. Burial at sea had been a simpler matter, for it entailed only sewing the body into a canvas shroud and pitching it into the deep. On land, death imposed the dismal chores of grave-digging and coffin-making. Young David Hobbs, whose carpentry skills had been employed up to this point in building accommodation for the living immigrants, now turned his hand to housing the dead. He could have had no idea how hard he would work over the ensuing weeks – day and night – building coffins.

For Elizabeth Wade's suicide was the first death on land, but there were many more to come.

21–22 AUGUST: THE SEARCH FOR A DOCTOR

Meanwhile, back in Brisbane, Dr Ballow was desperately trying to find a medical man to help Dr Mallon. But to his dismay, a volunteer was impossible to find. Besides Ballow and Mallon, there were four medicos in the vicinity of Brisbane and Ipswich. Of these men, one could not be contacted, and the others refused the plea for help.

It wasn't surprising that no one wanted the job. At best, it would disrupt their professional practice and isolate them from their families for an indefinite (and probably long) period. At worst, it could kill them.

At least some members of the community saw their reluctance as perfectly reasonable. As a reporter for the *Moreton Bay Courier* wrote:

> The want of zeal may be traced to the fact, that there is no certain provision for the surviving families of those who may be cut off by disease in the performance of such dangerous duties; and although we should join in admiration of any man who would voluntarily risk his life for the preservation of those of others, it must be remembered that there are grave and solemn duties which every man owes to those dependent upon him for support.

The doctors had 'wives, children, or other helpless relatives in their care' who would be left destitute by their death, and, the reporter went on:

it would be hard to condemn any man who gave his first care to his own family. Whilst we appreciate and honour the devotion of those who have exposed themselves to death in the performance of their professional duties, we cannot say that he who has no prospect of his family being provided for, ought to be blamed for being careful of his life.[128]

Understandable as the doctors' refusal was, it left Dr Ballow in a difficult position. It was not his duty to take over care of the quarantine station himself. In fact, he did not even hold a permanent government-appointed position as health officer in Moreton Bay; Captain Wickham had asked him to *act* in the role when the *Emigrant*'s arrival created the need. Typically, when a ship was quarantined, it was the health officer's role to appoint another doctor to look after the sick, while he kept himself available to fulfil his other duties such as meeting and inspecting incoming ships, liaising with the government and attending to public health. It was by no means expected that Dr Ballow should serve as a clinician at the station. But the lack of volunteers left him with little choice. He could wait for a replacement to arrive from Sydney – a three-day journey by steamship, by which time the death toll would have skyrocketed – or he could go himself. He chose to offer himself.

Dr Ballow stepped up with a clear lack of enthusiasm. In a letter addressed to Captain Wickham, he made it plain that he was volunteering, 'although not holding at present any regular appointment as Health Officer or Colonial Surgeon, by virtue of which my services could be officially required'.[129] He pointed out that absenting himself from Brisbane would harm his own private practice, noting that he had several midwifery and other cases that would have to be referred to another doctor.

The task would be not only a sacrifice as far as business was concerned, but also downright unpleasant. 'The quarantine station also being of a very considerable distance from Brisbane,' Ballow wrote, 'and having no proper accommodation, to afford shelter from the inclemencies of the weather, together with the vast amount of sickness prevailing there, will render the duty a very arduous and disagreeable one.'

But uppermost in Dr Ballow's mind must have been the significant risk to his own health. With fever tearing through the quarantine station, he had every reason to worry.

DR DAVID BALLOW

Dr David Keith Ballow was well known to Captain Wickham. Brisbane was a small town and the men moved in the same circles. Only six years apart in age, both were Scots who had grown up in Leith. They had sat on committees together, served as police magistrates together, and interacted often in their professional lives during their years in Moreton Bay. But concerned as he must have been about the danger into which Ballow was about to place himself, Wickham would have understood, as Ballow himself did, the call of duty.

Dr Ballow was the resident surgeon of the Moreton Bay District Hospital, as well as police magistrate and district coroner. Having worked in Brisbane since its convict days, Ballow was one of the town's longest-standing residents – and one of the most respected.

The doctor was a colourful, larger-than-life figure – 'rather a good-looking jolly Scotsman'.[130] He was born on 27 October 1804 at Montrose, the eldest son of John and Marjory (née Sparks) Ballow. By the time he was seven years old, the family had moved to Leith, the port town that serviced Edinburgh. It was there that

David's younger siblings, Marjory junior and William Douglass, were born. His father, John Ballow, was a cloth merchant who lived and worked on the Shore, in a house that overlooked the Water of Leith.

Ballow's childhood and young adulthood are poorly documented. His family must have been reasonably affluent, for the boy was well educated. In a time when medical practitioners could be trained by apprenticeships to local surgeons, only the prosperous and well connected went to university. Like George Mitchell and Patrick Walsh Mallon, David Ballow received his training in Edinburgh, in one of the most prestigious medical schools in the country at the time.

He graduated with a Licentiate from the Royal College of Surgeons at the age of 28 in 1832 – four years after Dr Mallon. By 1836, he had arrived in the New South Wales town of Sydney. He was appointed medical clerk, a government position that paid the healthy but not extravagant salary of £128 2s.

Dr Ballow was capable and conscientious and, it seems, charismatic and ambitious. Only a few months after his appointment as medical clerk in Sydney, he was also appointed as district surgeon of Invermein (later known as Scone). With convict servants assigned to him as footman and valet, Ballow lived in relative comfort in the Hunter River region.

As district surgeon, Dr Ballow was responsible for the medical care of convicts and free settlers in his district. The role was an important one. It was also, at times, a role that might have presented ethical challenges for a man whose professional calling was to heal and protect the sick.

One of his unpleasant duties was to supervise convict floggings. Times were harsh. Although change was afoot, discipline of convicts was still excessive and cruel, and punishments brutal.

But as district surgeon, Dr Ballow would have had to get used to any distaste he might have felt, for it was part of his job to make sure convicts survived their punishments.

On 21 October 1837, David Keith Ballow married Margaret Campbell McArthur in the Presbyterian Church of Scotland in Sydney. Ballow's bride was an attractive young woman who, at only 16 years old, was less than half her husband's age. Margaret was the youngest daughter of the late Captain Donald McArthur, a military man of moderate wealth and social status.

Margaret had arrived in the colony of New South Wales as an assisted immigrant on the *Canton* in 1835, accompanied by her widowed mother, two of her brothers and their wives, and two sisters. Another sister would migrate two years later. (Two other brothers had died as young men in Edinburgh.)

On her arrival in Sydney, the future Mrs Ballow experienced a small taste of what the passengers of the *Emigrant* – and her own husband – would later endure. One of her fellow-passengers had come down with smallpox on the voyage, and the vessel was diverted on arrival to the quarantine station at Spring Cove. But the quarantine period was mercifully brief, for the disease had died out long before the *Canton* arrived in Sydney; the passengers were released within a few days. The family settled into life in New South Wales, and within a few years, all four McArthur girls had married well.

Less than two months after his marriage, Dr Ballow was appointed colonial assistant surgeon and transferred back to Sydney. Attending to prisoners continued to be a large part of his duties. His patients would have been the convicts on road gangs and in Hyde Park Barracks. He would have visited the Sydney Hospital in Macquarie Street and the crumbling old Sydney Gaol on George Street. Here, public hangings were held at the timber gallows that loomed over the gaol's stone walls. He would have supervised the administration of floggings and attended to the wounds of the victims afterwards.

Dr Ballow enjoyed great social status and mixed in exalted circles. He had position and a good income, but he also harboured ambition. He had a taste for a challenge.

The Ballows didn't stay long in Sydney. It seems that the doctor had too much pioneering spirit to settle in a city that was already well established; perhaps the idea of a new frontier that he could have a hand in shaping was too attractive to resist. Whatever the reason, on 22 March 1838 – only three months after moving to Sydney – David and Margaret Ballow boarded the brig *Isabella* and sailed to the convict establishment at Moreton Bay. The doctor had been appointed assistant colonial surgeon for the district.

When the Ballows arrived in Moreton Bay, the settlement was coming to the end of its convict era. In its heyday, it had housed around a thousand convicts; by the time Dr Ballow took up his appointment, numbers were down to only 300. He was the only doctor in the settlement.

It was Dr Ballow's job to tend the convicts and the military men who guarded them. Although the settlement was not as brutal as it had been a decade earlier, convicts were still flogged for misdemeanours. For neglecting their work, for insolence or stealing flour, a prisoner might receive 25 lashes. For repeatedly refusing to work, for threatening a constable, or for drunkenness, he could get 50 lashes. Prisoners who absconded or tried to abscond, stole food or rum, were repeatedly drunk and disorderly, or were violent, might be punished with 100 lashes or more.[131]

Floggings aside, the convicts and their minders kept Dr Ballow busy with a range of medical complaints. He attended to them in the Moreton Bay Convict Hospital, which was part of the complex of government buildings near the river, roughly where Queen Street meets William Street today. He treated cases of catarrh, rheumatism, asthma, pleurisy, fevers and haemorrhoids, gonorrhoea and syphilis.

The Moreton Bay Convict Hospital's role was to care for the convicts and government men; it was not responsible for the health of civilians, of whom there were few. But Dr Ballow, as a medical man with a strong sense of decency and duty, was unable to ignore the plight of sufferers who were ineligible for treatment at the hospital. He sought – and was granted – permission to borrow medicines from the hospital to treat these patients, and replace them later with stock he bought from Sydney, thus becoming Brisbane's first unofficial private practitioner of medicine.

The surgeon was well respected in the growing village of Brisbane. He was competent, conscientious and pragmatic. He attended to detail and correct procedure. His code of morality seems to have been conventional for a professional gentleman of the Victorian era: he believed in hard work, social responsibility and obedience to the law. To have tolerated the duty of attending floggings and hangings, Dr Ballow must have approved of – or at least accepted – the prevailing colonial attitudes to justice. He must have been able to overcome his surgeon's instincts to 'do no harm' in the interests of upholding the law, regardless of the cruelty of that law. He was a man of his times.

Dr Ballow was charitable but he was not a pushover. Convicts who misbehaved in his service could expect to be punished. When a convict servant of Ballow's drunkenly refused to obey orders, swore and attempted to strike him on the head with a saucepan, Ballow had the man taken to court, where he was sentenced to an iron-gang for 12 months. And when Ballow's servant Edward

Dwyer became drunk and abusive and absented himself without leave, Ballow had him charged and sentenced to a week in the lock-up.

But by the standards of the time, the surgeon was a fair master. He valued industry and rewarded those who, in his view, were deserving. Hannah Rigby was one of Dr Ballow's convict servants who would benefit from his benevolence. Hannah was an absconder and a repeat offender. An English-born embroiderer, she had been sentenced in 1821 to transportation for seven years for larceny. Two years after receiving her ticket of freedom, she was back in custody, having stolen 30 yards of ribbon. This time, she was sent to Moreton Bay. When her sentence expired and she returned to Sydney, Hannah immediately re-offended. She was sent straight back to Moreton Bay and assigned as a servant to Dr Ballow.

By then the government was winding down the penal settlement. The few remaining female convicts were returned to Sydney, but Hannah Rigby alone stayed on. Dr Ballow had found her conduct 'exemplary' and vowed that she had 'never given him any cause for distrust or complaint'.[132] He believed that her sentence should be remitted and asked the then Commandant, Lieutenant Owen Gorman, to petition on her behalf. The petition succeeded, and Hannah Rigby became a free woman. She stayed in the district after gaining her freedom – the only Moreton Bay female convict to do so.

When the government announced the closure of the Moreton Bay penal settlement in 1842, it looked as if the hospital would shut down with it. The government was looking to save money. But with some prisoners, government officials and military men remaining, Dr Ballow still had patients to keep him busy. Even during the convict times, some free men had begun to drift into

Moreton Bay. When the government opened Moreton Bay to free settlement, the trickle of settlers grew to a steady stream.

By this time, the Ballows were entrenched and had no intention of leaving. They lived in the surgeon's quarters: a cottage behind the hospital, on the bank of the river near present-day North Quay. Dr Ballow had thrown himself with gusto into life in the budding town of Brisbane. He had quickly become successful – professionally, financially and socially. He was committed to his community. He had seen the town grow from a population of about 300 white residents, most of whom were convicts, to almost a thousand free settlers. Land was being cleared for farming and business opportunities were opening up. The future looked exciting.

Once settled in Brisbane, Dr Ballow encouraged his sister to join him. In September 1841, Marjory Ballow sailed from Dundee to Sydney and thence to Moreton Bay. She arrived in late January 1842, and six months later was married to John Kent, the deputy assistant commissary general: an ill-fated man. (Much later, poor Marjory would have to endure the suicides of both her husband and son.)

In 1843, the government held its first sale of land in what would later become the state of Queensland. Dr Ballow bought land on the river bank in the area that is now Eagle Street.

As the population of Brisbane grew, so did the demand for medical services. Dr Ballow was no longer the only medical practitioner. The homeopath Dr Stephen Simpson had arrived in the district in 1841 and acted as colonial surgeon when Dr Ballow returned briefly to Sydney. Simpson gave up practice the following year and became commissioner of Crown Lands for Moreton Bay, acting as administrator until the arrival of Captain Wickham. Simpson's arrival in the colony was soon followed by the appearance of Dr Kearsey Cannan, who began practising in Queen Street in 1842. Glasgow-trained William McTaggart Dorsey moved to Moreton Bay in 1842 and built up a medical practice at Limestone (Ipswich). Dr William Hobbs and Dr Patrick Mallon joined the fraternity at Moreton Bay in 1849.

Not all patients could afford medical attention. With this in mind, residents of Moreton Bay met in 1844 to establish the Moreton Bay Benevolent Society, whose charitable purpose was to 'relieve the poor, the distressed and the aged'.[133] With Dr Ballow as its treasurer, the society funded treatment for paupers through donations from settlers.

In a practice that is astonishing today, that charity published the names of its beneficiaries, along with the dates of their admission and discharge and even their diagnoses, in the local newspaper. In 1845 and 1846, the society gave charity to 18 patients for the treatment of conditions such as ulcers, dyspepsia, rheumatism, syphilis, *prurigo scroti* (itchy rash of the scrotum), *fistula uranitis*, pyrosis (heartburn), tuberculosis and gonorrhoea. These details were all printed in the *Moreton Bay Courier*.

The life of a colonial surgeon in the frontier town was far from dull. Dr Ballow treated infectious diseases, snakebites, broken limbs and gunshot wounds; and as the settlement grew, he delivered babies, attended to the ailments of old age, and treated victims of violence, accident, and attempted suicide. He even tended a man who had been attacked by a shark while swimming in the river. And if this wasn't excitement enough, he also served as district coroner. As the only medical man in the district when he arrived, Dr Ballow had acted unofficially as coroner for years until his appointment was formalised in 1848.

Ballow's skills in the rough-and-ready settlement were in demand. His duties as surgeon and coroner were not for the faint-hearted. But Dr Ballow didn't quail before grisly tasks; on the contrary, he had just the personality to handle the challenges of his job. He was courageous, confident in his considerable abilities, and astonishingly energetic. Nothing was too hard for him.

In Brisbane's early days, the Indigenous groups of Moreton Bay outnumbered white settlers. For the most part, relations between Indigenous and European people had been initially cordial, but now and then, disputes arose and conflict became violent. In late May 1840, the assistant surveyor Granville William Chetwynd Stapylton – a notoriously difficult man – and two convict labourers were measuring out the land near Mt Lindsay, when a group of Aboriginal men set upon them. Stapylton and the convict William Tuck were speared and bludgeoned to death; the other convict, James Dunlop, was seriously wounded.

The rest of Stapylton's party returned to the camp later that day to find the surveyor and Tuck murdered and Dunlop unconscious. They fled to Brisbane to fetch the commandant of the settlement – Owen Gorman – and Dr Ballow. About a week passed between the attack and the arrival of Ballow and the commandant upon the scene, and by this time, Dunlop was close to death. Dr Ballow dressed his wounds and attended to the bodies of the murdered men, which were in a dreadful state. Stapylton's arms were gone, and his right foot had been broken off near the ankle joint. His skull lay a few yards away from his torso. His partly burned body had been eaten, possibly by native dogs. Dr Ballow could identify the surveyor only by the colour of the hair on the detached head. The body of the prisoner Tuck was in a 'highly putrid state, much charred by the fire, and was torn and disfigured in many parts by the birds of prey'.[134]

Dr Ballow had the gruesome job of conducting the autopsies.

Two men were later captured for the killings, tried and sentenced to death. Merridio and Nengavil were tried for the murder of Tuck alone, for Stapylton's body had been mutilated so badly that it was impossible to determine the cause of his death. In Queensland's first public execution, Merridio and Nengavil were hanged from Brisbane's convict-operated windmill. Dr Ballow, as colonial assistant surgeon, was a witness at the morbid event; it was his job to certify that the prisoners were dead.

In a town with such a small population, the Ballows would have known most of the inhabitants. When tragedy struck them, it must have affected Dr Ballow personally. As a devout Anglican, the doctor would have been thrown into contact with the 'pioneer' Anglican Minister John Gregor, who was a Scot like himself.

John Gregor's brother, Andrew, had settled on the Pine River, 35 miles north of Brisbane. Neither John nor his brother Andrew was well adapted to life in the wild north. They faced many difficulties, not least of which was the strained relations between white settlers and Indigenous groups in the area. These relations had deteriorated since 1842, when shepherds had massacred up to 60 Aboriginal visitors to Kilcoy Station in a horrific mass poisoning. A long campaign of retribution culminated in a coordinated attack, by men from local Aboriginal groups, on Gregor's station in October 1846. The attackers killed Andrew Gregor and Mary Shannon, the pregnant wife of his servant.

Dr Ballow conducted autopsies on the victims. It must have been an appalling task. According to the *Cornwall Chronicle*:

the head and face of Mr. Gregor were covered with blood; the left eye had been driven from the orbit, and there were numberless fractures of the skull, more particularly one on the left side, extending from the orbit to behind the ear, and another on the right side, through which the brain protruded. The head and face of the murdered woman were also covered with blood, and on the left side there was a large open wound extending from near the orbit to behind the ear, exposing the brain, which appeared to have been inflicted by a tomahawk.[135]

Eight years later, a warrior of the Dalla people would be sentenced to death for the murder of Andrew Gregor and a further killing in 1847. His name was Dundalli. An exceptionally charismatic man, Dundalli was one of the most respected Indigenous lawmen in the district whose attempts to conduct peaceful negotiations with the white settlers had been frustrated. This leader of resistance to white domination was eventually hanged in a horrifying botched execution.

Dr Ballow also conducted an inquest into the brutal murder of the sawyer Robert Cox. In 1848, pieces of Cox's dismembered body had been found scattered around Kangaroo Point on the morning after he had been drinking with friends at Sutton's Bush Inn. Cox had been overheard talking about a lucrative job he had just finished, and it was rumoured that he had been slain for his money. The inn's cook, William Fyfe, was found guilty of the murder. He was hanged in Sydney, although protesting his innocence until the end. Years later, a rumour went about that the prominent public figure Patrick Mayne had confessed to the murder on his deathbed.[136] His story has become one of Brisbane's most enigmatic and notorious legends.

1848 also saw Dr Ballow taking on the office of police magistrate. As Brisbane grew, so did the range of the doctor's interests. With no children of his own, Dr Ballow channelled his seemingly boundless energy into the community. In 1848 he was elected to the North Brisbane's local Church of England school board. The following year he became treasurer of the committee for Brisbane's newly formed School of Arts: a society for 'intellectual recreation and instruction', whose purpose was to 'furnish opportunities for the discussion of subjects connected with arts, sciences, and general literature; and to provide a library and reading-room for its members'.[137]

Dr Ballow's interests were not even limited to medical practice, justice, education and the arts. He was also a keen horticulturalist who produced 'healthy and vigorous' crops of sugar and cotton. In 1849 – a year in which Ballow threw himself into a breathtaking range of endeavours – he was appointed to the founding committee of a newly established (but short-lived) Moreton Bay Sugar Company.

The Ballows were committed Christians. They worshipped in a rough Church of England church that sat behind the convict lumber yard on the corner of Queen Street and North Quay: a small, simple brick building known as 'St John's'. Before long the congregation had outgrown its primitive little church and sought to build a new one. In 1848 Ballow was appointed as a trustee to superintend the building of a new church in Brisbane – once more, in the company of Captain Wickham. The following year, the Crown granted land to the church. The new church would, in time, be built – but not until Dr Ballow was no longer in a position to enjoy the fruits of his labours.

Since the closure of the penal settlement, the continued operation of the hospital at Moreton Bay had been under constant threat. In 1848, that threat came close to realisation. The government wanted to discharge the remaining patients, close the hospital, and transfer Dr Ballow to Van Diemen's Land. Dr Ballow objected. By now he was decidedly a Brisbane man. Captain Wickham supported him in his appeal against the hospital's closure. He wrote to the governor of New South Wales, who agreed to hand over the management of the hospital to a 'committee of gentlemen'.

A public meeting was held in May 1848 and a hospital committee was formed. Late that year, the former convict hospital became Brisbane's first public hospital: the Moreton Bay District Hospital. Dr Ballow was no longer a member of the Convict Medical Service. In 1849, he resigned from his position as treasurer to take up the role of resident surgeon at the new hospital. Dr Kearsey Cannan was to assist him as visiting surgeon.

Offering a salary of £25 per year plus accommodation, Dr Ballow's job was not a lucrative one. Rent on a humble two-bedroom cottage in Moreton Bay in 1849 could be as much as £12 per annum. As visiting surgeon, Dr Cannan was paid twice as much as his colleague the house surgeon. Money doesn't seem to have been a strong motivator for Dr Ballow. He was inspired more, it seems, by a sense of duty and the thrill of a challenge.

In 1849, Dr Ballow took on yet even more public duties. One was a position as surgeon to the newly established gaol. The other was as a member of the local Board of Immigration at Moreton Bay, along with Captain Wickham and William Duncan. The immigration board investigated complaints from passengers or crew when vessels arrived in the colony. Normally, the day after a ship arrived, a member of the board would inspect it before anyone else was allowed on board. He would interview all the immigrants and ask whether they had complaints about the crew, the captain, the surgeon or the ship. Serious complaints would be investigated and reported to the colonial secretary, who could impose fines for misconduct.

An immigration board had become necessary since Brisbane had begun attracting more free settlers directly from England.

When these vessels arrived, Dr Ballow, acting as health officer, boarded them with the customs officer to conduct the mandatory inspection. On finding typhus on board the *Fortitude* in 1849, Dr Ballow advised Captain Wickham to quarantine the immigrants at Moreton Island. Wickham sent tents for their accommodation and provisions to sustain them until they could be given a clean bill of health.

The people of the *Fortitude* were lucky. The death toll stopped at two, and the travellers were released to Brisbane after only two weeks at Moreton Island. Although the delay and discomfort of quarantine were inconvenient, their trials were trivial compared with the suffering of the *Emigrant*'s passengers, who would follow them into Moreton Bay 18 months later. When Dr Ballow issued instructions to the captain of the *Fortitude*, he could have had no inkling that the following year he would find himself dealing with a similar situation – a situation that would start in the same way, but have a tragically different end.

When the *Emigrant* sailed into Dr Ballow's life in August 1850, he was not quite 46 years old. His wife, Margaret, was only 29. The couple was comfortably settled in the community; they were highly regarded by members of their social set, financially secure, and rich with purpose. But their good fortune was about to come to an end.

23–26 AUGUST: AT THE QUARANTINE STATION

On 23[138] August, David Keith Ballow boarded the customs boat to Dunwich. Margaret Ballow's anxiety as she farewelled her husband can easily be imagined.

The doctor arrived to find the quarantine station in a dire state, with 68 patients in the hospital. The few days since his last visit had been eventful. Poor Elizabeth Wade had committed suicide, and typhus raged through the terrified and chaotic community. Dr Mitchell was still desperately ill, despite Robert Chapple's devoted care. But Dr Mallon's health had already improved and he offered his services as Dr Ballow's assistant.

In the few days since the drowning, death had already visited the settlement again. On 23 August, at 1.30 in the morning, typhus killed Joseph Rowe. Joseph was a single man; a 27-year-old labourer from Somersetshire. The fever had claimed him quickly; only eight days earlier he had been in good health.

Joseph's death was followed quickly by the demise of George Heuston (or Huiston). George was a 26-year-old labourer from Dr Mallon's home county of Tyrone. He had been helping to care for the sick on board the ship until he fell ill himself. Captain Kemp had hoped that removal to land would revive George Heuston, but his hopes had been dashed. 'When he went ashore a lease might have been taken of his life,' Kemp wrote sadly, 'but it took him off in a few hours.'

George Heuston died at six minutes past six in the evening of 24 August. Again, David Hobbs sawed and hammered and fashioned coffins. The two men were buried with Elizabeth Wade on a patch of land that sloped down to the sandy bay and commanded a glorious view of the glittering sea, a mile north of the quarantine station. Their names were inscribed on a 'humble wooden tablet'.[139]

By this time, Dr Ballow had taken charge of the station. He and Wickham had found, like Dr Mitchell had before them, that most of the immigrants were reluctant to put themselves in harm's way by helping the sick. In desperation, Wickham resorted to offering them the promise of daily wages for their services, to be paid when the quarantine was over. The doctors also found that help was given a little more freely when 'stimulants' – alcohol – were offered as a reward. With these inducements, they were able to enlist some volunteers.

Dr Ballow made plans to remove the healthy immigrants to the hills about a quarter of a mile north of the hospital. It seemed that matters *must* improve now. With two competent doctors and an army of helpers; with fresh air, supplies coming regularly from Brisbane on the *Aurora*, the separation of the sick from the healthy and the renewal of hope, it must have seemed impossible that the disease could continue to thrive. And indeed, for a few days there *was* a respite.

The immigrants settled into a routine. The workers kept busy. Hospital attendants toiled around the clock, at great risk to themselves. In fact, almost every hospital attendant or nurse fell ill at some point. Some recovered; others did not.

JOHN CLARKE FOOTE

From the moment the immigrants landed, John Clarke Foote took charge of the hospital, attending to patients day and night. He was a 28-year-old farmer who was travelling with his new wife, Mary Anne. The couple had been married only ten days when they had sailed from Plymouth on the honeymoon from Hell. They were emigrating as part of a larger group – with John's mother, Elizabeth; his brother, James; and his three unmarried sisters: Clarissa (aged 24), Lucy (17) and Harriet (13).

The Foote family would later prove to be an example of the assisted emigration scheme's success. The Footes were decent people: well educated, capable, pragmatic and kind.

John Clarke Foote was the eldest child of hatmaker and lay preacher Joseph Foote and his wife Elizabeth Clarke. He was born at Calne, Wiltshire, in 1822, and baptised two years later in the Wesleyan Methodist Church, Melksham. The family moved back to Gloucestershire, where John received his primary education at private school. He was 'of a studious turn of mind', having read widely to advance his education after leaving school. He had a particular interest in chemistry and liked to put it to practical use in tending to the sick. In later life, it was said of John Clarke Foote that 'countless persons had reason to be grateful to him for his kindly treatment of them during their periods of illness'.[140] It was this combination of knowledge, kindness and diligence that made John Clarke Foote so highly valued by the doctors and their charges at Dunwich.

The Foote family's story differed from the stories of many of their fellow-passengers. They were better off than most; throughout the 1830s and into the 1840s, Joseph had owned a freehold house and garden. The Foote name was held in high regard in the village.

John Clarke Foote's father and two brothers had emigrated before the rest of the family. Joseph, the patriarch, had sailed ahead to prepare the way for his wife and remaining children. He went as an agent of 'The Colonial Missionary Society', an organisation whose purpose was to promote the Congregationalist faith in the colonies, mainly amongst the white settlers. Back in Frampton, his wife had waited for news from her husband. His reports must have been favourable, for his sudden and premature death in Van Diemen's Land was not enough to discourage her or her grown children from undertaking the journey themselves. So it was that Elizabeth Foote, her five children aged from 13 to 29, and one daughter-in-law found themselves in Australia.

Elizabeth was 58 years old. It must have been hard, at her age, to tear herself away from her home country and start a new life in a strange land without her husband. But two of her sons were already living in Australia and the rest of her children were literate, resourceful and capable young adults who stood every chance of success in the colonies. Her sons John Clarke and James were farm labourers, and her two older daughters were dressmakers. There was every reason to expect they would find work in Australia and be able to support her in her widowhood. So it was that the Footes had found themselves aboard the *Emigrant*, bound for Moreton Bay.

It was a shame that Elizabeth, the matriarch, didn't live long enough to enjoy her children's success in the new colony. She died in May 1852, less than two years after her arrival. Her dreams had never really come to fruition, with her husband's death in Tasmania putting an end to hopes for a family reunion in Australia before they could even begin.

Her children, however, would thrive in their adopted home. They were intelligent, industrious, wise and philanthropic. They would succeed in business and public and family life, and become much-admired members of the community. In time, John Clarke would become a highly respected member of the Legislative Council, and James would serve terms as a member of the Queensland Legislative Assembly, alderman of Ipswich City Council, and mayor of Ipswich. But that was all in the future. Meanwhile, in 1850, they were simply counted as a blessing to the overworked doctors and the bewildered immigrants stranded at Dunwich.

INDUSTRY AT THE STATION

Care of the sick did not only involve administering medicines, washing and feeding the patients and soothing their fevers.

With so many inmates, the hospital had to operate like a proper institution, primitive though it was. There was food to be cooked, laundry to be done and stores to be managed.

Joseph Hall[141] and Ellen Walsh took over the washing for the hospital. This would have been an enormous and physically demanding job, given the inadequate facilities. Bedding and clothing had to be changed and aired regularly in the interests of hygiene. How the pair managed such a quantity of laundry in such circumstances is hard to imagine.

James Welsh (or Welch or Walsh) cooked for the hospital. Again, it was a mammoth task. In these early days of quarantine, there were up to 68 patients in the hospital and over 70 more convalescing – all needing to be fed, and all trying to keep clean and comfortable in accommodation that was barely more sophisticated than a campsite.

From the outset, John Farmer and Henry Lipscombe took charge of the stores. The *Aurora* brought supplies of bread, flour, meat, vegetables, tea, sugar and butter from Brisbane. She also brought bedding, oil, candles and utensils, and brandy, rum, wine, porter ale and beer for medicinal purposes. The supplies were lodged in the stores building where John Farmer and Henry Lipscombe organised them and 'judiciously and regularly' dispensed them as necessary.

Patrick Maunsell, the young Irishman from Limerick, continued to help the surgeons. Dr Ballow's praise for him was glowing. Mary Connor kept busy looking after the three Waterson orphans and the four youngest motherless Halletts: seven bewildered children. When Julia Chapple, the widow of James who had perished at sea, fell ill and languished in the quarantine hospital for seven weeks, her three small boys would have been in dire straits were it not for the kindness of some of the young female immigrants. Her eldest son was only six, and the youngest, one. Amelia Baker, a young married Englishwoman from Nailsea, and Emma Frith stepped in to fill the breach. Emma had recently lost her eight-month-old son. It must have broken her heart to look after another woman's one-year-old boy in place of her own.

The *Aurora* traversed the bay often. She brought over 371 live sheep, two dairy cows and some calves to keep the immigrants in milk and meat. James Foote took on the role of butcher and performed his duties to Ballow's satisfaction. A whole village was established on the island in a matter of days.

On 24 August, the *Moreton Bay Chronicle* reported that the immigrants would probably be released in 30 days – 30 days being the period of time after the last appearance of disease that must elapse before the community could be declared free of typhus. 'It is to be hoped,' the *Courier* sniped, 'that, as Dr. Ballow has now taken charge of the sick, his experience as a government surgeon will enable him to carry into effect those details of order and arrangement which must be so necessary under the unfortunate circumstances of the case, and which we fear have, from various causes, been as yet but indifferently attended to.'[142]

ISLAND LIFE

Meantime, those immigrants who were neither sick nor hard at work had little reason to complain. They were free to enjoy the offerings of this astonishingly beautiful island, with its white beaches, topaz bays, shady tangled forests; its dense ropey mangroves and grassy swamps. The island was abundant with wildlife: koalas, ducks and frogs, tortoises and wallabies, grey kangaroos, echidnas, bandicoots and possums. The birdlife alone was marvellous: the migratory waterbirds, sandpipers and kookaburras. The sea swarmed with life: turtles and rays, dolphins and dugongs. The humpback whales were journeying south with their newborn calves, passing by on the eastern side of the island – the ocean side – in view of any immigrants energetic enough to cross the island by foot.

Along with supplies of food, citizens of the mainland had sent various entertainments, and the immigrants amused themselves by reading newspapers, playing cricket and quoits and, as usual, with needlework and knitting. The men fished and the children attended school, though for those whose parents lay in hospital beds or on the ocean floor it must have been hard to concentrate. How Anne, Charlotte, Henry and George Hallett must have worried as their father deteriorated and their older brother James started showing signs of disease.

Meanwhile, those adventurous enough to stray from the camp-site might have laboured up the hills and explored the forests of eucalypts and grass trees to discover the ancient, pristine lakes that slept silently inland. The men traipsed through muddy swamplands, shooting ducks and finding fish for their dinners. Children roamed freely within the confines of the station; even five-year-olds like Samuel Brimble faced daily adventures.

The strict rules that had governed life at sea were almost certainly relaxed. In the quarantine station, no one had the authority to govern the immigrants' behaviour beyond requiring them to keep within the boundaries of the station. Neither Captain Kemp nor George Watson, superintendent of the station, could regulate the distribution of rations nor enforce any other sort of order. The surgeon-superintendent was incapacitated, and the matron dead. The immigrants were free to wander into the bush or on the beach – anywhere and anytime, so long as they kept within the restricted area. It is likely that the strict segregation of single males and single females was no longer observed. It was probably at the quarantine station that romantic relationships formed: relationships that would flourish and culminate in marriage when the ordeal was over.

Chapter 7

The tide of illness

Back in the hospital, the suffering went on.

Patients fell ill, trembled with fever and pain, vomited, ranted in their delirium, drifted into unconsciousness; eyes glazed over, chests bloomed with rashes, and sores turned gangrenous; and then fevers broke, and eyes cleared, and they rose, weak with fatigue and relief, from their beds.

In the hospital, the labour was intense but, remarkably, romance blossomed. The patients' cook, James Welsh, struck up a friendship with Ann Campbell, who was nursing at the hospital. Ann was an Irish girl of 19 from County Clare, and a Roman Catholic. James was English and Protestant, a mason's labourer from Somersetshire. The differences in their backgrounds faded to insignificance in the circumstances. Soon after their transfer to the mainland the pair would marry and have children. When they died more than 50 years later, they were buried in Cleveland, just across Moreton Bay from Dunwich where they had spent their first weeks in the colony.

For two days, death gave the settlement respite. Then on 27 August, typhus struck with renewed vigour. There were two fatalities on that day. One victim was Joanna Dwyer: a 33-year-old unmarried domestic servant and Roman Catholic from County Galway.

The other – tragically – was Joseph William Ball. Joseph, 44-year-old Londoner, third husband of Mary, father of Mary Ann and stepfather to the three Wade girls, had been the surgeon's faithful attendant. He had laboured selflessly throughout the voyage – even continuing to work after falling sick – and had been prostrate in the hospital since the immigrants had arrived at the quarantine station. Meanwhile, his wife Mary, who had suffered alongside him, was emerging from the clutches of fever. In less than a week she buried her only daughter and her husband. Her grief must have been terrible. To add to her anguish, her stepdaughter Mary Ann (Joseph's daughter), who had nursed her father faithfully as he lay dying, would soon show the signs of typhus herself.

The death toll mounted.

On 31 August – a Saturday – three more people died. They were John Connor, Henry Roberts and Elizabeth Brimble. Of John Connor, all that is known is that he was an unmarried labourer from County Clare, 28 years old, and a literate Roman Catholic. Henry Roberts was a cook from the *Emigrant*. His death was the second amongst the ship's crew – the supernumerary seaman James Lancaster having died at sea a month earlier. Another seaman by the name of Ward had been admitted to the hospital and recovered but – aside from Mrs Kemp – no other cases of illness have been recorded amongst non-passengers.

The other person to perish on that grim day was Elizabeth Brimble. Elizabeth was the 37-year-old wife of John Brimble from

Wiltshire, who had embarked on the voyage with their servant Sophia (now deceased) and three children, Lucy, Alfred and Samuel. Elizabeth's husband, John, was at this stage still in good health and able to care for their 12-year-old daughter and two sons, aged seven and five. His grief and dread as he watched his wife being lowered into the grave can only be imagined.

While the immigrants were making their temporary homes on Stradbroke Island, the barque lay at anchor in Moreton Bay. She could not be cleared to go on her way until 30 days had elapsed since the last outbreak of disease on board. Crew members who were sick would be taken ashore to the quarantine hospital, while the healthy seamen stayed strictly on board . . . and waited. For men accustomed to hard work and action, this inertia must have been deeply frustrating. For a sailor with a romantic attachment on the island, even more so.

Meanwhile, the police magistrate, Captain Wickham, was doing all he could to alleviate the immigrants' distress. He had written some weeks earlier to the colonial secretary in Sydney, asking for more tents to accommodate the remaining immigrants. The request had been passed on to the immigration agent, who agreed to send 12 tents from Sydney by steamer on the next voyage to Brisbane. On 1 September, the request was finally approved and the tents dispatched.

The tents would take almost a week to reach the island. That week was another difficult one, although numbers of new cases of typhus were decreasing and the hospital was beginning to look less frantic. On 3 September, patients in the hospital numbered 29: 17 men, nine women and three children. Six others were recovering and being treated as outpatients. One of the seriously ill men may have been James Real, 38-year-old labourer from Limerick. His wife, with her three teenagers and three young children, must have feared for his life. After all, her youngest, Patrick, was only five years old.[143]

But on this day, 3 September, the disease attacked with fresh savagery. Poor James Hallett, the eldest child in his family, died. As a teenager, James had barely had a chance to begin life. Only partially schooled, he could read but not write, and, at 15, had already been classed as an adult fit to work as a labourer. With his younger siblings, James had witnessed his mother's shocking death from 'apoplexy' on the voyage, and then his newborn brother's death a month later. And as his remaining siblings grieved for their brother, their father lingered on in the hospital. If James had lived and his father died, the care of his orphaned siblings might well have fallen to the young man. But this was not to be.

James died, and sometime during September his father, Charles, joined him in the grave. For a brief time, the Halletts had been a family of eight. Now both father and mother were dead, as was the newborn baby and the eldest son. There were four left: four children. Charles, at 13, was now the eldest in the family. His remaining siblings were 11-year-old James, seven-year-old Anne, and little George, who was only four. Mary Connor, who had been caring for the Waterson orphans since their parents fell ill, now took full responsibility for the Halletts as well. At only 20, she was looking after seven children who were all under the age of 14: seven frightened and grieving orphans.

News of the latest deaths travelled to Brisbane on the *Aurora* on 3 September. After the departure of the ketch from the quarantine station that very day, there were two more deaths. These were of two adult males: one who passed away in the afternoon and the other in the evening. Over the next three days, four more would die: three on 5 September and one the following day. The toll was now in the low thirties.

One of the victims on 5 September was Maria Trowbridge. Maria was 25 years old and hailed from Stratford in county Wiltshire. She left behind a husband, Josiah, and an unmarried sister, Martha Loder, who had emigrated with her. Maria's other sister, Catherine, had already died at sea as the *Emigrant* sailed through Bass Strait. Martha, at 18, was now alone. But she had formed a friendship with another emigrant, Francis Lyon, a 29-year-old shoemaker from Cranford. The pair would marry soon after their removal from quarantine; they would settle in Brisbane, have children, and enjoy a long life together. But in early September 1850, Martha's future happiness was only a dream. First, she had to farewell another sister, and then pray anxiously for Francis' recovery as he too fell ill with the fever.

Maria's widower, Josiah Trowbridge, would recover, but suffering would revisit him in later life. Shortly after his arrival on the mainland – on 11 December 1850, only three months after his wife's death – Josiah Trowbridge would remarry. His second wife was Frances Frith, whom he had met during the ordeal of emigration. Frances was an Englishwoman with two small children. Her husband, Robert, died sometime during the period of quarantine. No doubt, arriving alone in the colony with two toddlers, Frances felt she needed a husband. Josiah gave her a home and at least six more children. After a spell in Ipswich, they eventually settled in New South Wales.

Josiah Trowbridge's life would end in tragedy. He had been one of the witnesses in the inquiry into Elizabeth Wade's suicide by drowning at Dunwich, and he would take his own life in the same way almost 50 years later. In 1898, his body was fished out of the canal at Leichhardt. His coat, vest and hat were found underneath the bridge near the place where his body had been found floating; in the pocket of his trousers was a note thanking his son and his wife for their kindness to him, and expressing the hope that they would never do as he did. Josiah was 70 years old and had been living with his son, a caretaker at the Town Hall. Witnesses had observed his 'nervous prostration' and melancholia in the days leading up to his suicide. Josiah himself had written that 'he was in so much trouble that he could not resist it'. [144]

But this was a separate tragedy in a distant time and place. Meanwhile, in 1850 on Stradbroke Island, the suffering went on.

On the same day as Maria Trowbridge's death, two other adults passed away. The following day, another followed them to the grave. The deaths were piling up so thick and fast that the surgeon's reports to the mainland gave no names but only numbers. Of the deaths between 3 and 6 September, the unnamed victims may have been Charles Hallett, Robert Frith, John Hector, James Syrett (or Synott or Siret) and James Real. [145]

John Hector was a 23-year-old Irish labourer whose history is unknown. James Syrett was only 21 years of age. He was a Church of England labourer from Buckinghamshire, England, who was travelling to New South Wales with his 18-year-old wife, Jane. Tragically, James' young widow would survive him by only a matter of weeks.

James Real was a humble tenant farmer from Pallasgreen, Limerick. The 38-year-old left behind a wife and six children aged between five and 18. Despite their early disadvantages, Real's fatherless children would go on to achieve extraordinary success. His youngest son, Patrick, would in time become a household name.

As the captain and crew of the *Emigrant* sat in limbo in the bay, and the community at Dunwich stumbled from one tragedy to the next, the people of Brisbane were asking questions. How could such a disaster have happened? *The Moreton Bay Courier* noted that the 'unhappy condition' of the passengers of the government-sponsored ship *Emigrant* showed a 'striking contrast to the state of the passengers who came in the private emigrant ships *Fortitude, Chaseley,* and *Lima*'.[146] The reporter called for a government inquiry.

The immigrants at Dunwich and the crew on the barque may have been physically isolated but they were not cut off from the outside world altogether. Along with supplies of food, medicines, utensils and other essentials, the *Aurora* brought them newspapers. Every report about their ordeal in the *Moreton Bay Courier* made its way back to the island. Captain Kemp read the report in which the unhappy fate of his barque was contrasted with the private emigrant ships and was deeply offended. The implied criticism enraged him.

After striving so hard, showing his passengers every kindness, seeing his *own wife* fall ill, and helplessly watching as so many of the people under his care died, he felt he was now being blamed for the outbreak. It was the final straw. Captain Kemp took up his pen and addressed the *Moreton Bay Courier* in the strongest of terms. He would brook no criticism of the ship, her surgeon-superintendent, or himself.

'As far as regards the ship *Emigrant*,' he wrote, 'she was acknowledged by the authorities in Sydney last year as a most eligible ship for the conveyance of passengers, both as regards her spacious 'tween—decks and her sailing qualities'. On that previous voyage, moreover, 'I had on board 50 souls more than this year, viz., 326 instead of 276; and only one adult died during the passage, and that of consumption, although measles prevailed throughout the whole of the children, 117 in number.'

Kemp pointed out that he had been in charge of ships for 18 years, in ships 'full and crowded', including two trips to Sydney during which he lost never more than one adult and two or three children. 'Even during the rage of typhus in Ireland and Liverpool, in '46 and '47,' he added, 'I went to Quebec with 500 on board; I lost but one, when there were vessels arriving with 150 deaths on board, not single instances, but numbers with upwards of 100.

'As far as regards the sickness,' Kemp fumed,

I presume you are aware what a fearful malady typhus is ashore, even where you can get away from it; but how much more so must it be on board ship, where there are no back doors to escape by, and where you can hardly get a second person to attend upon the sick! For almost certain everyone who attends falls, which has been the case on board my ship. The surgeon at times could scarcely get anyone to attend; 'twas only by the utmost persuasion such could be done.

Kemp went on to describe the course of the disease since its first outbreak, adding that 'Dr Mitchell himself, after superintending the whole both night and day, was attacked the day we arrived here; he has been laid down ever since, and very near death's door, and still lingers.

'As for the true origin of the sickness,' he speculated, 'I believe there is no possibility of ascertaining, but it often occurs from people who have been rather scant of provisions . . . being placed upon full allowance; also the changes of climate will, I believe, often have a similar effect.'

As to the proposed inquiry, the captain responded bitterly.

You wish the thing to be diligently inquired into, I make no doubt but such will be the case, or it will be different from any voyage I have made under the Commissioners, which have been generally sifted so closely as almost to make the commander of a ship feel himself degraded to hear questions put to some who are in no way fit to answer them. However, I am happy to say I never yet had fault found.[147]

7–19 SEPTEMBER: THE GRIM REAPER PERSISTS

The longed-for tents arrived on 7 September. More than three weeks after their arrival in quarantine, the immigrants finally had a little more protection – rudimentary as it was – from the elements. They received the tents with relief, for the weather had been inclement. If sickness, fear of death, and inadequate housing weren't enough to endure, they had also to contend with storms. On 9 September 'violent squalls' and heavy rain attacked Moreton Bay from the south. The rain that had been heartily welcomed in Brisbane and up the Logan River was received with far less enthusiasm by the immigrants huddled in their leaky huts and canvas lean-tos. But some relief – however pitiful – was at hand.

'The tents that were sent down have been very beneficial to the immigrants,' announced the *Moreton Bay Courier*, 'and the arrangements of the surgeon in charge have been very satisfactory. Dr. Ballow had hopes that none but convalescents would be remaining in about a week.'[148] By this time there were 20 inpatients in the hospital (ten men, seven women and three children) and five outpatients. No new cases had broken out on board the ship, and Captain Kemp hoped that he might soon be able to offload his cargo and sail away from Moreton Bay.

Poor Dr Mitchell suffered still in a hospital bed, day after long feverish day. Dr Ballow continued on in robust health. Dr Mallon had fully recovered and was labouring hard alongside him. The surgeons worked around the clock with little regard for their own comfort. The immigrants were all too aware of the risks the surgeons were taking to care for them, and were humbly grateful for their sacrifice.

By the end of the day on 9 September, the running total of deaths since the voyage had begun had reached the mid-thirties. But the Grim Reaper had not finished with the travellers.

On 10 September, Esther (or Hester) Farmer died. She was the wife of brave John Farmer, one of the few men whom Captain Kemp had praised for willingly offering his help to the sick on board, and the only hospital attendant not to have fallen ill. Since their arrival at the quarantine ground, John had been working 'most satisfactorily' as a storekeeper. The Farmers had seven children, all of whom would miraculously survive the ordeal – though at least one (20-year-old Thomas) spent some time in the hospital with typhus.

Esther's death was followed by a blessed respite. Two days passed without casualties.

On 13 September, just as it seemed that a corner had been turned, the fever struck again: two new cases were admitted to hospital. One would recover and the other would not. One of these patients was John Shears, who had been helping in the hospital. He was an unmarried 25-year-old butcher from Sandford in Somersetshire. John would go on to live to the age of 90. He would spend his life in country Queensland and celebrate his golden wedding anniversary in 1913. An inaccurate obituary in 1915 would announce that John 'arrived in Queensland in the year 1849 in the first immigrant ship, known as "The Old Emigrant." Three hundred embarked, but owing to sickness only 60 saw "the new land."'[149]

The other invalid to be admitted to the hospital that day was Mary Ann Ball. Mary Ann had been attending her father, Joseph Ball, in the hospital up until his death. Mary Ann's suffering so far had been dreadful: since leaving London, she had lived through her father's death, her stepsister's suicide and her stepmother's illness. Now her own life hung in the balance.

A few days later, the doctors admitted another new case to the hospital: a young man who, up to that point 'had been entirely separated from the sick'.[150] To doctors Ballow and Mallon, it must have seemed that nothing would stop the spread of disease. Their efforts were frustrated again and again. By this time, 16 patients were still occupying hospital beds.

Meanwhile, in Brisbane, the citizens wanted answers. *Why?* How had this disaster happened? Rumour had it that the *Emigrant*'s cargo on her last voyage was responsible. The ship had previously carried guano, some of the remaining traces of which, it was alleged, had fermented in the hold. The public demanded an investigation, and they would soon be gratified. But before the inquiry could begin, death would deliver another blow – perhaps the heaviest of all – to the desolate community.

19 SEPTEMBER: THE FATE OF DR MITCHELL

George Mitchell had been wretched with the fever for weeks. The grim details of his decline have not been documented but can be imagined: the fever and chills, the cough, the headache that flared up with the light, the nausea, vomiting and diarrhoea, the joint and muscle pains and the rosy rash. The delirium, the ulcers, the gangrene and the coma.

The disease had first attacked George at the end of the voyage and, although he had received the most devoted care, he had weakened with every day that had passed. On 19 September,[151] after almost six weeks of suffering, George Mitchell died. His death was sadly lamented by Captain Kemp and the immigrants, to whose care he had applied himself for as long as he was able.

Dr Mitchell's body was interred on a slight rise beneath the trees, in sight of the white arc of the beach and the turquoise waters of Moreton Bay. His grave is an obelisk that bears age-blemished plaques on two of its four sides. The plaque on the north side reads:

SACRED

TO

THE MEMORY OF

GEORGE MITCHELL

LATE SURGEON SUPERINTENDENT

OF THE SHIP "EMIGRANT,"

who well and fearlessly combated

for many weeks a deadly malady

to which he fell a victim

15th[152] September 1850

Aged 25 years

On its opposite side is the inscription:

AROUND THIS STONE

ARE INTERRED

THE MORTAL REMAINS

OF

TWENTY-SIX IMMIGRANTS,

WHO

SEEKING IN THIS LAND

AN EARTHLY HOME,

HAVE FOUND, ELSEWHERE,

WE TRUST,

A BETTER COUNTRY.

In earlier days, a third plaque on Mitchell's grave gave testimony to the 'unwearied kindness' of Captain and Mrs Kemp. The fate of this memorial to the Kemps is unknown. It is long gone from its original site at Dunwich, as is the 'humble wooden tablet' that once named the dead.

It can be assumed that the money Dr George Mitchell had willed to his mother eventually reached her in County Armagh. The government owed the late Dr Mitchell's estate ten shillings for each immigrant who was alive when the vessel was brought to anchor at the quarantine station. With the head count at that point being 261, Dr Mitchell's estate was entitled to £130 10s. Dr Mitchell owed Captain Kemp £30, which he requested in his will that the emigration agent pay. The balance would go to his mother, Jane Mitchell of Clady Beg.

In the space of only seven months, Jane Mitchell had lost both her husband and her eldest son. At least she had no reason to add undue financial stress to her woes; in addition to George's bequest, Jane's landlord, the Earl of Charlemont, had the decency to return cash to Mrs Mitchell, being 'the difference between the increased and former rent of the late Alexander Mitchell's holding in Clady Beg'.[153]

Jane lived at Clady Beg until her death in 1876, when she was in her seventy-fourth year. She lived to see most of her children grow to adulthood and marry. Several of her children produced offspring of their own, and several remained in the district. Her second youngest, Alexander, married, had ten children, and emigrated to Canada. He lived and died in Ontario, producing generations of citizens of Canada and the United States of America.[154]

On the same day that Dr Mitchell died, young Jane Syrett, aged only 18, followed her recently deceased husband to the grave. David Hobbs got to work building more coffins. The men dug more graves. They buried Jane Syrett near the other immigrants in an unmarked plot, and added her name to the wooden tablet that listed the dead.

21 SEPTEMBER: DESERTERS

Out on the ship, no new cases of fever had been reported for some time. Hopes that the *Emigrant* might soon be able to move on were growing stronger. She was not quite ready to sail yet, however; the barque was required to remain in the bay for 30 days after the last appearance of disease on board. All being well, that period would expire on the 28th of the month.

Excitement must have run high on board. After the three-month hellish voyage, the crew had been locked in limbo for another month on the bay. For men who thrived on adventure and action, the waiting was a torment. For two seamen, it was intolerable.

James Hall and Charles Young had had enough. On 21 September, the *Moreton Bay Courier* reported that two seamen had absconded from the ship and were 'probably' on Stradbroke Island. James Hall was born in Liverpool in 1831, the son of a painter, Joseph Hall, and Elizabeth Hall (née Maddon). During the passage, James had formed an illicit relationship with one of the passengers of the *Emigrant*: Mary Ann Mahoney, the 19-year-old English girl who had witnessed Elizabeth Wade's final hours. Perhaps James Hall had jumped ship because he'd had enough of the confinement. Perhaps he had set out in pursuit of Mary Ann. Perhaps the thought of his imminent departure from Moreton Bay with the *Emigrant* – never to see Mary Ann again – was too much to bear.

In any case, the two young seamen deserted the ship and presumably made their way to the island. Before long, they were captured. They were tried before the Brisbane Bench on 11 November 1850 for 'absenting themselves without leave' from the ship. The men pleaded guilty and were sentenced to 14 days of hard labour in the 'common gaol' of Brisbane.

For James Hall, the two-week sentence was probably worth enduring. Once he had served his time, he was a free man; by then, the *Emigrant* had left without him. He would marry Mary Ann Mahoney in Brisbane's Church of England parish of St John on 25 March 1851, before the witnesses Francis Lyon and his new wife Martha (née Loder), both fellow-passengers. The pair would settle in South Brisbane and produce a large family. Of their ten children, two died in early childhood. James spent most of his working life at sea, eventually becoming a master mariner for Queensland's coastal ships.

After a six-month illness, James Hall died at his home on 11 March 1895, of 'mental worry, atheromatous arteries and cerebral haemorrhage'. At the time of his death at age 64, James was registered as a clerk. James' widow, Mary Ann, died at her home ten years later, aged 74.

20–27 SEPTEMBER

By the time Dr Mitchell breathed his last, most of the hospital attendants had fallen ill. One of these was Mary Ann Ball: the daughter of the late Joseph William Ball. Having been admitted as a patient on 13 September, Mary Ann's decline was swift; she died exactly one week later. Mary Ann was 23 years old. Her stepmother Mary had now lost a daughter to the sea and a husband and a stepdaughter to typhus. She had barely recovered from the disease herself. From her once-large family, Mary Ball had only two stepdaughters left: Elizabeth Matilda Wade and Emma Wade.

Mary Ann's death, tragic as it was, marked something of a turning point. The virulence of the disease seemed to be waning at last. By this time only 12 patients remained in the hospital. New admissions were becoming less frequent. The community began to hope that the quarantine might be lifted by the end of the month.

But on 23 September, another young woman fell ill. Dr Ballow examined her and concluded that she was suffering from a 'determination of blood to the head'. The woman was a hospital attendant who had been caring for her fever-stricken sister. These two sisters were probably the two remaining Wade girls: Emma and Elizabeth Matilda. The next day, Dr Ballow reported the disastrous news: the girl was not in fact suffering from a determination of blood to the head, but typhus. If the new patient was indeed one of the Wade girls – and records show that they *were* in hospital at some time during the quarantine period – their stepmother must have been beside herself with worry.

The news was a blow to the whole community. A new case meant that the clock had to be set back again. A new case added at least another 30 days to the period of quarantine.

On the barque, however, the terrible episode was drawing to a close. No new cases having broken out on board the *Emigrant* for some time, she would soon be cleared for removal from quarantine. Before she could be granted pratique, however, she and her master must submit to an examination by the authorities.

On government ships, it was standard procedure for the captain to give a list of his passengers to the local immigration agent when the ship arrived in port. From this list, the amount of bounty to be paid for the passengers landed alive could be calculated. Under normal circumstances, the agent would board the vessel as it lay in port and question the immigrants. What was their occupation? Their religion? Could they read and write? Did they have relations in the colony? Had they been treated well on the voyage? Did they have any complaints?

These, however, were not normal circumstances. While a list of immigrants *had* been compiled on 10 August – when the ship arrived in Moreton Bay – the usual thorough interrogation had been delayed by the *Emigrant*'s long quarantine. But now that the fever was abating, the time had come to complete the paperwork.

On 25 September, Captain Wickham sailed once again across Moreton Bay to the quarantine station, this time in company with Mr William Duncan, the sub-collector of customs, and Dr Kearsey Cannan, Brisbane's acting health officer. Their purpose was not only to conduct the customary interviews with the immigrants but also to investigate the cause of the epidemic. *The Moreton Bay Courier* was about to be satisfied.

Over the next couple of days, these authorities interviewed Captain Kemp and the crew on the barque, and quizzed all the emigrants in the quarantine station except for those laid low with illness. The hospital was still busy, its beds occupied by about ten men, women and children. The matron's daughter, Fanny Burberow may have been one of the patients, along with Thomas Bloxam. The Irish weaver Thomas had lost his wife at sea and was facing the task of bringing three children (John, Anne and Thomas junior) to the colony alone – if he survived.

While these patients were spared interrogation, the rest of the immigrants were grilled about the voyage. Complaints about a ship's captain or surgeon-superintendent were taken seriously. If a government investigation revealed that the men in charge of a vessel were negligent or incompetent or abused their power, it could impose heavy fines and end a career at sea. But not one complaint was registered against Captain Kemp or his deceased surgeon-superintendent. The passengers spoke of them both in glowing terms. They gave testimony to the 'kind and attentive manner in which Dr Mitchell performed his duties', and praised Captain Kemp's efforts to 'afford them every indulgence and comfort which their circumstances could admit of'.

Normally when an immigrant ship arrived in port, the passengers were allowed to stay on board for two weeks under the care of the surgeon-superintendent. During these so-called 'lay days' the colonial government provided for the newcomers until they found jobs and accommodation. In cases of extended quarantine, questions arose as to who was responsible for the immigrants' care, and whether the colonial government owed the shipowner 'demurrage' for the extra time it had the use of the ship. For these reasons, it was important to determine the cause of the outbreak. If the vessel was at fault, the shipowner might be liable.

But as to the cause of this outbreak, Dr Cannan could find no reason to blame Dr Mitchell, the captain, or his ship. There was nothing to suggest that the disease 'arose from any want of cleanliness, or from any neglect of duty in the part of the late surgeon-superintendent'.[155]

He reported that both Captain Kemp and Dr Mitchell had complained about the 'objectionable' state of the water closets, the entrance to them being from the berth deck instead of the upper deck, which caused an 'extremely offensive' smell to be directed to the steerage quarters below. This complaint, however, he dismissed as a cause of disease. An unknown hand noted beside his remarks that 'no other arrangements will do for the females, though they will constantly complain'.

Dr Cannan concluded that the disease could only have been introduced onto the ship by some of the immigrants.

The *Moreton Bay Courier* was quick to retract the doubts it had hinted at earlier about Captain Kemp and the *Emigrant*. The journalist was effusive in his praise of Kemp's and Dr Mitchell's 'unwearied assiduity and patient kindness'.

The *Courier* went on:

But there was one on board upon whom no official responsibility devolved, and who was yet, to use the language of Scott, 'a ministering angel' to the sick. Mrs. Kemp, the captain's wife, has indeed earned golden opinions from all sorts of people. This lady, as appears by the statements of all the witnesses examined, was unremitting in her charitable attentions to the passengers, and even when suffering from fatigue and exhaustion, devoted herself with a singular and rare humanity to the alleviation of the sorrows and sufferings of others. Her personal attentions, under the most trying and dangerous circumstances, are acknowledged with gratitude and blessings by the immigrants, and, weak and unworthy as any praise from us may be for such 'noble' conduct, we gladly place on record here our tribute of respect for the disinterested exertions of this brave and good woman.[156]

The *Moreton Bay Courier* revealed Dr Cannan's conclusion that the disease had been brought on board by some of the immigrants. It could not resist adding that 'the disease broke out amongst the Irish immigrants, and it is suspected that they may have brought the germs of the disorder on board with them'.[157]

With that, Captain Wickham released the ship from quarantine. She would soon be able to offload her remaining cargo onto the *Aurora* for conveyance to Brisbane. Within a couple of days, Captain Kemp had brought the ship up to anchorage just off the mouth of the Brisbane River.[158] They had left the quarantine station behind but still had business to conclude in Moreton Bay. Before long, he and his crew would be free to resume their lives. But the immigrants at Dunwich would not.

During the inquiry, not one amongst the crew or passengers had raised a single complaint against the captain. But it seems that there were some who were not completely satisfied with their lot. Two seamen had already absconded from the ship, and on 26 September, two more would desert. Perhaps they had had enough of the seafaring life and preferred the idea of settling in Brisbane; knowing that the ship's departure was imminent, they had only a short window of opportunity left in which they could escape. The presence of the government men and the to-ing and fro-ing of vessels between Brisbane, Dunwich and the *Emigrant* may have provided enough distraction to enable them to flee.

The two absconders were seamen John Owens and Robert Walker. They would be captured eventually and brought before the Brisbane Bench. By the time their cases came to trial, however – on 12 November – the complainant, Captain Kemp, was long gone. The pair was more fortunate than James Hall and Young, who were tried and sentenced the day before them; Owen's and Walker's cases were dismissed and the men set free without charge.

26 September was an eventful day. While Captain Wickham and Dr Cannan were quizzing the emigrants, and the seamen Owens and Walker were making their bid for freedom, the trage-dies in the quarantine station continued to unfold.

In the early hours of the morning, typhus struck yet another blow to a family who had already suffered far too much. For the previous three weeks – since the death of their father – the four Hallett children had been under the Irishwoman Mary Connor's care. They had lost their mother, an infant brother, their father and their eldest brother. But death hadn't finished with the Hallett family. On 26 September at 3am, Henry Hallett, aged 11, passed away. From a family of eight, only three remained: Charles, who was 13, seven-year-old Anne, and four-year-old George.

Mary Connor now had only six children to care for: the three English Protestants from the Hallett family, and the three Watersons, Irish Catholics like herself.

Then the sun rose over the island and brought with it yet another death. At seven o'clock in the morning on 26 September, Thomas Coleman took his final breath. Coleman was 37 years old, an unmarried labourer from Somersetshire. He had been helping with the hospital's washing – a task that was every bit as dangerous as tending to patients directly, although Coleman wouldn't have known it. Infected lice would secrete themselves in the patients' bedding and clothes and leap onto new hosts who handled the laundry. At least one of them found its way to Thomas Coleman and introduced the disease into his blood.

There was to be no rest yet for poor David Hobbs, who set to work building two more coffins. By this time, he had made 21 or more. His mental health would suffer in later life – and no wonder.

On the next day – 27 September – the hospital admitted another man. Dr Mallon wrote with a hint of despair: 'the man admitted this day has not been exposed to contagion since the 28th August on which day his wife died'. The man was probably John Brimble, whose wife Elizabeth had actually died on 31 August.[159] It was an anxious time for his three children, Lucy (12), Alfred (seven) and Samuel (five) as they waited to see whether they would join the ranks of the orphaned. At least they had extended family on board. If their father should die, their second cousin, 21-year-old Andrew, and his wife Louisa, who had two small children of their own, would surely have taken them into the fold.

Even with John Brimble's admission, there were now only 11 remaining in the hospital: ten cases of fever and one of 'debility'. All of them were men. Although patient numbers were dwindling, each new case was a fresh blow to the immigrants, and a further frustration to the potential employers who waited anxiously in Brisbane to bolster their workforce. Every new case meant further delays.

John Brimble would recover. But for him and his family, there were terrible times ahead.

28–29 SEPTEMBER: A BRUTAL DEATH

Typhus is an unpredictable malady. It can lie dormant for weeks and attack out of the blue just when it seems that all danger is past.

On 28 September, a woman was admitted to hospital who had had no contact with the disease since she had attended a patient who had died, some three weeks earlier. Some – like Dr Mallon – picked up the illness immediately on contact but shrugged it off in a matter of days. Others, like the 'aged' John Farmer who laboured day and night to care for the sick, seemed immune. Age, gender and constitution seemed of little conse-quence; thus far the disease had felled strong young men as easily as it had slain small children and older women. For some, like Julia Chapple, typhus had caused a long period of prostration followed by recovery. For poor George Mitchell, it had meted out a slow and wretched death.

But for Dr Ballow, the death that typhus delivered was swift and brutal. On 23 September, the Scottish doctor was still attending to the sick. By the next day, Dr Mallon had taken over as surgeon in charge, for Dr Ballow had become one of the patients. Mallon applied remedies as he saw fit, and Dr Ballow appeared to rally. On 28 September, the *Moreton Bay Courier* reported that Dr Ballow had 'at length been laid up, but we have reason to hope that the attack is not a dangerous one, and that the Doctor will soon be restored to a state of convalescence'.[160]

The *Courier* was wrong. The case was a dangerous one indeed. Dr Ballow soon sank into delirium and by half past 11 the next morning – Sunday 29 September – he was dead.

Brisbane was shocked. David Keith Ballow had been an impressive character, and one of the town's most respected pioneers. He had been prominent not only in the medical world but in philanthropy, the church, the justice system and the arts, and had taken a keen interest in agriculture and education. The news of Dr Ballow's death was received by the citizens of Brisbane with great sorrow. As a mark of respect, they closed their businesses for the day.

Beside Dr Mitchell's grave in the Dunwich cemetery, a low sarcophagus sits in the shade of gum trees on the slope down towards the waters of the bay. A plaque on its north side proclaims:

Sacred to the Memory of
DAVID KEITH BALLOW,
LATE COLONIAL SURGEON, CORONER OF THE DISTRICT,
AND MAGISTRATE OF THE
TERRITORY, WHO IN THE DISCHARGE OF HIS DUTY AS
SURGEON SUPERINTENDENT
OF THE QUARANTINE STATION AT DUNWICH,
Fell, with many others whose graves are around,
a victim to typhus fever.

Born at Montrose October 27th, 1804. Died September 29th, 1850.
"Greater love hath no man that this, that a man lay down
his life for his friend"—15th chap. St. John, 13th verse.
THIS TOMB WAS ERECTED BY HIS AFFECTIONATE WIDOW,
MARGARET CAMPBELL BALLOW.

After her husband's death, Margaret Ballow had no reason to linger in Moreton Bay. She put all of her furniture and household effects up for sale – dining table, sofas, chairs, ottomans, bookcases, beds, bedding, china and glassware, engravings, books, near-new saddlery, firearms and kitchen utensils[161] – and made plans to return to her family.

On 17 December – only weeks after the quarantine period ended – Margaret Ballow boarded the *Eagle,* arriving in Sydney four days later. From Sydney, she went on to Portland (now in Victoria) to live near her sister Elizabeth Gallie. Some years later the two widowed sisters moved to St Kilda, where Margaret died in 1876. Although widowed at only 39 years of age, the 'dark, pretty and very pleasant'[162] young woman never remarried.

Dr Ballow's sacrifice has long been publicly recognised. Shortly before his death, he had campaigned for a new place of worship for the Church of England. Sadly, he didn't live to see the opening of St John's Church in William Street in 1854. To honour him, a memorial tablet of white marble was mounted bearing the inscription:

To the Memory of David Keith Ballow, late Colonial Assistant
Surgeon, Coroner of the District and a Magistrate of the Territory
who, on the arrival in this port of the ship "Emigrant," having
malignant typhus fever on board, with which the medical officer
of that vessel was seized and subsequently died, nobly undertook

*the duties of Surgeon Superintendent of the Quarantine Station, at
Dunwich, and fell himself a victim. Born at Montrose, Scotland,
17th October, 1804; died, Sept. 29th, 1850.*

St John's served the congregation for many years until, in 1910,
the Church of England opened a new cathedral in Ann Street. The
old church was dismantled and the memorial stone was moved
to the new premises. The plaque was never mounted in the new
cathedral; the memorial still lies, broken-down, in the basement
of the adjoining St Martin's House.

A plaque bearing the same inscription was mounted at the
entrance of 'Ballow Chambers' on Brisbane's Wickham Terrace.
The heritage-listed Ballow Chambers was built in 1924 for a group
of medical practitioners, on the site where medical practices had
existed since the 1870s. The building is a fitting memorial to a
medical man who had contributed in so many ways to the early
development of the town and died in the course of duty.

DR KEARSEY CANNAN

Dr Ballow's death left Dr Mallon in a difficult position. He was the
only medical man left on the island. His health was fully restored,
but as a sole practitioner he would have no respite. There were
still 11 patients in the hospital needing round-the-clock care.

In Dr Ballow's absence from Brisbane, Dr Kearsey Cannan had
been acting as the health officer for the district. With Dr Ballow's
death, responsibility for superintending the medical care at the
quarantine station became his. Dr Cannan was understandably
unwilling to make the same sacrifices as his late colleague. He
would not join Dr Mallon as a resident doctor on Stradbroke
Island, but visit only in his capacity as health officer on a few

separate occasions. He had already called on the station on 25 September during Dr Ballow's period of infirmity, and would visit again three days after his death, but on no occasion would he stay overnight on the island. He preferred to pitch a tent on the nearby Bird Island.

Bird Island was a tiny speck in Moreton Bay – a sandy and shrubby isle whose perimeter dropped abruptly into deep waters. It was barely large enough to pitch a tent, let alone provide fresh water. So tiny was the island that in recent years it has disappeared almost entirely into the sea, leaving only a glimpse of a shallow sandbar beneath the water's surface. Dr Cannan's willingness to endure the discomfort of Bird Island rather than risk prolonged exposure to the quarantine station says much about the virulence of the disease and the fear that it instilled.

Dr Ballow had been well known to Dr Cannan; they had worked together for nearly seven years at the Moreton Bay Hospital. Dr Cannan had been a visiting surgeon while Dr Ballow was resident surgeon. Cannan was an Englishman, born in London in 1815. His medical training had been through an apprenticeship in Kent. He had become a member of the Royal College of Surgeons in 1837 and, like both Ballow and Mallon, emigrated soon after completing his training. Cannan had practised in Sydney for a few years before moving to Moreton Bay in 1843 with his young wife and baby.

In 1849, when the position of surgeon to the new Brisbane Gaol had been created, Kearsey Cannan had competed with Dr Ballow for the job. His application had been rejected because Dr Ballow had a 'superior claim to appointment'. Now Dr Ballow, Cannan's colleague, rival and – presumably – friend, was no more.

It fell to the Police Magistrate Captain Wickham to find another doctor to help Dr Mallon. He appealed again to the medical fraternity of Brisbane and Ipswich but found no one willing to take the risk. He had no choice but to look further afield, and eventually received a response from Dr Frederick James Barton of Sydney. But Sydney was at least a three-day journey by steamship from Brisbane, and it would be almost three weeks before Dr Barton was able to take up his duties at the quarantine station.

In the meantime, disaster would strike again – but this time from a different quarter.

30 SEPTEMBER – 3 OCTOBER: THE CHILDREN

It was late afternoon – about 4pm on 30 September, and young Samuel Brimble was playing alone. Erroneous reports[163] claim that the five-year-old had been left unsupervised while his parents attended Dr Ballow's funeral service. In fact, by this time, Samuel's mother was already dead, and his father may have been in hospital. It is likely, however, that the funeral provided a distraction, and the boy, unobserved, wandered off alone to the beach to cook himself a potato. He lit a fire, and the flames caught hold of his clothing. When they eventually found him, the horrified immigrants rushed Samuel's badly burned but still living little body to the hospital. Eight hours later – at midnight – the boy passed away.

This time, David Hobbs had only a small coffin to build. Poor fever-stricken John Brimble, the gardener from Kingston Deverill, had lost his wife and his servant – who was also his cousin's daughter – and now his youngest child. The suffering seemed to have no end.

Samuel Brimble's death was followed by an outbreak of fever amongst the children. On 2 October, to Dr Mallon's dismay, an 18-month-old boy was admitted to the hospital with typhus.[164] Dr Mallon made no attempt to hide his frustration and disapproval, for the disease had spread to the boy as a result of his mother's foolishness. She had received clothes from the female hospital to repair – contrary to his orders. The surgeon's exasperation can be imagined.

The next day, another boy fell ill. He was Alfred Brimble, poor little Samuel's seven-year-old brother. By this stage there were 15 patients in the hospital, but Alfred Brimble's was the only malignant case. In time, both Alfred and his father would recover.

Some other children were not so lucky. Sometime during the long days of quarantine, four more children died. One was the baby daughter of William and Amelia Canning – their only child, who had been born at sea and was yet to be named. The other was the infant son – also unnamed – of Anne and Isaac Salisbury of Somersetshire, whose birth had been the first of the voyage and the bringer of such joy and false hope, such a long time ago. His life had spanned little more than the length of the voyage itself. The couple lost not only their newborn son but also their eight-year-old daughter, Mary Anne, to typhus while in quarantine. The Salisburys had embarked with five children and made the passage with six, but would begin their lives in Brisbane with only four.

Another child who slipped away was the infant Eliza Cummins. She was the daughter of Cornelius and Judith[165] Cummins (née Lawler). Not listed on the embarkation register, the little girl must have been born at sea. The Cummins family were Irish Catholics from Queen's County who were planning to reunite with two of Cornelius' uncles, then living in Bathurst. After Eliza's death, Cornelius and his wife were left with two-year-old Catherine and one-year-old Bridget.

The dates of these children's deaths have not been recorded. It is likely that they passed away during the early hectic days in quarantine, when Dr Mallon was ill and the daily reports were sketchy. But by the time typhus released its hold on the immigrants, these four children lay with its other victims in their sandy graves.

4–9 OCTOBER: KEMP'S DEPARTURE

Although the inquiry had cleared Captain Kemp and Dr Mitchell of any wrongdoing, some citizens of Brisbane were unconvinced. In early October, the editor of the *Moreton Bay Free Press* publicly questioned George Mitchell's fitness for the role of surgeon-superintendent.[166] Kemp, who was by then in Brisbane and preparing to put Moreton Bay behind him forever, responded swiftly and angrily. Dr Mitchell was both qualified and diligent, the captain stated, providing a brief outline of the surgeon's professional experience. 'As for the statement that the sanitary measures used on board the vessel were not sufficiently stringent, allow me to state that they were carried out to the utmost,' he added: 'whoever has informed the Editor of the *Free Press* to the contrary must be perfectly ignorant on the subject.'[167]

The Moreton Bay Courier was only too pleased to run Captain Kemp's letter, taking the opportunity to boast of its own factual and ethical superiority over its rival newspaper.

('We cannot suppose that our contemporary could have any reason for wilfully misstating this matter, unless it were merely for the purpose of contradiction, which we should be sorry to believe a sufficiently strong inducement to do such a wrong; but our readers will agree that, under the distressing circumstances of the case, such a statement ought not to have been published without the most diligent inquiry; and we now see that any such inquiry would have immediately elicited the truth.')[168]

The people of Brisbane had followed the drama of the *Emigrant* closely and were eager to acknowledge the heroism of some of the players. As the moment of the ship's departure drew near, the ladies and gentlemen of the Church of England made public their gratitude to the captain and his wife. They signed an address to Captain and Mrs Kemp, in which they expressed their appreciation of the Kemps' efforts to relieve and comfort the immigrants. They proposed to erect a tablet on Stradbroke Island with the inscription:[169]

SACRED
To the Memory of the Christian Charity
with which
CAPTAIN AND MRS. KEMP,
of
The Ship "Emigrant,"
Ministered
With unwearied Kindness
to
The last hours of those
Whose Graves
May be seen around.

The episode was all but over for Captain Kemp. Soon he would be on his way. But for the immigrants still in limbo on the island, time dragged on. On 5 October, Dr Mallon discharged four more males from the hospital but 11 patients remained: ten afflicted with fever and one with 'debility'. Dr Mallon continued to work as the sole medical practitioner, supported by his hospital attendants. Mary Connor carried on caring for the six orphans; James Welsh cooked; John Farmer and Henry Lipscombe managed the store; Patrick Maunsell assisted Dr Mallon; James Foote slaughtered the sheep for the table and his brother John Clarke Foote administered medicines. In his periods of respite from coffin-making, the 'indefatigable' David Hobbs maintained and repaired the station's basic accommodation.

In Brisbane, the citizens anxiously awaited the release of their labourers and servants, impatient but sympathetic to their plight. *The Moreton Bay Courier*, acting on a suggestion from the community, invited the public to contribute books, newspapers and other amusements to the immigrants, 'as it is well known that despondency would be dangerous in their situation'.[170] Arrangements had already been made to send quoits and cricket bats and balls to the quarantine station. It was clear to all that an end to the exile was not imminent.

Meanwhile, Dr Mallon kept his ground 'manfully'. Despite the protracted nature of the ordeal, the doctor maintained his optimism. The number of patients was steady but by early October, Dr Mallon expected that there would be no further new cases. He was *almost* right.

In light of Dr Mallon's predictions, the government authorities began wrapping up official matters: paying Dr Mitchell's estate and settling the amounts owing to Captain Kemp and Mitchell's mother. Meanwhile, the *Emigrant* lay at anchor off St Helena Island. Having sent the last of her cargo up the river to Brisbane, Captain Kemp was ready to re-join her with his wife and young daughter. He had been paid a gratuity owed to him by the government as well as £198 for the sails, awnings, spirits and timber that he had supplied to the quarantine station. The ship had finally been granted pratique and was free to leave. On 9 October, Kemp weighed the anchor and set sail. It must have been with relief that he put the nightmare behind him.

The *Emigrant* set off to the north in search of guano, a powerful fertiliser that in 1850 was in great demand in the western world. In his quest for this much-coveted resource, however, Kemp would be disappointed.

9–24 OCTOBER: THE FINAL BLOW

By 9 October – almost two months after their arrival at the quarantine station – all 12 patients in the hospital appeared to be recuperating well, and those outside of the hospital bore a 'healthy appearance'. No new cases of fever had presented in a week, although one man who had previously convalesced was readmitted on 8 October with an abscess. Even David Hobbs had had a break; no more coffins had been needed since Samuel Brimble's death on 30 September, more than a week earlier.

The death toll stood at 47.

In another three days, Dr Mallon was hopeful enough to declare – cautiously – that the quarantine ground was free from fever. The 12 patients in the hospital had improved further and were sitting up and moving about within the precincts of the hospital.

The next day, however – 13 October – gave him cause to reconsider. One of the male hospital attendants had been complaining of illness since the previous evening. He had already suffered through the fever, having landed with the 'most malignant form of the disease', and had been discharged on 20 August. Dr Mallon regarded the man's symptoms as 'suspicious' but was not convinced that he had typhus. To his relief, the man had recovered by the following day.

Time passed and spring enveloped the immigrants in its antipodean warmth. More days went by with no new cases. Hopes soared. Immigrants began to look forward with real expectations that their purgatory would soon be at an end.

And then: the final blow. Andrew Brimble got sick.

On 16 October, Dr Mallon examined the young labourer from Kingston Deverill, who had not been exposed to the contagion for a full two weeks, and found, to his deep dismay, that the young man had a fresh case of typhus. The doctor admitted him to the hospital. On the next day, Dr Mallon discharged ten patients – five men and five women – who had been convalescing from fever. Only three patients remained: one with an abscess, one with 'debility', and Andrew Brimble. In his *Daily Return of the Sick*, Dr Mallon wrote, with apprehension: 'the case admitted yesterday is not of a mild nature it is malignant'.

Andrew Brimble, at only 21, had a wife and two small children. The past six months had been cruel to his family. Andrew's sister, Sophia, had died on the voyage; his father's cousin, John, had lost his wife and young son, Samuel, in quarantine. Miraculously, Andrew's own children had survived: two-year-old Emily and the infant William who had been born on the barque as she lay at anchor in Moreton Bay.

And as if mocking the pitiful group of outcasts for daring to hope, fate even turned the weather against them.

Spring was well underway and brought with it the violent storms of the subtropics. On 19 October, the waves clawed at the beaches on the far eastern side of the island, the waters of the bay churned inky and white-tipped, and the wretched little settlement cowered under the force of the wind. The heavens opened up and drenched the quarantine station. Rain poured in through the roof of the hospital onto the patients.

Next day, one of the female patients who had been discharged a few days earlier was readmitted, her condition worsened by her exposure to the storm.

It had been a trying time for Dr Mallon, having to contend with a succession of dashed hopes and take full responsibility for the patients under the most taxing conditions. With Dr Ballow now lying in his grave, Dr Mallon had been running the hospital alone. The government had engaged Dr Frederick James Barton of Sydney to help out, but the wait for his arrival had been long.

DR FREDERICK BARTON

Dr Barton was a young man. The third of four sons of a shipbuilder, he was born in Rotherhithe, Surrey, on 16 August, 1825. Frederick had studied medicine in England and had become a member of the Royal College of Surgeons at the end of 1847. He had emigrated the following year, setting off from Plymouth on the *Waverly* in September 1848 and arriving at Port Jackson in December. When he took the commission at the quarantine station at Dunwich, Barton was the same age as the late George Mitchell: only 25.

Dr Barton would become known as a humble man, and a hard worker with a passion for scientific knowledge. In 1850 he was untested and ready to take risks. He accepted the government's generous terms of two guineas a day for two months, with rations, and passage paid to and from Brisbane.[171]

Dr Barton arrived in Brisbane on the *Eagle* on 19 October. A few days later – almost too late – he would make his way to Dunwich. He would not arrive until after the final tragedy struck.

Andrew Brimble went downhill fast. After six days in hospital, during which he had endured the violence of the storm, poor Andrew expired. His death on 22 October was the forty-eighth of the *Emigrant* disaster. It was also the last.

The events of the past six months having made the fragility of life only too clear, Andrew Brimble's grieving widow was loath to delay her infant son's baptism. A new Anglican priest, Henry Offley Irwin, had arrived in Moreton Bay on the *Eagle* earlier that month to take charge of the Parish of St John. Only two days after Andrew's death, Rev. Irwin sailed across Moreton Bay to baptise Andrew and Louisa's child in the quarantine station. Although the baby had been initially named William, Louisa had him baptised *Andrew.*

Drs Barton and Cannan reached the island on 24 October. By this time, three patients still remained in hospital, one young female hospital attendant having been admitted that day with a mild case of fever. Dr Cannan visited with the purpose of ascertaining whether some of the immigrants – those who had not been afflicted and had had 'sufficient time out of reach of infection' – might soon be removed to Brisbane. In the meantime, Captain Wickham assured the colonial secretary, lists would be prepared of clothing and other articles to be destroyed, along with an estimate of their value.

By the end of October, three patients still remained. The one typhus case, a female hospital attendant, was progressing well. On 5 November, Captain Wickham was confident enough that the epidemic had finally burned itself out to write to the colonial secretary explaining his plans to transfer the immigrants to the mainland. If no further cases of illness should emerge in the next 14 days, he wrote, he would arrange to ferry them to Brisbane in batches, starting with those who had not been sick or had been the greatest length of time free from infection.

And at last the disease had been beaten. Typhus and other maladies had claimed the lives of 48, including two surgeons, a cook and a seaman. Twenty-six of the passengers and the two men who had tended them lay beneath the sandy soil of Stradbroke Island; the others rested on the ocean bed.

The weather continued stormy, the island lashed by wind and lightning and rain. But the fever had broken. The health of the immigrants held out.

12–29 NOVEMBER: EVACUATION AT LAST

On 12 November, 35 of the immigrants – all adults – boarded the boat that would take them at last to Brisbane. The skies were still wet and squally. The passage must have been choppy and unpleasant, as if the elements were conspiring to throw up obstacles to the bitter end; and what joy those people must have felt when their feet finally touched land!

The island community was abuzz as the remaining immigrants gathered up their children and their meagre possessions and prepared to leave. As they readied themselves to leave their loved ones behind in sandy graves, the Brimbles must have faced the next chapter in their story with heavy hearts. And Patrick Real, as a small child, could not possibly know the extent of the struggle his widowed mother would face in caring for six children alone. But there is no doubt that for the six orphans – three Halletts and three Watersons – the joy of a new beginning was overshadowed by the sorrow of their loss.

One more drama was still to come – and this one, final event was an occasion of joy. On 14 November, Elizabeth Lipscombe gave birth to a healthy boy. He was the first child of Elizabeth and Henry, a young Anglican couple from Surrey, England. Henry was a brickmaker who had been helping out in the stores of the quarantine ground. The couple would name their son George *Stradbrook* Lipscombe.

A second batch of immigrants – 50 men, women and children – arrived in Brisbane on the evening of 15 November. Four days later, Captain Wickham wrote to the colonial secretary declaring with undisguised joy that Dr Mallon had reported all of the immigrants in quarantine to be 'perfectly healthy' and that Dr Cannan had given instructions for their removal.

'No time will be lost in bringing the remainder to Brisbane,' he wrote. He reminded the colonial secretary of the difficulty that the medical men had had in getting attendants for the sick, and the promise of financial reward that he had been obliged to offer in order to procure helpers. 'The reluctance shown by the majority of the immigrants to act as hospital attendants and nurses can scarcely be wondered at,' he wrote, 'with only one or two exceptions, those who have undertaken such duties have been attacked by the fever, and in several instances, have fallen victim to its virulence.' Wickham promised to forward a list of helpers due some remuneration as soon as the quarantine station had been evacuated.

Forty-eight more immigrants landed in Brisbane on 20 November. Only half of the original number remained.

Before the final contingent could be transferred to the mainland, the *Moreton Bay Courier* published a touching tribute to Dr Mallon, written by the immigrants as they realised that their period in quarantine was coming to a close.

QUARANTINE STATION,
Stradbroke Island, Nov. 11, 1850.

SIR,-We, the undersigned immigrants, deem it a duty incumbent on us to acknowledge your services as surgeon in charge at the Quarantine Station, for your unprecedented and indefatigable exertions on our behalf thus rendered you dear to us. We therefore take the opportunity of recording our acknowledgment of your unceasing attention in the discharge of your professional duties towards us, and beg to say you have merited the name of an ornament to your profession, which we consider you justly entitled to, for by your zeal and experience the progress of that awful malady was retarded which put a period to the existence of gentlemen of your profession (whom we deeply lament), as well as many of our fellow immigrants, during your long and dangerous stay at the Quarantine station. We now, being on the eve of our departure, approach you with feelings of deep respect and gratitude, and wish you may be long spared to step forward, when called upon by duty, in aid of the distressed. We therefore bid you a kindly adieu, and remain. DEAR SIR,

Your obedient faithful friends,
[Signed by 137 of the Immigrants.]

Dr Mallon was moved by their gratitude. The experience had been no less traumatic for him than for his charges; he had witnessed the cruel deaths of two colleagues and more than two dozen others: men, women and children. He had endured physical discomfort in the course of his duty but had applied himself to it with unstinting kindness. His effectiveness had been limited not by shortcomings of his own but only by the paucity of medical knowledge at the time.

Each loss of life must have wounded Dr Mallon, and he was anxious not to take too much credit for the lives saved. With humility, he reminded his friends that their survival was not the result of his ministrations alone; they had the late Dr Ballow, a benevolent government, and God to thank for their good fortune. His letter of reply to the immigrants was published beneath theirs in the *Moreton Bay Courier*.

QUARANTINE STATION,
Stradbroke Island, Moreton Bay, 11th Nov., 1850.

MY DEAR IMMIGRANTS,-I am in receipt of your kind address of last evening. Indeed it is consoling to me, after the perils, shocks, and storms experienced on this field during the three months, to read your breathings of pure and unaffected gratitude. But permit me to say that our success is chiefly attributable, under the blessings of Divine Providence, to the alacrity you evinced in carrying on the wise and sanitary, though stringent measures which my late and much lamented colleague thought proper to adopt to ensure your safety. And the bountiful liberality, care, and attention bestowed by a parental government to your wants, is another source contributable in the greatest degree to your present health and condition. And now I have the pleasing duty to return you my sincere thanks for the kind feelings expressed towards me; and as I have known you so long in affliction, my innermost wishes are, that each and all of you may long enjoy all the health, happiness, and prosperity which the sunny land of Australia can afford.

I remain,

DEAR IMMIGRANTS,

Your faithful friend,

P. W. MALLON[172]

And then on 29 November, 195 days after departing from Plymouth, the last party of immigrants set out from Dunwich and sailed across Moreton Bay to their final destination. They crossed the sandbar at the mouth of the Brisbane River, passed the swampy, low-lying islands, and meandered some 15 miles along the river's course. Past the mudflats, the scenery changed, and the mangroves and gums gave way to green banks and more familiar introduced vegetation; here and there were cultivated gardens, and homes, and 'birds of strange plumage'.[173] Then within a mile of the town the river curved around suddenly, its sheer rocky banks rising on each side, and delivered the grateful travellers to the bustling precinct of Queen's Wharf.

Part 4

O'er separate paths

"The Land! The Land!"
Hymn of thanksgiving on arrival.

Tune – Evening Hymn, or, Old Hundredth.

WHAT welcome sound salutes our ears?
What speck across the main appears?
Rejoice! rejoice! ye pilgrim band;
The pilot shouts, 'The land! the land!'
Oh, echo back the joyful voice;
Break into singing, and rejoice;
Let bounding heart, and grasping hand,
Announce to all, 'The land! the land!'
Yes, the long pilgrimage is done;
The peril past, the land is won.
Then let us thank the Gracious Hand
Which brings us safe to land! to land!
And, Christian friends, tho' here below
O'er separate paths we each one go,
We shall, ere long, on fairer strand,
Together hail 'The land! the land!'
Then once more here your voices raise;
Together sing, give thanks and praise:
Commit to God's most gracious hand
Your way; and then 'To land! to land!'

Chapter 8

Moving on: life, death and change

THE TRAGEDY OF THE KEMPS

Captain William Henry Kemp sailed away from Moreton Bay on 9 October 1850, leaving behind a sadly depleted, sorrowing and still fearful community. What a range of emotions must have accompanied his departure. The bonds that tragedy and fear can forge are deep, and must have been painful to break. On the other hand, Kemp's life and the lives of his wife and child had been spared, and after two months of waiting – of inaction and dread – it was time, at last, to move on; it must have been with enormous relief that he weighed the anchor and set sail.

He sailed north to search for guano. When his quest proved fruitless, Kemp filled his ship with turtles instead and brought them back to New South Wales.

In mid-November, Kemp's presence was required in Brisbane for the trials of the deserters from his ship: James Hall, Charles Young, John Owens and Robert Walker. Desertion of their seamen was a common problem for ships' commanders. The life of a sailor was difficult and dangerous, and the attraction of life in the colonies – especially during gold-rush years – was a temptation that many found impossible to resist. On Captain Kemp's 1849 voyage to Australia on the *Emigrant*, 13 of his men had jumped ship at Port Jackson and Callao. It was by no means a reflection on Captain Kemp's ability or popularity with his crew. Despite legislation that made desertion of crew illegal, by 1852 sailors were deserting in Australian ports at rates that were considered in the British Parliament to constitute an emergency.[174]

Captain Kemp was not interested in settling the score. He had put Moreton Bay behind him, and instead of returning to Brisbane for the trial of the deserters, he made for Sydney. His plan was to sail from Sydney to Hokianga in New Zealand, where he would load up with timber spars to take back to England. But while he was in Sydney, there was more trouble from his crew. A man named Lindsay and a boy named Thornton visited the ship as it lay at anchor, after which time Kemp caught them ferrying four of his seamen ashore. Furious with Lindsay for using 'strong persuasion' to entice his men away, Kemp ignored his pleas for forgiveness and reported the incident to the Water Police. When Lindsay and Thornton were dragged before the Magistrate Captain Browne, Kemp vowed to have them punished severely for helping his seamen to desert.

The court found, however, that there were 'extenuating circumstances'.[175] Moreover, Lindsay had a clean record and a family to support. And as for the boy: he protested his innocence, maintaining that he had merely helped to row the boat. Kind-hearted Kemp relented. Lindsay was fined only 40 shillings and Thornton five. Not only did Captain Kemp withdraw his plea for severity, but he paid half of Lindsay's fine!

Kemp sailed to Hokianga as planned and collected his timber. From there he sailed to Hobart and then Adelaide (where his crew caused him further grief by getting into a fight), and on to Hokianga via Port Jackson. From Hokianga he made the long journey back to England, bearing a cargo of great planks of New Zealand timber. On board was what Kemp believed to be the largest plank in the world: a piece of Tasmanian blue gum measuring 148 feet. The captain also conveyed back to England some curious specimens of natural history, including the rare 'Parson Bird', whose black plumage and two white feathers under its neck lent the bird its name.[176] Kemp reached Plymouth early in 1852 and continued on to Portsmouth to deliver his cargo.

By this time, he was an experienced and well-respected commander with a first-class certificate as a mariner, but his formal qualification had been awarded under the older, voluntary licensing scheme. In 1851, the United Kingdom had introduced regulations that made it compulsory for new masters and mates to pass an examination before they could command merchant vessels. Those already serving in this capacity were exempt if they had valid certificates proving prior service. When, after his long absence, the captain returned home, he chose to upgrade his certification. While in Portsmouth in March 1852, Kemp took the opportunity to exchange his first-class certificate for a 'Certificate of Competency' as master under the new scheme.

Captain Kemp never returned to Moreton Bay, although he *did* take another fateful trip to Australia. In 1852, after only a couple of months back in his native country, he set off from Liverpool again in the *Emigrant*. Kemp arrived in Port Phillip in August with his wife, daughter and maidservant, some merchandise, a handful of cabin passengers and 50 or so in steerage. Unlike the previous expedition, this voyage was not government sponsored; his passengers were paying customers. And happily, this passage was without incident.

In fact, it was such a success that the passengers were moved to make public their appreciation of the captain and his wife. The cabin passengers wrote to the *Argus*:

> Dear Sir, the undersigned, Cabin passengers on board the ship *Emigrant,* under your command from Liverpool to Port Phillip cannot take our leave of you without expressing our sincere thanks for your extreme kindness and general disposition to promote the comfort and welfare of all on board during the voyage. We have to acknowledge with gratitude Mrs Kemp's unwearied kindness and attention to all. In conclusion, we wish you, Mrs Kemp, and daughter every success and happiness in future prosecution of your voyage and future career.[177]

The steerage passengers were similarly effusive in their praise. His passengers' gratitude must have been balm to the captain, whose competence had been unfairly questioned by some members of the press after his previous distressing voyage to Australia.

From Port Phillip, Captain Kemp, his family and a handful of his passengers sailed on to Port Jackson. He and his wife, Frances Sarah, had decided to settle in Sydney. They took a house in Upper Fort Street, opposite the flagstaff in the maritime district close to the harbour. Kemp found work commanding the clipper barque *Sydney Packet*, ferrying passengers and light freight between Sydney and Melbourne.

The barque was due to leave Port Jackson on 22 December. For some reason, its departure was delayed. Perhaps it was because a seaman of the vessel had been charged with stealing from a passenger, or perhaps it was because the barque was being offered for sale and the conditions had changed; whatever the reason, at the last minute a new departure date was set. A new notice in the paper advised that the *Sydney Packet* was expected to clear customs on 24 December and set sail on Christmas Day.

So it was that instead of being en route to Melbourne on Christmas Eve as he might have been, Captain Kemp was at home with his wife. When they went to bed that night, they neglected to put out the candle on the bedside. Just before midnight, the flame leapt onto the bed curtains and set them alight. The fire consumed poor Frances Sarah and scorched her husband's arms as he tried to beat off the flames. He set off an alarm that roused the neighbourhood; the police came running. They quickly subdued the blaze and saved the house. Only the bed and some pieces of furniture were damaged.

But both Captain Kemp and his wife were seriously injured. Frances Sarah was so debilitated that she couldn't speak. She suffered for two weeks before dying on 8 January, 1853. She was 40 years old.[178]

Captain Kemp returned to England. How to care for his almost eight-year-old daughter was a serious concern for a man whose career meant long months away from home. But before the year was out, he had married again. Kemp's second wife was a 41-year-old widow from Yarmouth named Elizabeth Burcham. The daughter of a master mariner, she would understand the seafaring life.

Kemp was master of the *Emigrant* for a few more years, until the ship was sold to the Portuguese. He was still registered as a master mariner at least until 1858. By 1861 he had died, leaving his daughter in the care of her stepmother. The women lived in the slums of London's East End and subsisted on Elizabeth Kemp's 'private legacy'.

Kemp's daughter, Fanny Hannah Kemp, never married. After her stepmother's death, she lived on the charity of friends in a terrace house at 20 Phillips Road, Hackney. She fell ill with tuberculosis and languished for six months before passing away on 2 November 1872. She died one month before her twenty-eighth birthday.

A COSTLY BUSINESS

Back in Moreton Bay, the immigrants settled into their new lives. The residents of Brisbane had been almost as eager to see the newcomers' release from quarantine as had the immigrants themselves. They had been looking forward to strengthening their workforce for a long time. And so by Christmas all of the new arrivals had found employment.

Starting their lives afresh in the colony, they put the horrors of the past six months behind them. But the episode was not over for Captain Wickham; he still had debts to settle, wages to pay, and the remnants of the quarantine station to liquidate.

Dr Mitchell's estate had been settled. As for Dr Ballow's estate, Captain Wickham had firm opinions. Initially Dr Ballow's widow had been paid only £51 9s for his 37 days of service at the quarantine station – a lower rate than the other surgeons had received. Margaret Ballow had written to Captain Wickham asking that her late husband be paid a rate equal to Doctors Mallon and Barton: that is, two guineas (£2 2s) per day. Captain Wickham agreed and urged the colonial secretary to pay the highest possible allowance to Dr Ballow's widow. He reminded his superior that the doctor had undertaken the duty of caring for the sick at Dunwich after all other medical officers in the district had refused it. He pointed out also that Dr Ballow had abandoned a lucrative private practice to accept this most arduous and dangerous appointment, and that he had done so out of a 'high sense of duty and humanity'.

Because of Dr Ballow's death, Captain Wickham wrote, his widow had 'been reduced from comfort and plenty to a state of dependence on her relatives'.[179]

It was only fair, Wickham argued, that Dr Ballow should be paid as well as Drs Mallon and Barton had been. Dr Ballow's contribution had been, after all, 'not of an ordinary nature'.

The colonial secretary agreed. The red tape took some time, but almost a year after his death Dr Ballow's widow was informed that a sum of £38 17s would be deposited into her late husband's account.[180]

To encourage immigrants to help out at the quarantine station, Captain Wickham had been obliged to offer them financial incentive. With the ordeal over, it was time to honour those promises. Wickham wrote to the colonial secretary, listing the names of those helpers he judged deserving. These were the hospital attendants, the laundry workers, the nurses, cooks, storekeepers, butchers and the carpenter. There were 21 in all, and each – except for Mary Connor, who was rewarded with a passage to Sydney – was paid one shilling and sixpence per day.

The protracted quarantine had been an expensive business. The guards were paid two shillings and sixpence per day as well as their 'indulgences', and Captain Kemp was reimbursed for the sails and timbers that had been taken from the ship to fashion accommodation. The immigrants were reimbursed for the clothing that had had to be destroyed to reduce the risk of infection.

From various storekeepers in Brisbane the government had purchased bread, flour, meat, vegetables, tea, sugar and sheep, as well as butter, soap, brandy, rum, wines, porter ale and beer, two 'milch cows' and calves, milk, bedding, oil, candles, stores, utensils and other articles. Large amounts of wine, spirits, porter and ale had been purchased for the station. Captain Wickham defended the massive bill for 'stimulants'; the doctors had needed them for medicinal purposes. Alcohol had also been provided to the healthy as a reward for their services. Without such rewards, Wickham added, they might not have been induced to help.

What to do with the deserted quarantine station was another problem. The immigration agent, Francis Merewether, recommended that items such as the iron bedsteads should be taken to Brisbane and kept in storage there, ready to be returned to the quarantine station as soon as they were needed again. The wooden buildings, erected from the ship's fittings so dutifully by David Hobbs only months earlier, were taken apart. The timber was taken to Brisbane where, Merewether argued, it could be used by the government or sold.

BRISBANE GROWS

The immigrants newly delivered from the horrors of quarantine integrated quickly into the community. Brisbane was teetering on the brink of change. The *Emigrant* had been the fifth ship in the recent wave of immigration that had swept new settlers into the town. A census conducted in March 1851 found the non-Indigenous population of Brisbane alone to be over 2500.

The growing population injected new life into the Moreton Bay region and kick-started development. Earlier in the year, the first Circuit Court had been proclaimed in Brisbane, a Customs House had been built, and the first land sales had been held in Ipswich, Drayton and Warwick. Over the ensuing years, more churches of various denominations would spring up, a Moreton Bay Amateur Musical Society would be established, a School of Arts would open, more immigrant ships would arrive, banks and a stock exchange would be built, exports of wool and cotton would be shipped directly from Brisbane, the township of Cleveland would be proclaimed, and development would spread to the north. Brisbane would suffer floods and an influenza epidemic. White settlers would come to outnumber the Indigenous people, taking over their land, disregarding their laws, and destroying their culture, their health and their livelihood.

The citizens of Brisbane began to feel disadvantaged by the town's distance from the administrative hub of Sydney. With decisions being made 500 miles away, they were frustrated by their lack of representation in government and the perceived neglect with which they were treated. They began to agitate for separation.

The first public meeting to discuss the issue was held in Brisbane only a few months after the *Emigrant's* passengers were released from quarantine. But it would be another eight years before the concept would become a reality.

On 6 June, 1859, Queen Victoria signed the document that would establish Queensland as a colony. At the end of that year, a crowd of some 4,000 people thronged the streets of Brisbane to celebrate the birth of the new colony and watch the swearing-in of Sir George Ferguson Bowen as its first governor.

By this time, Captain John Clements Wickham had served as the senior administrator in the growing settlement for 16 years. His first wife had died in 1852, leaving him with two sons and a daughter. Five years later he had remarried. As the town had developed, his responsibilities had grown along with his salary. In 1857, Wickham's position had been upgraded to government resident, and he was obliged to give up the role of police magistrate.

When self-government became imminent, Wickham refused the post of colonial treasurer that was offered to him. Instead, he sought to retire with a pension from the New South Wales

Government; he was, after all, 61 years old. The New South Wales Government, however, rejected his request on the grounds that any remuneration due to him was now the responsibility of the new Queensland Government. Although the governor supported Wickham's petition, and despite his long and successful period of service, the Queensland Government refused to pay him a pension.

Embittered and no longer financially secure, Wickham left Australia for England in 1860. His youngest child – a son by his second wife – was born on the voyage. Wickham settled in the South of France, where the cost of living suited his circumstances better. He died from a stroke on 6 January 1864, at the age of 65, and was buried at Biarritz.

In the meantime, Dr Frederick James Barton – whose services Wickham had secured just as the period of quarantine was coming to an end – had settled in Brisbane. His initial contract had guaranteed him work for only two months, but Barton would see out the rest of his life in the district.

Dr Ballow's death had left the Brisbane Hospital without a resident surgeon. Dr William Hobbs had relieved Dr Ballow in the position during the period of the *Emigrant*'s quarantine, but he returned to private practice when the business was over. In 1851, the Moreton Bay District Hospital was re-established as the Brisbane General Hospital. In January of that year, the committee of the Brisbane Hospital elected Frederick Barton as its new resident surgeon. He served on and off as resident surgeon until early 1863, when he fell ill with 'consumption'.

The 38-year-old suffered for six months, during which time he was attended by his colleague Dr Kearsey Cannan. He passed away on 30 August 1863, leaving a grieving widow with three small daughters. According to his obituary, Barton was:

one of the most modest and unassuming men who ever filled a public office . . . benevolent almost to a fault, kind in his demeanor [sic], a thorough gentleman in his deportment, an ardent student, a loving husband, an excellent father, and an ever-faithful friend, the late house surgeon of the Brisbane Hospital had claims upon our esteem and respect which few could hope to equal, and none could hope to surpass.[181]

Dr Cannan, in contrast, lived a long and colourful life. Like Dr Barton, he embedded himself firmly into Brisbane life and never sought to leave. Late in 1850, Dr Cannan resubmitted an application for the position as visiting surgeon to Brisbane Gaol – a position that had been left vacant by Ballow's death. Dr Cannan had competed with Dr Ballow for the job the previous year and had lost to his better-qualified rival. This time, unopposed, Dr Cannan was granted the position.

Over the following years, Dr Cannan would be appointed coroner for the district of Brisbane, surgeon of the Brisbane contingent of the newly formed Queensland Volunteer Rifle Brigade, and a member of the Immigration Board. When a lunatic asylum was established at Woogaroo (now Goodna) in 1864, Dr Cannan became its first full-time medical superintendent. He lost the position a few years later when an enquiry found him to be a 'muddling administrator'.[182] His skill as a doctor, however, was highly regarded, and Dr Cannan retained a connection with the asylum as visiting surgeon. In the meantime, he had also acted as police magistrate at Woogaroo and had been appointed the district registrar for births, deaths and marriages. He was the first president of the short-lived Queensland Medical Society when it was founded in 1871.

The first *official* private practitioner in Brisbane (although

Dr Ballow attended some private patients during the convict era), Dr Cannan was more interested in his patients' welfare than their money. He treated many of his patients for free. He has been described as hardworking and 'reasonably competent'[183] for his times. Well liked and respected by his community, it is said that Cannan's 'tolerant, kindly and attractive personality made an early Australian community a little more civilized and enjoyable'.[184] Kearsey Cannan caught the flu in 1894 and died of bronchitis, leaving behind his wife and four surviving children. He was 79 years old, and had practised medicine right up to the end.

THE TROUBLES AND TRIUMPHS OF DR MALLON

While Dr Ballow's heroism has been rightly acknowledged, public recognition for the noble deeds of that other Brisbane doctor, Patrick Walsh Mallon, has been sadly lacking. Dr Mallon's self-lessness and courage were equal to those of his worthy colleague. And yet the good fortune that allowed him to survive the ordeal seems to have rendered his heroism less noteworthy in the eyes of history.

Dr Mallon's constitution was as remarkable as his compassion. Only days after falling ill with the dreaded fever, he had recovered and got immediately back on his feet to tend the sick and dying in quarantine. His skill and dedication were not unappreciated by the immigrants. 'We now, being on the eve of our departure, approach you with feelings of deep respect and gratitude,' they had written, as the ordeal drew to a close, 'and wish you may be long spared to step forward, when called upon by duty, in aid of the distressed.'[185]

Just as the immigrants had wished it, Patrick Walsh Mallon was indeed *long spared to step forward, when called upon by duty, in aid of the distressed.* And although his sojourn in Moreton Bay was all but over, his career in medicine would endure.

Mallon's time in Moreton Bay had been riddled with strife. He had arrived in April 1849 and after practising for less than a year had been forced by the courts to return funds to a plaintiff over a disputed charge for his services. Only months after this incident he had risked his life and endured three months of physical and emotional suffering at Dunwich quarantine station. The episode had interrupted an ongoing legal dispute with a former patient. When he returned to Brisbane with the last of the immigrants in late November 1850 and resumed his practice, he also resumed the legal battle that had begun the previous year. In the latter part of 1849, Dr Mallon had attended an innkeeper in Drayton who later disputed the doctor's charges and refused to pay his bill. By 1851, Dr Mallon was still waiting for his payment. In September of that year, he took the matter to court.

Dr Mallon had charged the innkeeper for his medical attendance and the expenses of the journey. The defendant – the innkeeper, Dr Mallon's patient – challenged the charge on the grounds that the doctor had journeyed to Drayton in order to buy a horse from him, but had stayed unbidden to treat his illness. Far from agreeing to pay his medical bills, the patient sought to charge Dr Mallon for accommodation at the inn. The case was tried in the Supreme Court, which meant that Dr Mallon had to make the three-day journey by sea to Sydney once more. For Dr Mallon, the case was worth pursuing; the judge rejected the innkeeper's demand for board and ordered him to pay the bill (minus £14 for the purchase of the horse).

Moreton Bay had offered Dr Mallon little but trouble: two court cases and an extended period in quarantine – a time of ceaseless drudgery, discomfort and dread of death. Moreover, it appears that for the period of his service in the north he had left his children in the care of others – possibly his late wife's family – in New South Wales. He must have missed them; one can imagine that witnessing the death of so many infants might have made him feel the absence of his own children more keenly. In any case, it was not long before Dr Mallon chose to give up on the place soon to be known as Queensland and return to the district where he had made a name for himself in the 1830s: the Dungog/Maitland region.

By the end of 1851, he had resumed practice and returned with vigour to his old life. It was a life that was notable for his involvement in public service, education and philanthropy.

By the beginning of 1852, Dr Mallon had become a donor to (and presumably an attendant surgeon at) the Maitland Hospital. He was outspoken in his support of ethics and justice; he was not afraid to stand up for what he believed was right. But he was not infallible, and neither was his career without embarrassments.

In February 1852, the behaviour of his servant, Catherine Cody, aroused Mallon's suspicions. She had been in his service for a few months. From the beginning, she had had bouts of illness but after two months she appeared to recover. The doctor suspected she had borne a child and done away with it. On searching his home for traces of a child, he 'discovered in the water closet on his premises, some bones, some human hair, and some small pieces of bombazine, leading him to the conclusion that the child had been thrown in there, wrapped up in the bombazine.'[186]

Dr Mallon reported his suspicions to the authorities. Police arrested Cody and opened an investigation. Witnesses who had known the servant before her employment with Dr Mallon refuted the suggestion that she might have been pregnant.

Then it was determined that the bones he had discovered were those of a cat! The matter was dropped, but the editor of *The Maitland Mercury and Hunter River General Advertiser* could not resist adding his opinion to the report: 'Before preferring so serious a charge against the young woman, Dr. Mallon was surely bound to have thoroughly satisfied himself that the bones found were those of an infant.'[187]

Dr Mallon was clearly not above an occasional lapse of judgement. His unwise property investments in the 1830s and '40s attest to this. His legal disputes in Moreton Bay – two in less than two years – also suggest a character whose undeniably noble intentions and desire to further the public good were perhaps undermined by a want of diplomacy. There can be no doubt, however, of his strong sense of public duty and justice. He was human: skilled, principled, courageous and imperfect.

Dr Mallon settled in Dungog and married Elizabeth Angela Wright (sometimes known as Angela) on 17 January 1854. Elizabeth, like Mallon's first wife, was a Church of England woman. Despite his Catholic faith, Mallon and his bride were married in the Church of England at Dungog.[188] The new Mrs Mallon was 20 years younger than her husband, being only about 26 at the time of the wedding.

The pair went on to have a large family: Olivia (born 1855), Patrick (1857), Charles Henry (1859), Susan Eliza (1860), Frances Theresa (Fanny, born 1862), Thomas Bailey (1864), and Mary Veronica (1869). There were also two girls and a boy who died in infancy: Jane (1856-1857), Mary (1866-1867) and Walter (1873–1875). Although Patrick and Elizabeth wed in the Church of England, their children appear to have been brought up as Catholics. When Elizabeth died in 1909, she was buried, like her husband, in the Catholic section of the Rookwood Cemetery.

By 1859, the family had moved from their home in Dungog to Port Stephens. In his new home, Patrick Mallon threw himself into public life, delivering lectures on a range of topics: chemistry, optics and the evils of drink. At the Port Stephens School of Arts, he spoke about the 'Physiology of Man', and was 'very loudly applauded during his elaborate explanations of the human mechanism, showing minutely the principal features of our "fearful and wonderful" structure, and the beautiful adaptation of our organs to the work they have to perform'.[189]

In October 1860, Dr Mallon was employed as medical attendant at the brand-new Port Stephens Hospital and Benevolent Society, and the following year he became a magistrate in Stroud.

For Dr Mallon, 1865 was a terrible year. Following the death of a woman and her baby in childbirth, he was charged with 'wilfully killing and slaying one Mrs. Hill and child, wilful neglect, and unskilful treatment'.[190] The charges appear to have come to nothing, but the episode must have been devastating for a man of Dr Mallon's principles. The public embarrassment must also have been considerable, for the case 'caused a deal of excitement here, and the court was densely thronged throughout the whole of the two days'.

Perhaps it was the upsetting business of the court case that caused Dr Mallon to lose enthusiasm for practice in the district. In any case, he closed his doors and shifted his family to Sydney the following year. An advertisement in the *Freeman's Journal* announced that:

DR. P. W. MALLON, member Royal College of Surgeons, Licenciate of Midwifery, Royal College of Physicians, Edinburgh, Surgeon to the Holy Guild of St. Mary and St. Joseph, 1847 and 1848, has resumed practice in Sydney, and may be consulted at his residence and Dispensary, 105 Parramatta-street, opposite St. Benedict's Church.[191]

Dr Mallon would see out the rest of his days in Sydney, though in his later years he would move from his Parramatta Road home ('a pleasant, commodious 8-roomed house'[192]) to Isabella Street, Camperdown. He remained active in medicine and politics until at least the late 1870s. His signature on a petition for mercy in the sentencing of convicted murderer John Connors in 1867 shows that Mallon's compassion and humanity had not faded over the years. He continued to lend public support to his favoured causes and political candidates in his local area.

Religious tolerance appears to have been one of Dr Mallon's many virtues. The children of his first marriage seem to have been brought up, unlike their half-siblings, in the Church of England. Their mother's family clearly had an important influence in their lives; the children may have been at least partly raised by them. In the early years after his first wife's death, Dr Mallon would have found it difficult to care for the children and continue in medical practice. It is likely, given the social mores of the time, that the children were taken in by their maternal aunts or uncles.

Their father, however, remained an important part of their lives. He was a witness at the marriage of his daughter Catherine Mary to Thomas Hungerford, a prominent pastoralist and politician after whom the outback Queensland town of Hungerford was named.

Dr Mallon's eldest son, Arthur Wentworth Mallon, a poundkeeper, settled in the New South Wales town of Bingera.[193] His first wife, Mary Ann Clarke, died at a young age and, within two years of her death, Arthur married her sister. In time, he relocated to Western Australia, where he died in his sixty-fourth year.

The children of Dr Mallon's second marriage lived out their lives in New South Wales and fared, on average, not as well as those of his first. The eldest, Olivia, never married but survived to the great age of 85. Her sister, Mary Veronica, descended into a chronically drunken and abusive state and drove her miserable husband to file unsuccessfully for divorce. She would live to the age of 83. The others to attain some longevity were Patrick, who died at 68, and Susan Eliza, who died, unmarried, at 61. Fanny and Thomas Bailey both died in their thirties.

By the end of 1881, the doctor had begun to ail. He would endure an illness of 18 months before finally succumbing to 'cystitis and old age' on 6 April 1883. Patrick Walsh Mallon was buried in the Catholic section of Rookwood Cemetery, where he rests in the same grave as 17-month-old Walter, his youngest son.

Chapter 9

The fates of the immigrants

THE TRAGEDY OF THE MAUNSELLS

Catherine Maunsell – the first *Emigrant* passenger to show symptoms of typhus – settled in Brisbane. The 22-year-old domestic servant, who had left her home in County Limerick with her brother Patrick, recovered from the fever and went on to live to the good age – for Victorian times – of 71.

Catherine was one of several passengers of the *Emigrant* to marry a fellow-traveller. Her husband was James Cahill, a farm labourer from Tipperary, and a Roman Catholic like herself. Some relationships developed hastily, with the couples marrying soon after their release from quarantine. Others blossomed more slowly. Catherine and James' relationship was of the latter type; they did not wed until January 1854, a little over three years after their arrival in Moreton Bay. The pair went on to have a large family: seven sons and three daughters, one of whom died in infancy.

Like so many poor young Irish folk of their generation, Catherine and her brother Patrick had ventured across the sea to pave the way for the rest of their family. And in spite of the traumatic start to their colonial venture, they must have concluded that the risk was worth taking.

Patrick and Catherine's sisters, Ellen and Honora, arrived in Sydney on the *Agincourt* on 4 March, 1852. During the voyage, 'fever' broke out and the ship was held in quarantine at Spring Cove. One can imagine the sisters' anxiety during this time; the *Emigrant* tragedy having apprised them fully of the danger of their situation. But they survived unscathed and all the immigrants were released within a few weeks. Ellen made her way to Queensland to witness Catherine's marriage to James Cahill.

Patrick and Catherine's brother, James, emigrated to Australia sometime during the early 1850s, leaving his wife, Alice, and their young son, Stephen, behind in Ireland. It was Patrick who paid the £22 to sponsor Alice and Stephen's passage so that they could reunite with James in Moreton Bay: a significant sum. At the same time, Patrick also sponsored his younger brother, John. In 1858, their parents, 21-year-old John and 13-year-old[194] sister, Margaret, also joined the family in the colony. Almost the whole Maunsell family was by then in Australia.

Immigration records state that James Maunsell (senior) was 62 when he arrived in Australia – though he was probably older – and his wife Catherine 52. When he died at his home in Charlotte St, Brisbane, in 1864, it was reported that James senior was the improbable age of 103, and that he had been 'a faithful servant to the late Earl of Clare, Mount Shannon, county of Limerick, Ireland, for 90 years'.[195]

Catherine's husband James Cahill fell ill with 'English cholera' in 1878 and died two days later. Catherine remained in their home at Harcourt Street, Fortitude Valley. She developed cancer in 1898, and died on Christmas Eve in 1900 from 'exhaustion'.

Catherine was buried in the Toowong Cemetery, after having spent 50 years in the colony. Seven of her children survived her.

While the Cahills led a private life, Catherine's brother, Patrick, was often in the public eye. Patrick Maunsell had shown a good deal of early promise. Dr Ballow had commended him highly for his 'constant attendance' on the surgeons during the quarantine ordeal. Afterwards, Patrick was due to be paid one shilling and six pence per day for his services but it was Captain Wickham's view that he deserved more. He was a hard worker with a strong sense of family commitment and civic duty. But there was to be no happy ending for Patrick.

Soon after his arrival in Brisbane, he secured work as a servant for Henry Twiss, publican at the Logan Hotel in South Brisbane. By late 1851 he had been appointed police constable.[196] In the rough environment of Brisbane Town, the job – arresting drunks and breaking up fights – was a thankless one. Patrick performed his duties diligently, but by the beginning of 1853 he had left the force.

By this time, the young Irishman had saved enough money to buy land, establish his own business and sponsor the immigration of his family. In 1853, he acquired a publican's licence, and by the following year he was running the Queen's Head Hotel. In 1855, however, he sold the hotel and announced his intention to leave the district 'for some time'.[197] Whether he did actually leave is unknown; by 1857 he was back in Brisbane.

Patrick launched himself into the property market. In 1857 he owned both a 'four-roomed cottage, with detached kitchen containing a servant's apartment and brick oven'[198] in Charlotte Street and 78 acres at Kedron Brook. But Patrick was unsettled; once again he bought property, then within months offloaded it and left the district. This time, he offered both the cottage in Charlotte Street and a farm at Kedron Brook to let.

Patrick travelled to Sydney, where he married Margaret Sweeney at St Mary's Cathedral. Margaret was an Irish girl who, like her husband, hailed from Limerick. Soon after their marriage, the couple was back in Brisbane. They continued to let out the Charlotte Street cottage, offering 'board and lodging, with all the advantages of a comfortable home'[199] to four single men, while Patrick worked as a gardener.

Soon they started a family of their own. Their first son, James, was born in 1860. In all, they would have six children: James, Catherine, Ellen (who died in her third year in 1867), Edward John, Stephen Michael and Helen. Patrick's property portfolio and fortunes grew. By 1866 his wife was advertising for a servant and by 1867 he was seeking tenants for the 'European Boarding House' in Charlotte Street, a property that boasted 12 rooms and 'water laid on'.[200]

Patrick was a pillar of the community – and yet he had enemies. In October of 1867, a fire broke out in his 'European Boarding House', which had been unoccupied for ten days. Neighbours sounded the bell to summon the fire brigade, and managed to douse the fire before it did much damage. The fire brigade ascertained that the blaze had broken out in the roof at the back of the house, in an unusual spot, leading them to conclude that the fire had been deliberately lit by a 'malicious person'.[201] Fortunately – or perhaps suspiciously – the house had been insured by the Pacific Insurance Company for £300. The damage was negligible.

From 1868, Patrick lived on the corner of Grey Street and Melbourne Street in South Brisbane and worked variously as a gardener and a carpenter. As time wore on, the man who had showed so much potential as a youth gradually fell apart. In October 1873, he drank a glass of beer too many and assaulted his wife. Sergeant Barry of the Brisbane Police arrived at the

Maunsells' home just in time to witness Patrick punching Margaret repeatedly in the face. The sergeant took him into custody. At the City Police Court, Patrick was charged with serious assault and remanded for a few days until he could be brought before the Central Police Court. Margaret refused to testify against him. Patrick, who appeared penitent, pleaded guilty. 'No one could be more sorry than he was himself for what had occurred,' the *Brisbane Courier* reported. 'He had taken a glass of beer, but he did not intend to do so again.'[202]

Because of his previous good character and because his wife refused to prosecute, Patrick was released without charge – but with a stern warning from the judge.

This was the beginning of a downward slide. Despite his resolution to stay sober, Patrick couldn't keep away from the bottle. In June 1875, he was arrested for drunkenness and confined to the lock-up. He must have been quite pickled, for it wasn't until the next day that it was discovered his leg was broken.

Only a few months earlier Patrick had been implicated in a shady deal involving a Brisbane councillor. The Alderman David Grayson had sold a large quantity of timber to the council, contrary to the Municipality Act. Not only had he, in a conflict of interests, received payment for the timber from the council but he had charged a higher amount than had been agreed upon. And it was Patrick Maunsell who had collected the money on Mr Grayson's behalf. According to the prosecution at Grayson's trial, Patrick was 'either a "go between", and acted in a manner highly wrong, or else did a friendly turn for the defendant'.[203] Since Patrick Maunsell had nominated Mr Grayson for council two years earlier, it might be inferred that the men were more than passing acquaintances. (Grayson was found guilty and fined £75 but defaulted on the fine and was sent to prison.)

Over the next few years, Patrick Maunsell lived with his wife and some of his children at his brother's place at Kedron Brook. He also owned property in South Brisbane. By this time, he appeared to have amassed considerable wealth, mostly from rents on his properties. But his material riches did not make him happy. Patrick was a heavy drinker, and a violent one.

From November 1880, however, he gave up the drink. At around this time, some unknown 'melancholy news' prompted Patrick and his family to move back to Grey Street. A couple of months later, a deep depression settled upon his spirits. His acquaintances noticed that Patrick's state of mind seemed altered; he was distracted and restless, and failed to recognise them when passing them in the street. He was seen often pacing on his verandah.

On 5 February at half past three in the afternoon, Margaret Maunsell took two of her children shopping in North Brisbane. She left her 11-year-old son, Stephen, at home with his father.

Margaret left Patrick pacing up and down on their verandah. Ten minutes later, Patrick summoned young Stephen and sent him out to buy tobacco. *You need not be in a hurry,* Patrick told him, and gave him a penny. As he was leaving, Stephen saw his father shut the windows and the front door and go out to the kitchen. He assumed that Patrick was going out.

Aitchison the tobacconist was a short walk away, across Victoria Bridge into Queen Street. The boy was gone for about 20 minutes; when he returned, the verandah was empty and the front door was locked. He went around the back. The back door was also locked, but he found the keys lying in the back yard. Stephen picked up the keys and tried them in the back door, but the door would not budge. He left the keys in the kitchen and went around to the front to wait for his mother.

Margaret returned a little after five o'clock. She found the house locked up and her son, Stephen, waiting on the verandah. The boy explained that he had been unable to get in, and fetched the key for her. Margaret opened the door and went in.

The front room was just as she had left it, except that the window was shut. She went into the bedroom. The room was dim but Margaret could make out the shape of her husband on the floor. Thinking that he might have had a fit, she knelt and took hold of his hand. It was then that she saw the blood.

Appalled, Margaret hurried out to raise the alarm. Outside, Sergeant Grimes happened to be passing by and heard her cries. Margaret called him in, and together the pair rushed back to the gruesome scene. The sergeant found Patrick Maunsell lying on his back in a pool of blood. The man was stripped to the waist and blood saturated his upper body. Grimes lifted Patrick's head and saw that his throat was cut. The wound was about two inches long and very deep; the jugular vein had been severed. Patrick was dead.

A blood-stained knife lay under the body's right arm. There was no sign of struggle; the room was in perfect order. Sergeant Grimes sent for a doctor, and Dr O'Doherty arrived sometime before six o'clock. By then the body was cold. The doctor had no doubt that death had been caused by the wound to the throat, and he said as much at the inquest three days later.

At the Magisterial Inquiry, it was concluded that Patrick Maunsell had committed suicide by cutting his own throat.

Patrick's suicide may not have been committed impulsively in a drunken state. It appears to have been planned. Five days before his death, on 31 January, Patrick had made a will. He bequeathed his property in South Brisbane to his eldest daughter, Kate, a dressmaker. Patrick also asked his trustees to sell off his property in North Brisbane and with the proceeds pay £150 to his son, Thomas, £50 to his sister Catherine Cahill and £100 to her child, who was also his godchild. He also bequeathed £50 to his youngest sister, Margaret. The rest of the proceeds were to be distributed amongst his wife and other children, with the younger children's share to be invested and the income to be used for their maintenance and education.

And yet – Patrick's estate amounted to less than £50.

Patrick was buried in the Toowong Cemetery on 7 February. Much of his property – including two large boarding houses and two cottages – was offered up for sale at auction. For a man whose selflessness and strength as a young emigrant were so admirable, this descent into alcoholism and depression and debt was pitiful and puzzling. Even more puzzling are the generous bequests made in Patrick's will, considering the dire state of his finances. Had his debts been called in during the few days between making the will and his suicide? Was he deluding himself about the value of his estate? Was he pretending to his family that he was ignorant of his financial collapse? We will never know.

After Patrick's death, his widow advertised rooms in her Grey Street home for the accommodation with board of 'two young ladies engaged in business'.[204] She lived for another 35 years. She died suddenly in April 1916 in the Coorparoo home of her unmarried daughter, Ellen, at the age of 85. Margaret was buried at Toowong Cemetery with the remains of her husband. Both lie beneath the weeds and between tumbled-down headstones of fellow-Catholics, in sadly neglected unmarked graves.

THE TRAVAILS OF THE BLOXAMS

The passengers of the *Emigrant* began their colonial lives in appalling conditions at Dunwich. Some of them would end their days in exactly the same place, enduring hardship of quite another kind.

John Bloxam[205] was 14 when his family left their home in County Galway to make a new life in Australia. He travelled with his father, Thomas; his mother, Fanny; and his younger siblings, Ann and Thomas junior. Like most of their fellow-travellers, the family suffered loss on the voyage. Thirty-two-year-old Fanny had died of typhus on 5 August, just as the barque entered Bass Strait. Her widower, an illiterate weaver, was also stricken by the fever but recovered at the quarantine station.

The family settled in Queensland. The widower lived at Moggill Creek and, in time, his daughter joined him there with her husband and children. Thomas junior moved north but died suddenly of an aneurysm at only 45 during a trip to Brisbane.

The eldest Bloxam child, 14-year-old John, didn't linger in the district with his father and siblings upon their arrival. He seems to have had trouble settling anywhere. Initially he found work on Gracemere Station, Rockhampton, as a stockman; later he worked as a horse driver, farmhand and cook in Roma, Toowoomba, Blackall, Ipswich and Indooroopilly. He married in Rockhampton and raised three children. But by 1900, the restless John had left his wife, Ellen, and returned to the south, where his sister still lived. By then John was 65 years old and earning only five shillings a week. His outraged wife had John hauled all the way back to face the court in Rockhampton to answer to charges of desertion. The police magistrate seems to have regarded John as a pitiful case. He remarked that out of his meagre wage, he could not 'spare much', and that he did not think that, considering his age, John was in a position even to keep himself. 'I think it is a great pity that a man of your age should have been brought all this way from Laidley for nothing,' he added.[206]

When his sister Ann died, John Bloxam became the last surviving member of his immediate family. Having parted from his wife, he had no one left to care for him. In 1905, he was admitted to the Benevolent Asylum that had been established in 1867 on the site of the former quarantine grounds at Dunwich. Intended to accommodate the elderly and infirm, the Dunwich Benevolent Asylum actually became a dumping ground for drunks, the disabled and, occasionally, lepers. It was poorly funded and overcrowded; by 1901 the asylum was home to over 1000 inmates.

John Bloxam's first spell at the Benevolent Asylum was brief, but he would return for a longer stay some years later. We can only imagine his feelings as he returned to Dunwich as an old man. If any memories of his 14-year-old life had survived, he would have noticed major changes to the settlement. As the white-haired, bearded gent stepped off the steamer *Otter* onto a timber jetty, which had been built as an extension from the original stone causeway, he would have found himself in a small village that included a police station and lock-up, a visitor centre, a public hall, a bakery, kitchen, laundry and recreational facilities, a dairy and a piggery. His property would have been surrendered upon entry and stored away in the 'swag room' for safekeeping, for inmates were allowed few personal possessions. Like the other residents, John would have been given trousers, flannel shirts with 'Dunwich Benevolent Asylum' stamped on the back, blucher boots, socks, a coat, overcoat and a slouch hat to wear.

Inmates needing medical care were separated into distinct wards, each housing patients of different classifications: the inebriates, the infirm, and the 'Asiatics'. Those whose conditions were in any way distasteful were sent to the 'foul ward'. Otherwise inmates lived in dormitory-style accommodation, with some

of the men housed in tents in the 'men's camp', on the site later
known as Mitchell Park. John Bloxam may well have ended his
days in this Dunwich institution in a tent, in conditions not much
better than those of his first days in Australia.

The residents of the Benevolent Asylum were outcasts, regarded
with contempt and permitted little personal freedom. They dined
together in a mess hall, on food that was often cold and unap-
petising. The institution was highly regimented, with inflexible
rules and routines that might have reminded John Bloxam of the
shipboard days of his youth. There were set meal times and set
bed times and rules governing cleaning and personal hygiene.
Fraternising between the male and female inmates was strongly
discouraged.

John's wife had died back in 1908, three years after his first
admission to the asylum. John lingered on alone for another
20 years and was still an inmate when he died of 'senility' at the
age of 94. He was buried in the Dunwich cemetery, not far from
the graves of his fellow emigrants who had died in quarantine
after sharing the dreadful voyage from England with him 78 years
earlier.

John Bloxam was not the only *Emigrant* passenger to return
to Dunwich in his final days. There were others, like 20-year-old
Michael Quinlan, who, having emigrated 50 years earlier seeking
fortune and happiness, died as penniless and alone as they had
been upon arrival in the colony.

MARY GORMAN AND JOHN TOLMAN:
STRUGGLES AND STRIFE
Only a handful of the *Emigrant's* passengers died within five years
of their arrival. One of these was James Tolman. He and his brother

John had emigrated from Moorlinch, in County Somerset. James was a 23-year-old Church of England farm labourer. His brother was three years his senior. James had fallen ill with typhus at the end of the voyage and had been transferred on arrival to the quarantine station hospital, where he took many weeks to recover. His brother had also survived a bout of the fever.

John Tolman was amongst the men who had carried the drowned body of Elizabeth Wade out of the sea. He was not to know, on that terrible day, that his brother James would soon suffer a similar fate. Shortly after his arrival in Moreton Bay, James found work with Mr John Collins at his Moondoolun (or Mundoolun) sheep station in the Logan District. His career as a station hand was brief. In July 1852, James Tolman's body was found in the Logan River. He had been trying to cross the river on horseback when he was swept away by floodwaters and drowned. His horse was found, close to death from exhaustion, on an island downstream, where the current had wedged it between the trunks of two trees.

James' brother, John, would go on to live a long and eventful life in Queensland. If the authorities had sought only to attract immigrants who would work and reproduce, they would have been highly satisfied with John Gorman. If they had hoped that their immigrants would also have shown good moral character, they might have been left scratching their heads.

In September 1853, three years after her father died of typhus in sight of land, Mary Gorman married John Tolman. Mary was only 12 years old during the passage and 15 at her wedding. Her husband was 14 years her senior. The pair married at Nindooinbah (near Beaudesert), settled in South Brisbane and had eight children over the next 17 years. John was a shipwright and worked as a carpenter on a prison hulk in Moreton Island. He had ambitions to build up his wealth through property investments, buying rental cottages in Cleveland and South Brisbane. But John overreached himself and was insolvent by 1867. Wallowing in debt, he was forced to sell his mortgaged rental properties and all of the furnishings within them.

In November 1870, a son was born to John and Mary Tolman: their eighth child, William Joseph Tolman. But these were not happy times for the family. Mary's health was failing; by then she had developed the uterine cancer that would slowly kill her. The baby died at only seven months of age. His mother, Mary Tolman, followed him to the grave a few months later. She was only 32 years old and had been sick for a long time. Mary's short life was full of heartbreak. Her father had died when she was just a child. She had married very young to a much older man and borne him eight children. She had endured the collapse of her husband's business and the death of her infant child.

John didn't grieve for long. He buried his wife at South Brisbane, and only eight months after her death – on 25 June 1872 – he married a young woman named Mary Jane Whiteford McKernan. John was a widower of about 47, and Mary Jane an Irish girl – and single mother – of 22.

Mary Jane had arrived in Moreton Bay in 1870 and fallen pregnant within months of her arrival. On 23 May 1871, she was delivered of an illegitimate son whom she named Walter Edwin Patrick Whiteford. When the child was born, Mary Jane was living in the Servants' Home in Ann Street, an institution where young immigrant women could stay in relative safety while they sought work. Here the girls were given accommodation and training in domestic activities to help them gain employment as servants.

The Servants' Home was in the seedy vicinity of Queen's Wharf, where sailors came and went, drunks and criminals prowled, and predators took advantage of young immigrant women who arrived fresh from the United Kingdom. As a shipwright, John would have spent a lot of time in the wharf district. It may have been there that he met the young Irishwoman.

A question mark hangs over Walter's paternity. In later life, both John Tolman and Walter would claim a father/son relationship. If this was true, John would appear to be a predator who adulterously impregnated a naïve young immigrant while his sick wife was carrying his child. On balance, however, it appears that John brought Mary Jane's illegitimate child up as his own, although he was *not* Walter's biological father. [207]

In 1872, John was a newly widowed man with seven children, and Mary Jane was a young single woman, alone with a baby. Their union would have seemed mutually beneficial, despite the age gap. But John was no saint, and his relationship with Mary Jane was tumultuous. By mid-1878, the pair had separated and Mary Jane had taken custody of their four children. John declared publicly in the *Brisbane Courier* that he would not be responsible for his wife's debts. A few weeks later he was before the courts on assault charges.

The couple had been living apart for about a month when Mary Jane visited her husband's home at Kangaroo Point to see her stepdaughters. Tolman came home at about half past five that evening and told her that 'he did not want any rows'. A short time later, one of his daughters 'came and pushed her about'. Mary Jane complained that her husband was a 'mean old wretch to stand by and see his wife assaulted.' John threatened to break her jaw. His wife picked up a plate and swore that if he hit her, she would defend herself. John ordered her to put down the plate and when she did, he grasped her by the throat with one hand and punched her in the face with the other.

He beat her for ten minutes, until her eyes were black and swollen and her face and clothing covered with the blood that poured from her nose and mouth. Mary Jane fled to the local police constable, who took her to Dr Hobbs. The doctor found that the excessive flow of blood had been caused by her husband's attempt to strangle her. The police constable questioned John Tolman, who explained that he had beaten his wife because she had 'aggravated him'. Mary Jane was hospitalised and her husband arrested. John Tolman was tried, found guilty, and fined £5.

Mary Jane had violent tendencies of her own. More than once she came before the Brisbane courts, accused of drunkenness, disorderly behaviour and using indecent language. On one of these occasions she complained of feeling sick but the hospital refused to admit her because of her violent conduct on a previous visit.[208]

The pair reconciled. They produced three more children – their last daughter, born in 1888, dying in infancy. In about 1894, John, his wife and young daughters moved north to Thursday Island, where some of John's older sons were working in the pearling industry.

Late in life, asthma started to get the better of John Tolman. In 1896, he was admitted as a patient to the Benevolent Asylum at Dunwich, which by then had been established in the grounds of the Quarantine Station. John's wife Mary Jane was a heavy drinker; it may have been owing to her chronic alcoholism and poor health that she was unable to support an aging husband whose own health was failing. John was 72 when he was admitted. By then, he was estranged from some of the children of his first marriage. He had no property and hardly a cent to his name.

Being more than 20 years older than his second wife, John might not have expected to outlive her, but this was not to be. Less than six months after his admission to the Benevolent Asylum,

Mary Jane died on Thursday Island from chronic alcoholism, anasarca (oedema) and heart failure. She was only 47[209] and her youngest child was 12. John lived at the asylum until 1900, taking a few brief periods of leave during those four years. He passed away in Townsville in 1907, from 'senile exhaustion' and heart failure, aged 83.

A SUCCESS STORY – THE REALS

Several of the *Emigrant*'s passengers went on to achieve eminence: the Footes, for example, and the Fogartys, one of whom became a well-respected member of Legislative Assembly and Toowoomba's first Labor member of the Queensland Parliament. But perhaps the most impressive story is Patrick Real's. His achievements, considering his humble beginnings, are astonishing.

Patrick Real was only five years old when his family made the voyage to Australia. He was the youngest of the six children of James and Ellen Real: poor Irish Catholics – tenant farmers – from Pallasgreen, Limerick. James died in quarantine. His death left his 37-year-old widow to care for their six children, aged from four to 18, alone.

Ellen never remarried. She took her children to Ipswich and did her best to give them a good upbringing. Although alone and in straitened circumstances, Ellen raised a family of formidable and varied talents. Amongst her progeny were successful businessmen, landowners, a mayor of Ipswich, and a highly respected nun – the 'Head Superior' at Monte Sant' Angelo in North Sydney.

But the highest achiever of the Real family was without doubt the youngest: Patrick.

The Reals were literate people, and Ellen saw to it that Patrick received some education. But times were hard. At the age of 12,

Patrick had to leave school for the workforce to help support the family. He was apprenticed to two different carpenters. It was said that Patrick was 'a thoroughly good workman – that he had a hearty dislike of all "scamping," and an intense respect for honest work and duty conscientiously done'.[210] For a time, Patrick worked at the Ipswich railway workshops. But he loved politics and debating, and he was bright, ambitious and determined. He was not destined to live a small or insignificant life.

As a young man, Patrick decided he wanted a career in the law. He continued working to support himself while also furthering his education. A priest who taught in the local Catholic school recognised his ability and tutored him in Latin and Greek. As for his legal studies: Real taught himself, using the textbooks and standard works recommended by the board of examiners. In 1874, he passed all his exams and was called to the Bar.

Patrick's career in the law was long and impressive. From private practice to public office, he distinguished himself as a man of ability and integrity. From poor fatherless immigrant, Patrick Real rose to become one of the highest-earning barristers of his time. In the 1880s, he served as crown prosecutor for the Central District Court. In 1890, he became acting judge in the District Court of Queensland, and went on to become a judge in Queensland's Supreme Court. In 1903, Patrick Real was appointed Senior Puisne Judge of the Supreme Court of Queensland.

Patrick Real had an abiding regard for the importance of education. His own struggles to attain a good education inspired in him a desire to ease the way for others. He became a member of the Board of Advice for the Queensland Public Library, and served on a Royal Commission that paved the way for the establishment of a Queensland university.

In 1879, Real married Anne Catherine Thynne. The couple had four children: three daughters and a son. Patrick was known as a committed family man, devoted to his mother, his wife, children and grandchildren.

He appears to have retained lifelong connections with some of his fellow emigrants. Charles O'Brien was a 25-year-old Irishman who brought his wife, Anne, and two young children to Moreton Bay on the *Emigrant*. He had settled in Brisbane and owned a succession of pubs in Fortitude Valley. But fire, an adverse economic climate, and a readiness to extend credit to his customers led to repeated insolvencies for O'Brien. In his later years, he was financially ruined. He managed to secure a job as caretaker in the Supreme Court, which provided him with accommodation in the attached cottage as well as an income.

O'Brien's obituary in 1900 drew attention to his friendship with two men who had been fellow-passengers of the *Emigrant* and had become prominent lawyers: T.M. Slattery of New South Wales, and His Honour, Mr Justice Real. O'Brien's connection with Patrick Real may have helped him to get the caretaker's job. Real had been a small child and O'Brien a man on the voyage to Australia, but given their common backgrounds, the length and traumatic nature of their shared experiences, and the small population of Queensland, it is not at all surprising that the Real and O'Brien families maintained contact. Neither would it be out of character for Real, out of loyalty, to grant a favour to a family friend in his old age.

Real's physical appearance was as impressive as his character. He was 191cm tall and lean, with black hair and blue eyes and a husky voice. He has been described as 'quick-tempered' and 'prone to rash and imprudent statements'.[211] But for his integrity, learning and generosity, the man was much admired.

His obituary read:

So far as stature goes he was a Saul among judges, but he was big mentally as well as physically, and his head though so high above the common level, was as full as more than half a century's arduous labour and study had been able to store it. It might not perhaps, have had that polish which comes from a more favoured early life than fell to him, or, from a University training, but he possessed that which neither the one nor the other can give but may improve – a large and fruitful mind.[212]

Patrick Real retired in 1922, after campaigning unsuccessfully against the compulsory retirement of judges. He died on 10 June 1928. Upon his death, Dr Duhig, the archbishop of Brisbane, eulogised that 'From beginning to end the life of Patrick Real was unblemished. Humble in its origin, noble in its conception of duty, scrupulously faithful in performing its allotted task, it was a life that might be summed up in the words of Holy Writ: "Simple, upright, and God-fearing".'[213]

Patrick Real was buried with his wife in the Toowong Cemetery. His grave sits broken and neglected on the hillside. The headstone is blackened and stained with age and its epitaph is barely legible. The cross that once stood proudly upon the plinth has tumbled from its base and lies in pieces on a bed of dried twigs and leaf litter. It gives no hint of the great success in his career and personal life that was achieved, against all odds, by this remarkable man.

THE MIXED FORTUNES OF THE BRIMBLES

The decision to emigrate had devastated the Brimble families.

They had left England as a party of nine: John and Elizabeth with their three children; young Andrew and his pregnant wife with their two-year-old; and Andrew's sister Sophia.

John's losses had been immense. At 42, he was the eldest of the two Brimble families on the voyage. He had already lost two children – a son and a daughter – back in England. Then while in quarantine his wife had succumbed to typhus and his five-year-old son to burns. His cousin's daughter (and his servant) Sophia Brimble had passed away at sea, and his cousin's son Andrew had been felled by the fever in the last days of quarantine. The group that reached mainland Australia was much reduced. From the older family, only John, 12-year-old Lucy, and seven-year-old Alfred remained; from the younger family, there was only Louisa with her two-year-old daughter and newborn son.

John was a gardener. It appears that he didn't stay long in Moreton Bay; he took his children south, eventually settling in Pitt Street, Waterloo. In 1858 he married a widow, Elizabeth Sampson Barkly, who brought to the marriage children of her own. The pair produced two more sons – Samuel and Thomas – but their relationship was a disaster. By 1862, John was struggling to find work. Their children were taken into protective custody in the Randwick Asylum for destitute children. According to the records, their mother had deserted them and their father, an 'old man' (he would have been about 57), was unable to maintain them.[214] John and Elizabeth must have reconciled for Samuel and Thomas were released back into their parents' care in 1865. Nine years later, Elizabeth left her husband ('without cause', in his view) and John washed his hands of her.

By this time, John's daughter, Lucy Jane Brimble, was settled with a family of her own. In 1854, at the tender age of 16, Lucy had wed a farm labourer in Bathurst. Her husband, William Unwin, bought land near Millthorpe, and the pair established a property known as 'Green Hills Farm'. The Unwins adopted two sons and were well-respected members of their community.

Lucy's brother, Alfred, became a gardener like his father. He married at Botany in 1867, had six children, and moved back to Millthorpe where he lived to the age of 81.

In his later years, Lucy and Alfred's father, John, having parted from his second wife, seems to have followed his children to New South Wales' Central Western district and died in Guyong, New South Wales, in 1879. So completely estranged from Elizabeth Barkly was John by then that Lucy, who was the informant, refused to acknowledge the marriage on her father's death certificate, although she did list her half-brothers amongst his issue.

Lucy died in 1915, at the age of 77. At her funeral, Millthorpe mourned the loss of one of its oldest residents. 'But there was great comfort,' said the officiating minister, 'in the thought that her death was a happy release. Those who knew her were aware that it was her greatest desire to be in Christ walking with Him and living in Him.'[215]

Of the other Brimble family who came out on the *Emigrant*, only Louisa and her two small children had survived. In 1850 Louisa's daughter, Emily, was only two, and her son, Andrew, newborn. The prospect of life in the colony with two infants and no husband must have been daunting for the young widow. But she was not alone. Only two weeks after the *Emigrant* had sailed from Plymouth, Louisa's late husband's mother, brother and sister had embarked on a voyage of their own. Sarah Brimble and her grown children, Jonathon and Isabella, had followed Louisa and Andrew across the sea on the *Lord Stanley*. They had arrived in Sydney on 26 August, 1850, while their relatives still marked time in quarantine at Moreton Bay. Although Sarah and her adult children had arrived in New South Wales more than two weeks *after* Andrew and Louisa, they were already settled in Newcastle by the time Louisa was released from Dunwich.

Louisa made her way south to join her late husband's family in Newcastle. She may have travelled with John Brimble and his children, although they parted ways sometime later when he set off inland. The young widow didn't stay single for long. On 10 January, 1853, she married another Englishman – James May – at Christ Church in Newcastle. Her marriage was part of a triple wedding ceremony; her late husband's brother, Jonathon, and sister, Isabella, took their vows on the same day. With her second husband, Louisa went on to have ten more children.

Louisa's two children by Andrew Brimble – Emily and Andrew – grew up in Newcastle, married and had children of their own. Andrew junior's life had begun in the midst of tragedy, and heartbreak would dog him throughout his life. Of the four children he fathered, only one would reach old age. A daughter, Elizabeth, died at 18, and a son, Andrew Jonathon, of bronchitis as a baby. Caroline Sophia, Andrew's youngest daughter, perished in horrific circumstances. When she was only six years old, the girl was crushed by a coal truck at the Stockton Company's estate. Her body was taken home in such an 'awful state of mutilation' that at the inquest 'the injuries when described made several jurymen most uncomfortable'.[216] The doctor amputated three limbs but the poor child died shortly afterward.

Andrew himself lived to the age of 69. He died in April 1920 and is buried with his wife in the Church of England section of Stockton Cemetery.

Interestingly – and perhaps coincidentally – the Brimbles had settled not far from their long-estranged relation, William Bramble (as he was known by then), who had arrived in the colony as a convict back in 1821. By the time his cousins had made their way to Newcastle, William was living in nearby Raymond Terrace. There is no evidence to suggest that William re-united with his Brimble family. He had gained his certificate of freedom in 1832, married, bought land and fathered 11 children in all.

William spent much of his life at odds with the law. Most of his offences were minor or were thrown out of court: cattle stealing, stealing geese, shooting and stealing a bullock.

Then his crimes took on a more serious nature. After his first wife's death, he married Mary Ireland (née Sullivan) in Stroud. The same year the pair separated, and a couple of months later he attacked Mary with a knife. Her daughter and son were present and, trying to restrain their stepfather, got into a tussle with him. In the struggle, William Bramble's stepson, John Ireland, received a gash on the thigh. Bramble was arrested and charged with attempting to murder his wife and wounding his stepson and stepdaughter. By the time the matter went to court, the charges had been down-graded, and Bramble was found guilty only of inflicting grievous bodily harm. The court heard that 'Bramble was a good fellow, except when in a temper'.[217] Because of his age and previous 'good character', mercy was shown, and the prisoner was sentenced to two years in Maitland Gaol with hard labour. William Bramble lived into his eighties, dying at the home of his daughter in 1887.

MARY BALL AND THE TRIALS OF THE WADE GIRLS

The Balls and Wades had embarked as a blended family of six. By the time they set foot in Brisbane, only three remained.

Typhus had claimed the lives of Mary Ball's husband and stepdaughter; it had temporarily stricken her two Wade step-daughters – Elizabeth Matilda and Emma – and Mary herself, and it had driven her only daughter to suicide. At only 41, she had not only outlived an infant son and daughter and a teenaged daughter and stepdaughter, but two of her three husbands. After her failed first marriage so many years earlier, she had closed the door to her past and bigamously wed John Wade; when she had lost him, she had made a life with Joseph Ball. Now she was widowed again – but she would not be alone for long. Mary was nothing if not resilient.

On 9 August, 1851, Mary Ball married a farmer in Moreton Bay: a bachelor named Edward Wheeler. The couple settled in South Brisbane and lived a quiet life. Mary died in her South Brisbane home on 15 December 1868, after suffering from 'gastric fevers' for three weeks. Her only blood relation left in the colony was her brother, William, who was living in Gympie. He had emigrated about three years after Mary's terrible journey, and spent ten years in Victoria before joining Mary in Queensland. Evidence suggests that Mary's stepdaughters maintained a strong relationship with her and her brother.

Mary's last husband, Edward, had predeceased her by a year or two.[218] Probably unknown to her, her first husband, Frederick Whittenbury, had died in 1865. When she had married Edward Wheeler, Frederick had still been alive and legally her spouse – making Mary a bigamist three times over. Frederick, journeyman carpenter, died in the grim Union Workhouse at Hackney. Unlike Mary, he had never raised himself out of penury, nor escaped the squalor of London's East End.

When Mary died, her stepdaughters, Elizabeth Matilda Wade and Emma Wade, lost one of their last remaining connections with their old lives. They had only each other – and Mary's brother William Shanks – left in their adopted home. Like so many of their contemporaries, they had suffered tremendous loss.

A mother, two fathers, two stepsisters and two half-siblings had died before they even began their lives in the new one.

Together they had pinned their hopes on emigration, and together they had endured discomfort, illness, fear and grief. Together they settled in Brisbane, found husbands, and embarked on new lives. Little wonder that they remained close throughout their lives. But one sister was more fortunate than the other.

Elizabeth was one of the lucky female emigrants who, at first, appeared to achieve exactly what she had set out to find: prosperity and a dependable husband. Blacksmith William Qualtrough was born on the Isle of Man and had emigrated to Australia the year before Elizabeth. The pair married on 12 April 1851, in Brisbane's parish of St John. Elizabeth's sister, Emma, witnessed the marriage alongside George Heirdsfield, who would become *her* husband on 28 June the same year.

William Qualtrough was successful in business and a solid, honest, well-respected citizen. He and his wife prospered and bought up land in Cleveland, South Brisbane and the area now known as Woolloongabba. The Qualtroughs lived in a timber home in Stanley Street, where Elizabeth lovingly tended her garden. They produced three sons: William, Walter Henry and Alfred. But it wasn't all plain sailing. William senior died too young from heart disease at only 46. The eldest son, also William, had a drinking problem and died from cirrhosis and a stomach haemorrhage at 29.

Elizabeth had another worry: her beloved younger sister, Emma, had made a poor choice of partner. George Heirdsfield was a Londoner, an ex-convict who, in 1836, had been sentenced to seven years' transportation in New South Wales for stealing a four-shilling handkerchief. He was a poor Protestant lad; a 'stockman's boy'; small, fair-haired, freckled and tattooed.

He served his time in Sydney until he received a ticket of leave in 1841.

Despite his humble beginnings, George was literate, and he had just enough business acumen in the early days to support a wife and six children and purchase land. It started off well enough. By 1864, the Heirdsfields lived in Fortitude Valley, in a six-roomed brick house with attached four-roomed cottage on the corner of Wickham and Brunswick Streets. But then the cracks started to appear. George was a drinker and a poor money manager.

'He was always drinking,' George's daughter, Lucy Hendle said later, 'and we could not put up with it, because we are not drunkards ourselves.'[219]

According to his sister-in-law, Elizabeth Qualtrough, George 'never had any money'. He was constantly borrowing from her husband. In 1866, Heirdsfield transferred the deeds for his cottage to William Qualtrough in lieu of money that he owed and some extra cash. The Qualtroughs agreed that the Heirdsfields could continue to live there rent-free during Emma's lifetime if George paid the rates. According to Elizabeth Qualtrough, her husband had arranged the transfer to protect the Heirdsfield children from their father's excesses; he believed his alcoholic brother-in-law was in danger of losing the property.

George, Emma and their family lived in the cottage rent-free as agreed, and when William Qualtrough senior died four years later, in 1870, the land was willed to Elizabeth. 'I feel thankful that I have done right to Heirdsfield's wife and children,' Qualtrough was heard to say before he died.[220] Qualtrough's act of generosity would later trigger a bitter legal dispute between the two families.

As well as putting up with a spendthrift, alcoholic husband and raising six children, Emma Rosetta (as she was known by then)

Heirdsfield suffered from rheumatism. She died on 4 February 1875, at 51.[221]

It appears that George Heirdsfield and some of his children remained in the cottage after Emma's death. Meanwhile, George's drinking problem wasn't getting any better. His alcoholism was such a problem that he was periodically sent to the Benevolent Asylum at Dunwich to dry out. He was admitted to the asylum on at least six occasions during the last eight years of his life. He died there, intestate, in 1890 – on the same site as the quarantine ground in which his late wife had been confined decades before. The eldest Heirdsfield boy, George, died a month later.

After George Heirdsfield's death in 1890, Elizabeth Qualtrough sold the Brunswick Street property. From then on, things got ugly. George Heirdsfield's daughter Lucy initiated a law suit, claiming her father had never *sold* the property to William Qualtrough, but that the deeds had only been transferred to him in trust for her and her siblings.

The case was heard in the Supreme Court in 1899. It was complicated by the fact that Elizabeth had bought houses for Lucy and her sister with funds from the sale, but had refused to hand over Lucy's deeds. After much deliberation, the jury ruled in Elizabeth Qualtrough's favour, deciding that George Heirdsfield had indeed sold the land to Qualtrough and *not* transferred it to be held in trust for Heirdsfield's children. But they *did* order Elizabeth to hand over the deeds to Lucy's home.

Lucy and William appealed the court's decision, but their case was dismissed. It is interesting to note that one of the judges who handled the appeal was *Mr Justice Real*. This was Patrick Real, the small boy on the ill-fated *Emigrant* voyage who went on to become a well-known judge – the child who had lost his father in quarantine.

Elizabeth had been devoted to her younger sister, and the Heirdsfield family's dysfunction caused her much bitterness and grief. Elizabeth's love for Emma guided her behaviour. It came out in the trial that she had given George junior money 'because he had brought up and educated his sister Lizzie to be good to his mother'. She added that she had also agreed to give William Heirdsfield a small consideration – £100 – only because she was persuaded to do so by his brother. Otherwise she would 'not have given him a penny, because he was a bad boy to his mother'.

A cerebral haemorrhage carried Elizabeth Matilda Qualtrough off in 1903. She died in her Stanley Street home and was buried in the South Brisbane Cemetery (Dutton Park) with her husband and son William. Walter joined them in the grave in 1910. Their resting place, marked by an impressive headstone – not ostentatious, but more substantial and taller than its neighbours – lies near the base of a slope down to the Brisbane River. The cemetery is in a mild state of disrepair: overgrown and blanketed with leaf litter and twigs, its headstones age-mottled and its graves sunken and cracked; but it is shaded and beautiful – a peaceful place of eternal rest.

MARY CONNOR AND THE PLIGHT OF THE ORPHANS

For most of the emigrants, the last day of quarantine marked the end of seven months' torment. They left the island with relief, thankful to have survived and eager to forget. Their plans to build new lives in Moreton Bay had been put on hold for too long already and they were impatient to get started. For them, the worst was over.

For six orphans, however, the misery had only just begun.

On 4 December 1850, a sorry little group of children clustered on the wharf alongside the Brisbane River. Mary Connor, the plucky, kind and barely literate young Irishwoman from County Limerick, was their protector.

The children were the remaining members of two families: the Irish Catholic Watersons and the English Protestant Halletts. The Waterson children were Patrick (aged eight), Edward (six) and Elizabeth (two); the Halletts were Charles (aged 13), Ann (seven) and George (four). The poor little Hallett children had lost not only their parents, but three brothers as well. With the exception of Charles Hallett, who could read a little but not write, none of the children had much education, and none had a single relation in the colony. What was more, they were penniless.

Mary Connor was kind and resourceful, but she was a 20-year-old single woman; it would be impossible for her to raise six children on her own, even if that was her wish. But the new settlement of Moreton Bay had no facilities to care for orphans. They had to be sent to Sydney.

In Captain Wickham's report to the colonial secretary, he had initially recommended that Mary Connor should be paid one shilling and sixpence per day – like the other helpers – for looking after the children during the quarantine period and part of the voyage. Later, he changed his mind. It transpired that Mary had plans to travel to Sydney to join her uncle and aunt in Campbelltown. It was decided that if the government paid for Mary's passage to Sydney, she could consider herself sufficiently rewarded for her kindness. The government did not see fit to pay for the luxury of a cabin; steerage was considered good enough for Mary.

Mary accepted the terms. So it was that the young Irishwoman was there to shepherd six wretched orphans onto the *Eagle* on that stormy summer's day. What trepidation they must have felt, once more setting foot upon the unsteady deck of an ocean-going vessel. How they must have dreaded descending into the pit of the steerage quarters. But this voyage was to be quite different from the nightmare trip of recent memory; the *Eagle* was a wooden paddle steamer, much smaller than the *Emigrant*, and her journey would be shorter. The *Eagle*'s passengers were few: besides Mary and the orphans there were seven gentlemen, one lady, and 18 in steerage.[222]

The voyage took three days. The party arrived in Sydney on 7 December, but it took a further couple of weeks to settle the children into their respective orphanages: the Halletts into the Protestant Orphan School and the Watersons into the Catholic institution. Then Mary made her way to Campbelltown, the village some 30 miles west of Sydney, where her uncle and aunt were living.

On 21 June, 1852, Mary married Martin Payton (or Payten) in the Roman Catholic Church at Campbelltown. Martin was a farmer from King's County, Ireland; a man with a 'kindly nature' that made him 'popular with all classes'.[223] The couple took up farming land and made their home on the Camden Park Estate at Menangle. Their first child, Mary, was born soon after. Eleven more children followed, one of whom died in infancy.

Mary and her husband were well loved by their community. Mary was known as a 'remarkable wit' who, while doing her duty to her adopted country, was nevertheless staunchly loyal to her 'Faith and Fatherland'.[224] Her generosity and charitable spirit were much admired.

It is touching to note that although Mary surrendered the orphans in her charge to their respective institutions, she did not abandon them. Probably encouraged by his wife, some years after their marriage, Martin Payton took Patrick Waterson on as an indentured apprentice on his property at Camden. In 1861, Patrick was about 19 years old, although small and young-looking for his age. He was only four foot ten inches high and had a fair complexion, fair hair and blue eyes.

Patrick's life had not been easy. In 1850, when he was placed in 'care' with his siblings, New South Wales offered only three institutions for its orphans and destitute children: the Catholic Orphan School, the Protestant Orphan School, and the Female School of Industry (a privately run establishment intended to train girls as domestic servants).

Such institutions had no shortage of business. Since the 1820s they had been 'home' to a steady supply of children whose parents had died or were unable to provide for them. Convict women who were in no position to reject the sexual advances of their masters were compelled to give up their children to the orphan school. Until 1836, when the Catholic Orphan School was built (conveniently adjacent to the Female Factory, a prison and workhouse at Parramatta), the only orphan school had been a Protestant one, and all destitute children who were sent there had to take instruction in the Protestant faith regardless of the religion into which they had been born.

In the 1840s, the Depression and the gold rushes that enticed young men away from their families caused a dramatic increase in poverty and suffering. By 1850, mass immigration, unemployment and lack of social welfare created ever-worsening conditions, and Sydney's slums overflowed with poor and neglected children. The authorities believed that the best hope for these children would be to put them into spartan, highly regimented institutions. There was no reformatory system for children, and it was not unknown for police to send troublesome street kids to the orphan schools for 'correctional' purposes.

It was in this environment that the Hallett and Waterson children found themselves – the Halletts in the Protestant School and the Watersons in the Catholic one – where they would rub shoulders with the waifs of Sydney: some orphans like themselves, others neglected street kids; some unloved children of convict girls, others urchins abandoned by their fathers in favour of the gold fields; some made destitute by disease or unemployment or bereavement. These children, according to the authorities, inherited from their 'vicious and abandoned parents, a low physical organisation, blunted moral perceptions, and minds undeveloped from the want of instruction'. It was declared that: 'Their habits are dirty and repulsive, and their manners uncouth in the extreme.'[225]

The Catholic Orphan School was an especially dismal place. The government-funded orphanage had moved to new premises in Parramatta in 1844. The Georgian-style building rose three forbidding storeys above ground, with a basement below and an abutting wing for the superintendent and staff. On the ground floor was a schoolroom, the master's parlour and a storeroom; the children slept in dormitories on the two upper floors. To accommodate its growing population, in 1850 – just in time for the Watersons' arrival – another two-storey wing was added to the west.

The entire convict-built structure was walled in like a prison, surrounded on three sides by high sandstone walls and bounded on the fourth by the river. By 1851, the orphanage's grounds comprised about seven acres of poorly tended land and inadequate facilities.

The school was chronically understaffed. It was run by a matron who was assisted by the Sisters of Charity. The staff included a surgeon, a master, an assistant matron and four female servants; all were overworked and paid less than their Protestant counterparts. The master and the assistant matron doubled as teachers for the boys and girls respectively. School was compulsory for the orphans (though not for the general population) but the standard of education was poor and the results mediocre. In both Catholic and Protestant institutions, the schoolrooms were poorly furnished and equipped, and the teachers incompetent.

An investigation was conducted into the Orphan Schools in 1855. Its aim was to determine how well the institutions were reaching their goals, which were to restore the wretched children to physical and moral health by providing a 'cheerful and healthy' residence and nourishing and plentiful food, and by teaching the children good habits, values and religious mores. The aim was to turn the children into 'good and useful members of society'.[226] The commission found that the grim institutions had no hope of achieving these goals.

In the Roman Catholic Orphan School, children dined in the basement, in a room that was 'too small, unventilated and ill-supplied with furniture'. Due to a lack of chairs, the children stood for their meals. They ate with their fingers, and it was reported that 'the want of seats, of table-cloths, and knives and forks, tends greatly, not only to encourage habits of grossness, in taking food, but also to prevent the acquisition of civilized manners'.[227] The children ate only boiled food, since the kitchen had no facilities for baking, and while their food was sufficient in quantity, it was inferior in quality. The dining room was located so far from the kitchen that the food was usually eaten cold.

Conditions were crowded and unsanitary; the dormitories were overflowing and children sometimes slept two to a bed in unventilated, vermin-infested quarters on mattresses of straw. At night, they were locked into their dormitories. They slept in the same underclothes that they wore all day, changing their clothes only once a week. They were inadequately dressed, most of them lacking shoes and stockings, and clothed in 'peculiar and unbecoming' costumes that branded them with the 'badge of pauperism'.

It was a government principle that the orphanages were to be run according to strict economy. This translated to serious deprivation of items that would normally be considered necessities: bathroom facilities like a decent toilet and basins and towels and even water. Toilets were 'too small, too much exposed, and in filthy condition'. Boys washed in tubs in the cellar, and girls under a shed in the playground. The water was re-used; the last child to bathe did so in the same water as the first. The children bathed once or twice a week, depending on the season. The house was unclean, and the children and their clothing filthy.

The government expected the orphanages not only to operate frugally but to be self-sufficient. Children were put to work. The girls were responsible for the laundry and other household duties, while the boys worked in the kitchen or carted wood and water. A few boys helped in the garden but as they had no instruction, their efforts were largely unsuccessful.

The orphanage offered little in the way of leisure activities. The children were taught neither crafts nor gardening, and when it rained they were confined to the schoolroom. The effect of these conditions on the children was disturbing. Undernourished, overworked and unloved, they lacked the normal vigour and high spirits of children. The boys were 'dull and inert', uninterested in games, tired and sluggish. And cut off as they were from the rest of the world, the children who survived to adulthood were poorly equipped to adapt to society when they re-entered it. This was the environment into which the Waterson children were thrown.

It was an environment that many did not survive.

Poor little Elizabeth Waterson didn't last long. She was only three years old when she died in early November 1851, having been in the orphanage for less than a year. Her brother, Edward, followed her to the grave eight months later, in July, 1852. His age at death was recorded as four and a half although, according to his immigration records, he was closer to eight. Perhaps malnutrition had stunted his growth. There was no investigation into these premature deaths. No autopsy and no questions raised as to their cause. The little bodies were simply interred in St Patrick's Roman Catholic Cemetery at Parramatta, and the date of burial was noted in the parish register.

Patrick survived the orphanage but the damage inflicted by his childhood traumas seems to have left him ill-prepared for life.

The orphanage apprenticed Patrick out to Martin Payton when he was still a youth. For decades, the practice of acquiring apprentices from the orphan schools had been commonplace. Boys whose health and behaviour recommended them might be indentured as labourers, tailors, blacksmiths, shepherds or bakers; girls were typically sent out as domestic servants. The apprenticeship system was regulated by law, and those who were indentured were bound by strict conditions. The apprentice received payment at the end of the period of indenture, but if the apprentice misbehaved or absconded, he or she could be punished by law.

It seems likely that the kindly Paytons engaged Patrick Waterson out of interest in his welfare. But their kindness was not enough to save him. On 31 March, 1861, Patrick absconded and was believed to have headed towards Albury. As an indentured apprentice, Patrick was legally bound to his employer, and his desertion was a criminal act. His disappearance was the last definite report of Patrick Waterson of the *Emigrant*. He appears not to have been captured – or if he was, Martin Payton declined to press charges.

Patrick's fate is unknown. In 1864, a young Irish-born Catholic seaman by the name of Patrick Waterson was repeatedly getting himself into trouble. In June of that year he was found guilty of disobedience, and in August of desertion from the ship *Sandringham*. For both offences, he was gaoled with hard labour for four weeks. This man may not have been the same Patrick Waterson who lost his parents in the *Emigrant* tragedy; although his name, age, origin and religion match the orphan's, this miscreant was taller and darker-haired than the young man who had absconded from Martin Payton's farm. But the adolescent might have grown, and his hair darkened with the years as fair hair often does.

Perhaps the orphaned Patrick Waterson changed his name and lived a long and happy life. Perhaps he left the country. More likely, he was the seaman whose body was found floating in the Yarra River at Melbourne in October 1868. This young man, believed to be 22 years old, of unknown parentage, was a sailor attached to a Tasmanian schooner that plied the routes between Tasmania, New Zealand, Melbourne, Sydney and Adelaide – the *Martha and Lavinia*. He had left the schooner in a state 'not perfectly sober' on 11 October. He was last seen in the middle of that night, drunk, in Bourke Street in the company of a 'disreputable' woman. When his body was found on 19 October, it was judged to have been a week in the water. The verdict of his inquest was 'accidentally drowned'.[228]

Thus the entire Waterson family was extinguished.

Orphanages in the 19th century were dire places, but if you had to be an orphan, your odds of survival were slightly better if you were a Protestant.

The Protestant Orphan School was in Rydalmere, not far from the Catholic Orphan School. It officially opened in April 1850 – just as the *Emigrant* left Plymouth – when the Male and the Female Orphan Schools merged. Like the Catholic school, it was financed by the government – but it was better funded than its counterpart. In 1851, £17 5s 4d was spent annually on each child in the Protestant institution, compared with a mere £10 11s 6d per Catholic child.[229]

Harriott McKenny, the matron and executive officer in the Protestant School, was supported by a clerk, a schoolmaster, a surgeon, two female teachers, two laundresses, two nurses, four male servants, a hospital attendant and a barber. Compared with the Catholic institution, which employed only eight, the Protestant Orphan School was well staffed. And the staff were better paid.

The accommodation, when the bewildered Hallett children were admitted on 19 December 1850, was crowded, since the establishment that had been originally only intended to house girls was by then taking in male orphans as well. The dormitories were infested with bugs and smelled foul due to poor ventilation. The stench in the infant quarters was 'unbearable'. Girls and infants slept in iron bedsteads on mattresses stuffed with seaweed, flax or hair. The boys were not given linen in case they were tempted to tear their sheets to pieces. They slept in hammocks.

The Protestant children were fed better than the Catholics. They received meat twice a week and were given knives and forks with which to eat it. The boys ate, standing, on an open verandah, while the girls ate in a dining room. The manners of all the children were said to be 'extremely coarse' and their behaviour 'somewhat noisy and rude'.[230]

The Protestant orphans were just as poorly clothed and educated as the Catholics. The 1855 commission reported that boys in the Protestant School were not given boots because they preferred to go barefoot and were inclined to destroy boots if they were provided. Both girls and boys washed in large tubs in open sheds and bathed in the river. The toilets were filthy.

As far as conditions in their respective orphanages went, the Protestant Hallett children fared a little better than the Catholic Watersons. But their lives were by no means free from trouble.

On 21 April 1851, only four months after his arrival at the orphanage, little George Hallett died. He was only four years old.

By this time, his brother Charles had already been discharged and apprenticed to Dr Patrick Hill. Dr Hill was the surgeon at the Protestant Orphan School; he must have taken a liking to the 13-year-old boy in his care. He was the Colonial Surgeon of Parramatta and lived on a farm at Camden – not far from Mary Payton's home. It is tempting to think that Mary's interest in the orphan might have influenced her neighbour to take pity on him.

Dr Hill had an interest in mental illness and in 1852 became the first surgeon-superintendent of the Parramatta Lunatic Asylum. He died that same year. Dr Hill's benevolent nature inspired a poet to write, upon the doctor's death: 'The generous and the good have lost/The kind supporter and the friend,/Whose ready zeal was always shown/To aid each charitable end.'[231]

Once again, young Charles Hallett suffered the loss of an adult who may have been something of a protector to him.

Charles' movements over the next ten years are unknown. By 1862 he had moved to Mummel, near Goulburn, and married a Sydney-born girl named Martha Bott. The pair had 11 children and raised the ten who survived infancy in the Goulburn area. Charles lived a quiet and unremarkable life. A couple of minor brushes with the law were reported 1888, including the failure to send his children to school for the minimum prescribed number of days (a charge which was dismissed). It seems that schooling was not a high priority for Charles; he never did learn to write.

Charles may have moved to Goulburn to be closer to his one remaining relative: his sister, Ann (the 'e' had been dropped from her name by then). Unlike her brother, Ann Hallett *did* learn to read and write. This was probably a legacy of the extra schooling she had received during her three years in the orphanage. She left the home on 6 April 1854, when she was apprenticed to Jasper Tunn of Bungonia (near Goulburn) for six years. Anne was only about 11 when she was sent out to work.

Her master, Jasper Tunn, was a brute. An ex-convict and former coppersmith from London, he had been convicted of larceny in 1815 and sentenced to seven years' transportation in New South Wales. When he received his pardon in 1820, he wasn't finished with crime. In 1830, he was found guilty of a violent assault upon his wife, for which he was fined and 'bound to keep the peace' for a surety. Earlier that year he had been granted a publican's licence, and over the ensuing years he bought up land. Tunn's first wife died in 1832, and he remarried the same year. By the time Ann Hallett was assigned to him, the former convict was doing well for himself.

Tunn had no children by either of his wives. Jasper and his second wife, Sophia, referred to Ann as their 'adopted daughter' and re-named the 11-year-old girl Lucy. In 1860, disaster struck. Jasper's wife's clothing caught fire in the kitchen; she screamed for help and a neighbour came to her aid. The neighbour found Sophia on the floor in front of the fire with her dress ablaze. She doused the poor 57-year-old woman with buckets of water but it was too late; Sophia was badly burned and soon lapsed into unconsciousness. She died a short time later.

On his way to her funeral, Jasper Tunn was thrown from his

gig and run over. His injuries were serious enough to require surgical assistance. It was about this time, with her mistress dead and her master incapacitated, that Ann Hallett took the opportunity to escape. Apparently unable to tolerate her 'adopted father' any longer, Ann absconded in March 1860, only weeks before the end of her six-year apprenticeship.

Jasper Tunn expressed his outrage in the local paper. 'Whereas my adopted daughter, Lucy Tunn, otherwise Ann Hallett, having left my service before the expiration of her apprenticeship,' he wrote, 'this is to caution all persons against in any way employing or harbouring her after this notice, as I will prosecute anyone so offending.'[232]

To have risked her master's retribution so close to the termination of his legal rights over her, Ann must have been desperate. Or perhaps she had another reason to abscond. The year after her departure from the Tunn household, Ann married John Fox in the Wesleyan church at Goulburn. Ann was only 19 and her husband was ten years older. They were both living in Mummel, a village close to Goulburn, where John Fox worked as a farmer.[233]

That same year, Jasper Tunn sold his farm, moved in with a neighbour, and died suddenly in his bed. Meanwhile, Ann and John Fox settled in Junee and raised a large family. Ann's brother, Charles, joined her in the district, married her friend Martha Bott and brought his family up alongside Ann's. After a childhood deprived of love and comfort, and an adolescence bound to a violent bully, it seems that in adulthood, Ann might have found contentment at last. When her husband died in 1902, he was described in the local paper as 'one of the oldest and most respected farmers in the neighbourhood.'[234]

Charles Hallett died in 1909. By then, he had left the Goulburn district to live with his daughter and son-in-law, Elsie and

Abraham Jack Norman, at Marsfield. Charles was a widower and had been living on a pension for some time. He had always been a robust man but had lately begun complaining of chest pains.

In December 1909, terrible bush fires broke out at Marsfield and destroyed a number of cottages near the Normans' home. Charles Hallett and his son-in-law fought desperately in intense heat to try and save their property from destruction. Eventually, Charles staggered, exhausted, sighed 'Oh, Jack', and collapsed. His son-in-law caught him and lowered him to the ground. Charles died on 14 December from heart failure, leaving six grown children and no property whatsoever.

Ann lived for another nine years. She died on 6 February 1918 at the age of 76, an 'old and highly respected resident of old Junee'.[235] Nine grown-up sons and daughters survived her.

As for the kindly Mary Payton (née Connor): she lived to the age of 74. In 1903, she fell ill with a heart complaint. Three weeks later, she died from heart failure, endocarditis, and thrombosis of both femoral arteries. By then, Mary had been a widow for over 20 years. Her uncle, James, who had accompanied her on the voyage of the *Emigrant* 53 years earlier, lived on at Burrowa.

It was not common for newspapers to publish obituaries of humble old women, and yet Mary was so highly regarded that upon her death, the *Freeman's Journal* ran a lengthy article extolling her virtues. Mary was a 'fine example of Ireland's sterling daughters'[236] the paper proclaimed – and indeed she was. The compassion she had shown to six little orphans as a young woman was a trait that endured throughout her long and valuable life. For her kindness, charity and wit, Mary was greatly esteemed in her community. She had raised a large and respectable family and was mourned by her ten remaining children and countless grandchildren.

THE MISFORTUNES OF DAVID HOBBS AND MARY FARMER

The story of the *Emigrant* is the story of many heroes. The selfless Dr Mallon and the tragic Dr Ballow; the diligent Dr Mitchell and the compassionate Mrs Kemp. The men and women who risked their lives to serve in the quarantine hospital. Mary Connor, the unassuming, barely literate young Irishwoman who cared for six young orphans with no expectation of reward.

There was another hero: a young man whose deeds have gone largely unsung and whose life ended in lonely destitution. He was an Englishman – a young carpenter from Birmingham named David Hobbs. He had been one of the few men singled out for praise for his labours at the quarantine station. He had built huts to accommodate the living and coffins for the dead. He had toiled day and night at the heartbreaking task. Little wonder that he would eventually fall apart.

In the early days of January 1851, only a few weeks after the last of the emigrants was landed in Brisbane Town, police arrested a young man for 'bathing and exposing his person in the street'. The constable found the man 'quite naked', plunging into the water from the steps of the public landing place for the North Brisbane ferry. It was high summer and the man was drunk. When the constable arrested him and threw him into the lock-up, the prisoner used 'very bad language'.

The prisoner was an emigrant who claimed to have recently arrived in the country. His name was recorded in Court as 'James Corkan alias David Hobbs'. Police Magistrate Captain Wickham fined him 20 shillings, or 14 days' imprisonment if the funds could not be found. Since neither name – James Corkan nor David Hobbs – can be found in Brisbane Gaol's entry book, it can be assumed that he paid the fine. While it cannot be confirmed, it seems likely that this reveller was the young carpenter from Birmingham, recently arrived on the *Emigrant*.[237] David Hobbs' struggle with alcohol would be a lifelong burden.

From Moreton Bay, David soon made his way to Sydney. He was living there by 1 March 1852, when he wed Mary Farmer in the parish of St Lawrence. Mary was a 27-year-old domestic servant from Leicestershire. She too had come out from England on the tragic voyage of the *Emigrant* and was the daughter of none other than John Farmer, the 'aged married man' who had kept the store at the quarantine ground, and whom Captain Kemp had so admired for his constant attendance upon the sick. Mary was the eldest of seven children of Esther and John Farmer, and the only girl in the family. She had lost her mother to typhus at Dunwich. After their release from quarantine, John stayed in Moreton Bay for twelve months before moving his family to Sydney. About the time that his daughter married her fellow passenger, David Hobbs, John took some of his younger children with him to Victoria.

Later the same year, David Hobbs found himself in trouble with the law. A police sergeant was taking a 'disorderly' prisoner to the watch-house when David and his brother-in-law Thomas Farmer interfered. Hobbs and Farmer were charged with assault and required to pay a fine.

In the same year – 1852 – David and Mary's first child was born in Sydney. Her name was Mary Jane, and she lived for only a year. Her death was followed by the birth of another child, Thomas Henry, in 1854. This second child also died in infancy. Soon after Thomas' birth, the Hobbses moved to country Victoria, where David turned his hand to mining.

But his life was blighted by unrelenting tragedy. Of six children born to David and Mary, only one reached adulthood. In Ballarat in 1856, their son George Farmer Hobbs died of 'inflammation of the bowels' at the age of seven months. In the same year, Mary was delivered of another son, John James. Alfred was born in 1860 and died four months later with hydrocephalus. Eight years later, the 12-year-old John James would contract scarlet fever and die after four weeks of suffering. Only one child – a daughter named Jane, born around 1859 – remained.

By this time, David Hobbs had given up mining and become a schoolteacher. At some point he had injured his right elbow, a circumstance that might have prompted his career change. He began his training in 1866, and at the start of 1869 was given his first appointment as a qualified teacher at White Hills. The following year he resigned from this position, moved to Melbourne and took up a job as head teacher at a school in Brunswick.

Mary's father, John, had been living in Essendon in his final years. He had run a brickyard in Victoria and later worked as a carrier. But by the time the Hobbses moved to Melbourne, John was dead, having passed away in 1865 from 'congestion of the liver'.

It was about the time of their move to Melbourne that the Hobbs marriage began to break down. On 29 June 1871, a schoolteacher of Brunswick named David Hobbs publicly announced that he would not be responsible for any debts contracted by his wife, Mary Hobbs, after that date.[238] The pair may have reconciled briefly, but in 1876, David was citing 'illness and domestic troubles' as reasons for a lacklustre performance at work.[239]

By 1876, David had been appointed head teacher at the state school at Dunolly, north of Ballarat. He was declared by the local newspaper to be 'a very able teacher', whose departure five years later was 'regretted' by his sixth-class pupils.[240] The Department of Education, however, had a different view. During his teaching career, David had been rated by various inspectors as 'an average

assistant' and 'industrious, fairly smart, and shows good knowledge of approved methods'. But within months, he was charged
with 'neglect to impart instruction to pupil teachers' and fined
£5. He later complained that 'he had not had the same heart in his
work since the Department "robbed him of £50 a year"'.[241]

Worse was to come.

While at Dunolly, David had proved himself to be 'a very fair
teacher but inferior as an organiser and disciplinarian', 'industrious, generally useful', and 'satisfactory'. But he could not resist
the temptation to drink. Despite periods of temperance, in 1881
he fell off the wagon.

The department suspended David for drunkenness while they
investigated the matter. A report was filed in which he was criti-
cised for the faults in the teaching and managing of his school. But
they stopped short of dismissing him. The department decided
to give him one more chance, and sent him to a smaller school
where he might do less damage.

His next teaching post was even less successful. David was
stationed at the state school in the village of Darnum, West
Gippsland. At first, he was judged to be 'old-fashioned and hardworking', 'suitable for this school', and 'honest and painstaking',
but in 1883, the Education Department got wind that David was
drinking again. In his state of intoxication, he had failed to turn
up to work. There would be no more chances. He was dismissed
for intemperance and neglect of duty.

After his dismissal, David Hobbs seems to have gone to
pieces. He went immediately north to New South Wales, and on
20 September 1883 was admitted to the Maitland Gaol. His crime:
being of 'unsound mind'. He was discharged after two weeks, but
although he was in custody only briefly, this episode may have
been a taste of things to come.

It appears that throughout his adulthood, David alternated intervals of abstinence with periods of excess. When not giving in to the temptations of drink, he lectured about the evils of intemperance.[242] His life had been full of trials: the horrors of the voyage and quarantine; five dead children, a failed marriage, estrangement from his only living child, and an addiction to drink that had cost him his career. But after every setback, David recovered.

After his latest fall from grace, he eventually pulled himself together again and moved to Sydney. In the late 1880s, a David Hobbs, a 'reformed Infidel'[243] of Camperdown, was once more lecturing about the dangers of intemperance. The timeline and behaviour suggest that this was probably the same David Hobbs – the coffin-maker – from the *Emigrant*. The same man took on a number of government administrative positions in the early 1890s: inspector of nuisances, deputy inspector and deputy ranger of the Camperdown Public Park Trust and inspector of dairies. He resigned from public service in 1893.[244]

From April 1896, David had a brief spell in a Government Asylum for the Infirm and Destitute. Two years later he was struggling again. He was admitted to the Rookwood Benevolent Asylum on 17 September 1898, but discharged himself ten days later. His liberty was short-lived.

On 10 June, 1899, David Hobbs entered Rookwood Asylum for the last time. He was 72 years old[245] and had been in poor health for two years. He suffered from heart disease, a stricture of his urethra and recurrent cystitis. David died at 9.20 in the morning of 14 August, 1902. It appears that since the failure of his marriage, David had remained estranged from his wife and daughter. Since David had no family or friends to ease his final moments, it was left to the superintendent of the asylum to report his death. David was buried the next day at Rookwood.

Mary took her last breath a year later, on 6 August 1900. She had suffered for 13 weeks with 'senile decay' and 'paralysis' before passing away at the age of 76 in her home in Hawthorne.

Chapter 10

The lasting tragedy

Was the story of the *Emigrant* a saga of success or a tale of unmitigated tragedy? It depends on your criteria. The *government's* purpose in assisting immigration was to 'clean up' and develop the northern reaches of New South Wales by bolstering its workforce with young, skilled, respectable immigrants. The *emigrants'* aim was, of course, prosperity. They sought lucrative employment, health and happiness; they hoped for social advancement and long lives of comfort and good fortune.

Did either party, on the whole, achieve these goals?

From the government's point of view, the *Emigrant* was – despite the loss of life – a moderate triumph. In the short term, the residents of Moreton Bay and the newcomers were satisfied, for all of the emigrants found employment within a month of their arrival. In the long term, at least a hundred of them settled in the place that would soon become known as 'Queensland'; they started businesses, made homes, entered public life, and had children who did the same. At least 40 went south and built their lives in what would become the state of New South Wales, another 30 in Victoria, and a handful in South Australia. Many drifted into obscurity, their common names (all those Patricks and Michaels, Jameses and Johns, Marys, Annes and Catherines) making their movements hard to trace.

Only a handful died within a few years of arriving. Three of the six orphans were amongst the first to perish. But most of the emigrants did as they were expected to do: they worked, they married, they reproduced and they lived well and long.

Marriage was part of the plan for many of the single men and women who sailed to Australia. Some of the single passengers of the *Emigrant* found potential spouses before they even set foot on land. The long voyage and ordeal of quarantine had caused many friendships and several romances to blossom, despite the ban on fraternising between the sexes. In fact, at least *ten* marriages took place amongst the passengers within a few years of their arrival.

But for 48 individuals and their families, the voyage had tragic consequences. And for the survivors, the memories lingered.

One of the most colourful – and inaccurate – versions of the story was provided by Joseph Howe in the *Queenslander* 50 years after the ordeal.[246] A 23-year-old farmer from Somersetshire, Joseph had emigrated with his wife, Anne, and infant daughter, Julia. Joseph Howe was fond of a story – especially a story that he believed showed him in a good light. He was a name-dropper with a tendency for self-aggrandisement who did not trouble himself too much over the accuracy of his claims.

According to his sensational account, no less than *50* passengers had been consigned to a watery grave due to the outbreak of 'Black Fever' on board, and another *160* met their death while in quarantine. Howe claimed to be the only survivor to land with a living wife and child. 'One morning Howe saw four young women buried,' so the fanciful story went, 'and on more than one occasion he went out duck shooting with a friend in the morning, and saw that friend buried in the afternoon.'

While the details of Howe's story don't stand up to scrutiny (he also claimed that 'Dr Biller' was one of the victims), the horror he conveyed was real. And it was this horror that would linger in the memories – and shape the lives – of so many of the survivors.

In 1916, a woman named Mary Rhodes wrote a second-hand account of the *Emigrant's* story that was published in the *Brisbane Courier*. Her mother had been one of the quarantined passengers: an eight-year-old girl named Anne Fogarty who emigrated with her parents, John and Catherine, and her two brothers, Michael and John. The Fogartys (or Fogertys) were Roman Catholics from Tipperary. They settled in the Darling Downs and the children grew up to be well respected and prosperous; one of them (John) served five years as mayor of Toowoomba and was elected to Queensland's Legislative Assembly.

Anne Fogarty married Crown Lands Ranger Daniel Donovan in 1859 and passed on the story of the typhus outbreak to her children. As is often the case with family histories, the facts were distorted in the telling. The *Emigrant*, Anne's daughter Mary Rhodes reported incorrectly 66 years after the disaster, was the first free ship to enter Moreton Bay, after a voyage of six months. Typhus fever had broken out on board, 'owing to insanitary conditions and bad food and water'.[247]

In fact, the *Emigrant* was *not* the first 'free' ship; it was the fifth, and the second government-assisted ship. The voyage had lasted barely three months, not six. Typhus was spread by lice; insanitary conditions, and bad food and water had never been blamed for the outbreak. Whether the errors were in the flawed recollection of a child or in Mary's re-telling of her mother's story is neither here nor there. What is indisputable is that the trauma of the episode had lingered long in the young Anne Fogarty's memory. 'Many years afterwards,' wrote Mary Rhodes, 'my mother went to visit the graves of those she well remembered.'

A tragedy of another kind, though, is the stories of those whose lives were brief and unremembered.

A child had been born in the final hours of quarantine: the sixth child to be born during the ordeal of the voyage and quarantine. He was the son of Henry and Elizabeth Lipscombe, a young newlywed English couple from Surrey. Henry was a brickmaker who had managed the stores at Dunwich alongside John Farmer. When the child was born at Dunwich on 14 November, 1850, his parents named him *George Stradbrook Lipscombe*. His birth might have been seen as a symbol of hope, of a new beginning and a portent of the prosperous times to come.

After a brief period in Moreton Bay, the Lipscombe family settled in Sydney, produced six more children, and established a thriving brick-works. Henry served a term as mayor of Burwood, and his son, Henry George Lipscombe, was elected mayor of Enfield. Their lives were successful and productive.

But little George Stradbrook Lipscombe disappeared from history. He must have lived for at least 14 months, for a 'Mrs Lipscomb and child' sailed from Moreton Bay to Sydney in February 1852.[248] The only other evidence that he ever existed is the registration of his baptism and a note in the 'children of marriage' column on his father's death certificate: '1 male, dead'. George Stradbrook – the symbol of hope at the end of a protracted ordeal – probably died in infancy.

Epilogue

After the closure of the quarantine station, the Dunwich Benevolent Asylum operated on the site for 80 years. During that time, Dunwich also became the site of a lazaret for the isolation and treatment of leprosy patients. The lazaret operated from about 1891 until 1907, when it was relocated to Peel Island.

At the end of the 19th century and into the 20th, missions and schools for Aboriginal people of Moreton Bay came and went. Land at Amity was parcelled up and sold to new settlers. Fishing and dugong hunting continued to be major pastimes on the island; a dugong boiling down works was established and a fish canning works opened up.

In 1894, a barque carrying a cargo of explosives was wrecked on the shore of a narrow strip of land in the middle of Stradbroke Island. Salvage efforts included setting off explosives, which blew great holes in the sand dunes. Two years later, storms caused further erosion that split the island into two.

Point Lookout, on the ocean side of the north island, was

settled and a lighthouse erected; the population of North Stradbroke Island grew, and schools and churches sprang up. A jetty was built at Cleveland from which ferries departed for the island. Passenger services to Amity and, later, to Dunwich, were established.

In 1943, The Moongalba/Myora Aboriginal mission closed after 50 years of operation. Three years later, the Dunwich Benevolent Asylum closed and its 768 remaining inmates were moved to Sandgate, into a new facility known as 'Eventide'. The controversial closure caused job losses and upheavals for many inhabitants of Stradbroke Island. A few years later, a new industry arrived to take its place: sand mining. The business grew and moved further inland, causing damage to ecosystems and disrupting sites of cultural significance to the Nunukul and Goenpul people. Negotiations to end sand mining and return land titles to the Indigenous people are ongoing.

More than once during the last 70 years, the question of building a bridge to North Stradbroke Island has arisen. In the 1980s, plans to build a bridge almost came to fruition. The proposal met with strong opposition from residents and conservationists. Although the suggestion has come up from time to time, the island remains unbridged. Despite – or perhaps because of – this, tourism has flourished.

North Stradbroke Island's history is rich and colourful. Recognition of its significance is growing. In 1986, the Myora Aboriginal Cemetery was entered on the Australian National Heritage register. Large parts of North Stradbroke Island have been declared national parks. Conservation work is ongoing.

The historic cemetery at Dunwich lies just north of the area where once tents made from ships' sails and makeshift huts provided a rough home for 260 or so exhausted, frightened souls.

If you stand at the top of the incline you can see, between the pine and gum trees, the bright ripples of the bay. Back in 1853, just three years after the quarantine ended, a reporter from the *Moreton Bay Free Press* described the lovely scene: the azure sky, the blue sea, the fine sandy beach, and the consecrated ground where a 'humble wooden tablet' marked the resting place of the 26 'brave hearts', and two 'modest' tombstones honoured the memory of the surgeons.[249] Today the wooden tablet is long gone, but Dr Ballow's and Dr Mitchell's graves remain. And at the base of the hill, just west of a carpark, 26 small, mottled-white, unnamed crosses stand in two neat rows.

The descendants of those brave and desperate travellers who survived the ordeal have been scattered across Australia. A party of them gathered at Dunwich, Stradbroke Island, on Saturday 12 August 2000 to commemorate the 150th anniversary of the *Emigrant*'s arrival. Two years later, the mayor of Redland Shire unveiled a bronze plaque naming those passengers who died during the voyage or in quarantine, in the presence of more than 100 descendants, whose ancestors had sought and found, one way or another, 'a better country'.

Cast of characters

The passengers

The Bloxams

Thomas Bloxam (35), a weaver, and his wife Fanny (32) from County Galway, Ireland.

Their children: John, a 14-year-old labourer, Anne (12) and Thomas (10).

The Brimble families

There were two related Brimble families on the voyage, both from Kingston Deverill, Wiltshire, England.

The younger Brimble family: Andrew (21), a labourer and his wife Louisa (21), a domestic servant. Their daughter, Emily (two), and another child born at sea. Andrew's father was cousin to John Brimble, who was also on board the *Emigrant*. Andrew's sister, Sophia (17) was also on board, possibly as John's servant.

The older Brimble family: John (48), a gardener, travelling with his wife Elizabeth (37) and their three children, Lucy Ann (12), Alfred (seven) and Samuel (five). John's brother William had come to New South Wales as a convict in 1821.

The Burberows

Mary Burberow (or Barberow), a Londoner, a 56-year-old widow and matron of the voyage.

Mary's 18-year-old daughter Frances Jane Burberow (a governess).

Mary Connor

A kind and plucky 20-year-old Irish Catholic domestic servant from Limerick. Mary's uncle, James O'Connor, was also on board along with his wife and infant son.

The Farmer family

From East Langton, Leicestershire. John, at 49, described by Kemp as an 'aged married man' and praised for his tireless and selfless assistance in the ordeal.

John's wife Hester (or Esther), and seven children: Mary (25), Thomas (20), George (17), John Meadows (15), Frederick (11), Charles (10) and Benjamin (seven).

The Foote family

A highly respectable family from Gloucestershire, England. Their plans to join Rev. Joseph Foote in Van Diemen's Land had been scotched by his sudden death in 1848. On board the *Emigrant*:

Elizabeth, Rev. Foote's widow (58), and her children: James (22), dressmakers Clarissa (24) and Lucy (17), Harriet (13) and John Clarke Foote (29). Also John Clarke's wife Mary Anne (21).

The Frith families

There were two Frith families on the *Emigrant*, both from Swineshead, Lincolnshire.

William Frith (28) and his wife Emma (27) and their two sons, Edmund (five) and eight-month-old William (his name is given as William in some accounts and Henry in others).

The other Frith family: Robert Frith (30) and his wife Frances (27).

The Furphys

Euphemia Furphy (67), the oldest of the emigrants. From County Armagh, Ireland.

Her adult children: John (23) and his wife Matilda (22), and Euphemia's daughters Jane (28) and Elizabeth (26).

The Gormans
From Tipperary, Ireland. Daniel (39), his wife Mary (35) and their four children: Patrick (13), Mary (12), Denis (nine) and Thomas (seven).

The Halletts
From County Somerset, England. Charles (41) and his pregnant wife Hannah (43). Their six children: James (15), a labourer, Charles (13), Henry (11), Anne (seven) and George (four). A sixth child would be born at sea.

David Hobbs
David Hobbs, a hardworking 23-year-old carpenter from Birmingham, England.

The Lipscombes
Henry Lipscombe, a 22-year-old brickmaker and his wife Elizabeth (23) from Surrey, England.

The Loders
Three sisters: Martha Loder (18), Catherine Loder (15) and Maria Trowbridge née Loder (25), from County Wiltshire, England. Maria was married to Josiah Trowbridge, also a passenger on the voyage.

Mary Ann Mahoney
A 19-year-old domestic servant from London.

The Maunsells
Catherine Maunsell, a 22-year-old domestic servant from Mountshannon, Limerick, Ireland.

Her brother Patrick Maunsell, a 23-year-old gardener.

The Mearas
Timothy (38) and Mary (32 or 33) Meara: Irish Catholics from County Tipperary. Travelling with two sons: James (13) and John (10). A daughter, Mary, seems to have been born at sea.

The Reals
A family of high achievers, against all odds. From Pallasgreen, Limerick.

James (38), a labourer, and his wife Ellen (37). Their children: James (18, a labourer), Mary (16, a domestic servant), Kate (or Catherine, 14, a domestic servant), Michael (12), Ellen (eight) and Patrick (three).

The Salisburys
From Middle Chinnock in County Somerset, England.

Isaac (36), a farm labourer and his wife, Anne (34). Their children: Jane (13), Charlotte (11), John (10), Mary Anne (eight) and Eliza (five). A boy was born at sea on 23 April.

The Slatterys
Edmund, a 30-year-old shepherd, and Alice (28), from County Tipperary. Their children: five-year-old son Thomas and infant daughter Catherine.

The Tolmans
Two brothers from Moorlinch, County Somerset, England. John (26), a farm labourer. James (23), also a farm labourer.

The Wade/Ball family
Joseph William Ball, a diligent and selfless 44-year-old labourer/milkman/postman from London, and his Scottish-born wife Mary Ball (41).

Their adult daughters: Joseph's daughter Mary Ann Ball (23); Mary's daughter (Mary) Elizabeth Wade (18); Mary's step-daughters Elizabeth Matilda Wade (27); and Emma Wade (25).

Mary Ball (nee Shanks):
m 1. Frederick Whittenbury
– Mary Elizabeth Wade (born Whittenbury) known as Elizabeth Wade

m 2. John Wade
– children from John's first marriage: Ann, Charlotte, John, Elizabeth Matilda and Emma Wade
– children of Mary and John Wade: William (deceased) and Ellen (presumed deceased)

m 3. Joseph Ball
– child from Joseph's first marriage: Mary Ann

Family that departed England for Australia: Mary Ball, Joseph Ball, Elizabeth Wade, Elizabeth Matilda Wade, Emma Wade and Mary Ann Ball.

The Watersons
From Tipperary, Ireland. Henry (30), a labourer, travelling with

his wife Mary (26). Their children: Patrick (eight), Edward (six) and Elizabeth (two).

AT THE QUARANTINE STATION

Dr Patrick Walsh Mallon
Medical practitioner of Brisbane who volunteered to help at the quarantine station. An Irish Catholic from Dungannon, Ireland, in his early forties, a widower with two small children. A clever and courageous man with strong views and interests in politics, philanthropy, science and public health.

Dr David Keith Ballow
Acting health officer of Moreton Bay and pioneer of Brisbane who held official positions in many areas: medicine, agriculture, education and religion. Aged 45, born in Scotland. Had come to Brisbane as colonial assistant surgeon in 1838, and in 1850 was resident surgeon of Moreton Bay District Hospital. Married to Margaret Campbell McArthur. A well-known and respected figure in Brisbane.

Dr Kearsey Cannan
Visiting surgeon at the Moreton Bay District Hospital and acting health officer while Dr Ballow superintended the quarantine station.

Dr Frederick Barton
Arrived from Sydney at the end of the quarantine period to assist Dr Mallon after Dr Ballow's death. A young Englishman with a passionate interest in science.

Appendixes

The following is a list of those associated with the *Emigrant* who died on the 1850 voyage, at anchor or in the quarantine station. The list is in chronological order where date of death is known. Some dates were not recorded.

1. 2 May   **Baby Frith (William Frith**, son of William and Emma, sometimes recorded as Henry) – eight months old, of diarrhoea (was born 11 Aug 1849)
2. 24 May   **Hannah Hallett** (Somerset), died at sea of apoplexy
3. 25 May   **Mary Meara** (Tipperary), 32 yrs, died at sea of typhus, leaving three children
4. 3 June   **Catherine Slattery** (Tipperary), infant daughter of Edmund and Alley, died at sea
5. 18 June   **Baby Hallett** (born at sea, aged one month at death), died at sea of diarrhoea

6. 19 June   **Mary Burberow** (the matron), age 56, died at sea from fever and 'decay of nature'

7. 3 July   **Ann Cunningham** (Westmeath, Ireland), died of typhus at sea

8. 10 July   **Mary Waterson** (Tipperary), 26, mother of three children, died of typhus at sea

9. 15 July   **James Chapple** (Ermington, Devon), 31, (died 15 July according to Capt Kemp and on plaque; 18 July according to Mrs Kemp) died at sea of typhus

10. 22 July   **Ann Gleeson** (County Clare), 29, died at sea of typhus

11. 26 July   **Ann Charlton** (Leicester), 20, died at sea of typhus

12. 26 July   **George Hayward** died at sea of typhus

13. 28 July   **Sophia Brimble** (Wiltshire), 17, died at sea of typhus

14. 29 July   **Ann (or Mary) Connor** (Tipperary), 25, died at sea of typhus

15. 31 July   **James Lancaster** (supernumerary seaman), died at sea of typhus

16. 3 Aug   **Caroline Loder** (Wiltshire), 15, died at sea of typhus

17. 5 Aug   **Fanny Bloxam** (Galway), 32, died at sea of typhus

     8 Aug   Arrived in Moreton Bay.

18. 8 Aug   **Euphemia Furphy** (Armagh), 67, died at anchor in Moreton Bay of typhus

19. 10 Aug: **Henry Waterson** (Tipperary), 30, died at anchor in Moreton Bay of typhus

     12 Aug   Entered Moreton Bay but could not reach quarantine station immediately due to strong 'contrary winds'; anchored at Dunwich next day.

20. 13 Aug **Daniel Gorman** (Tipperary), 39, died at anchor off quarantine station of typhus

At quarantine station

21. 21 Aug **(Mary) Elizabeth Wade** (London), 19, drowned off quarantine station

22. 23 Aug **Joseph Rowe** (Somerset), 27, died in quarantine 1:30am of typhus

23. 24 Aug **George Heuston (Huiston)** died in quarantine at 6:06pm of typhus

24. 27 Aug **Johanna Dwyer** (Galway), 33, died in quarantine (27 or 28 Aug) of typhus

25. 27 Aug **Joseph William Ball** (London), 44, died in quarantine of typhus

26. 31 Aug **Elizabeth Brimble** (Wiltshire) died in quarantine of typhus

27. 31 Aug **John Connor** died in quarantine of typhus

28. 31 Aug **Henry Roberts** (cook on the *Emigrant*) died in quarantine of typhus

29. ? Sep **Charles Hallett** (Somerset), 41, died in quarantine of typhus

30. 3 Sep **James Hallett** (Somerset), 15, died in quarantine of typhus

31. 5 Sep **Maria Trowbridge** née Loder (Wiltshire), 25, died in quarantine of typhus (or 3 Sep)

32. 10 Sep **Hester (Esther) Farmer** (Leicestershire), 45, died in quarantine of typhus

33. 19 Sep **Jane Synott/Syrett/Siret** (Buckinghamshire), 18, died in quarantine of typhus

34. 19 Sep **Dr George Mitchell** (Armagh), 25, died in quarantine of typhus

35. 20 Sep **Mary Anne Ball** (London), 23, died in quarantine of typhus

36. 26 Sep **Henry Hallett** (Somerset), 11, died at in quarantine of typhus

37. 26 Sep **Thomas Coleman** (Somerset), 36, died at 7am in quarantine of typhus

38. 29 Sep **Dr David Keith Ballow** died at 11:30am in quarantine of typhus

39. 30 Sep **Samuel Brimble** (Wiltshire), five, died of burns in quarantine at 12pm

40. 22 Oct **Andrew Brimble** (Wiltshire), 21, died in quarantine of typhus

Dates of death unknown

41. **Infant boy Salisbury**, born on voyage, died on last days of the voyage

42. **Infant Eliza Cummins** of Queen's County died in quarantine; probably born on board

43. **Robert Frith** (Lincolnshire), 30, died in quarantine of typhus

44. **John Hector** (Limerick), 23, died in quarantine of typhus

45. **James Real** (Limerick), 38, died in quarantine of typhus

46. **Mary Ann Salisbury** (Somerset), eight, died in quarantine of typhus

47. **James Synott/Syrett/Siret** (Buckinghamshire), 21, died in quarantine of typhus

48. **Infant girl Canning**, born on board, died in quarantine

APPENDIX B: LIST OF MARRIAGES

Below is a list of *Emigrant* passengers who married fellow passengers. They are listed in chronological order. There may have been others.

1. **Catherine O'Brien** m. **Thomas Gleeson** 30 Nov 1850
   Thomas' wife had died from typhus on the voyage. He had two small daughters.
2. **Ann Campbell** m. **James Welsh (Welch/Walsh)** 2 Dec 1850
3. **Frances Frith** m. **Josiah Trowbridge** 11 Dec 1850
   Both had been widowed on the voyage.
4. **Martha Loder** m. **Francis Lyon** 23 Dec 1850
   Martha lost both of her sisters (Maria Trowbridge and Catherine Loder) at sea.
5. **Julia McMahon** m. **Thomas John Ryan** 27 Feb 1851
6. **Mary Ann Mahoney** m. **James Hall** (seaman) 25 March 1851
   James was one of four seamen who absconded from the ship while it was at anchor in Moreton Bay.
7. **Anne (Amelia) Sutton** m. **James Buckly (Buckley/Buckby/ Bugsby)** 8 May 1851
8. **Mary Farmer** m. **David Hobbs** 1 March 1852 (NSW)
   David Hobbs was a carpenter who made all the coffins in quarantine.
9. **Catherine Maunsell** m. **James Cahill** 6 Jan 1854
   Catherine was the first to fall ill with typhus on the voyage.
10. **Mary Gorman** m. **John Tolman** 1856
    Mary was only 12 on the voyage. Her father died at anchor near the quarantine station.

APPENDIX C: LIST OF THE HELPERS

Below were all to be paid 1 shilling 6 pence per day (except Mary Connor, who was given passage to Sydney in lieu of payment).

Hospital attendants
- John Clarke Foote (According to Captain Wickham he was 'active from the first landing of the Immigrants as principal in the hospital attending day and night administering the medicines and dressing the patients; the late Dr Ballow spoke in the highest terms of him for the great moral fortitude evinced in so trying a situation')
- John Shears/Shear (performed 'satisfactorily')
- George Willis/Wells (performed 'satisfactorily')
- James Buckley (performed 'satisfactorily')
- John Williams (performed 'satisfactorily')

Attendant on Dr Mitchell
- Robert Chapple

Washing for hospital
- Joseph Hall (Dr Ballow called him James Halls – possibly confusing him with seaman James Hall. He probably meant passenger Joseph Hall.)
- Ellen Welsh/Walsh

Hospital nurses
- Ann Campbell
- Ann Ford(e)
- Charlotte Hardwidge/Hartwich
- Eliza Daube

Hospital cooks
- James Welsh

Doctor's assistant
- Patrick Maunsell ('from the commencement in constant attendance on the surgeons and highly commended by Dr Ballow')

Storekeepers
- John Farmer ('judiciously and regularly served out to my satisfaction')
- Henry Lipscombe ('judiciously and regularly out to my satisfaction')

Butcher
- James Foote ('judiciously and regularly served out to my satisfaction')

Carpenter
- David Hobbs ('indefatigable, employed almost constantly at his trade erecting or repairing buildings, working frequently all night to complete coffins for the dead of which 27 were made by him')

In charge of orphans
- Mary Connor ('had charge of the Wattersons [sic] and Halletts [sic] children from the death of their parents and some time previous during their illness')

In charge of Mrs Chapple's children while she was in hospital for seven weeks
- Amelia Baker
- Emma Frith

Other:

- James Brennan/Braman/Beannan (one of Dr Mallon's assistants in the hospital; helped doctor try to revive Elizabeth Wade after her drowning; was a witness at the enquiry)

Acknowledgements

An enormous number of people and organisations helped me to research the story of the *Emigrant* and her passengers. My particular thanks go to the staff and committee of the North Stradbroke Island Museum on Minjerribah. I am also grateful to the staff of the State Libraries of QLD, NSW and Victoria, the State Archives of QLD, NSW and Victoria, the Toowoomba Local History Library, the Australian National Maritime Museum library, the Anglican Records and Archives Centre in Brisbane, Redland City Council, Campbelltown and Airds Historical Society, the QLD branch of the AMA and staff of St John's Cathedral in Brisbane.

I would also like to thank Susan Hunt for interpreting wills for me, and Daniel McDonald for helping me to discover the bizarre resuscitation practices of 1850. Thanks to Eddie Smith for research assistance and to Lucy Smith for feedback on my manuscript. A wholehearted thanks to Ann Wilson of Independent Ink for her professionalism and encouragement in bringing this book to fruition, and to the wonderful editors Samantha Sainsbury and Michele Perry for their extremely valuable advice on shaping the story.

I am grateful to descendants of the emigrants for providing access to their family histories: Jim Fenwick and Vicki Hails, Helen Crone, Kate van Barneveld, Pam and Kevin Hayes, Dorothy Mowat, Julie Bodycote, Laraine Dyer, Cynthia Foster and Peter Hodge. Jim Fenwick generously provided the photograph of the model of the *Emigrant* for the cover – the only image of the ship we have today. I owe a huge debt also to Elisabeth Mitchell, a descendant of George Mitchell's brother, whose existence I was thrilled to discover. Elisabeth's extensive research into her family history has provided me with most of what I know about Dr Mitchell's family.

Organisations and individuals in England have also helped me to research the backgrounds of the passengers and the conditions and regulations of 19th-century emigration. They include Ruth Bloom; the staff of Achievements family history researchers; the staff of the Plymouth and West Devon Record Office and from Books Boxes & Boats: Maritime and Archive Research in Liverpool; and staff of the Plymouth City Council Central Library, the British Library, the London Metropolitan Archives, the Wellcome Library, Medway Archives Centre, Brunel Institute, the National Maritime Museum and the National Railway Museum. In Scotland, staff of Edinburgh Old Town Association and the University of Edinburgh Library (Special Collections); and in Ireland, Fergus Brady of the Royal College of Physicians of Ireland and staff of Trinity College Dublin Archives, have all provided me with useful information. I am thankful to them all.

My research was built upon the excellent work of Kay Bothwell, whose book *The Voyage and Quarantine of the 'Emigrant': 1850* provided a wealth of information and directed me to a huge number of primary and secondary sources and family histories.

I am also grateful to Kerry O'Brien, descendant of *Emigrant* passengers Charles and Anne O'Brien, for his generous support of this project. And of course, for their never-ending love, care and encouragement, I thank my husband, Steve, my parents, John and Jeanette Paterson, and my children, Lucy and Eddie.

Endnotes

PART 1

1 Text from a sampler of 1854: 'The Emigrants Farewell and The Emigrants Prayer', held at the Powerhouse Museum: http://www. powerhousemuseum.com/collection/database/?irn=172770#ix-zz4Yv9dJRmj. Its origin is uncertain; according to the *Armagh Guardian* of 11 May, 1852, it was written by Miss Mary Atkinson of Couragh (see *Irish Emigration Database*, http://www.dippam. ac.uk/ied/records/38950).

2 Jewitt, L.F.W. (1873) *A History of Plymouth*. London: Simpkin, Marshall & Co. [Retrieved from the Internet Archive]

3 Possibly in Falkirk, where her parents were married.

4 Brayshay, M. (1980, Dec): Government Assisted Emigration from Plymouth in the nineteenth century. *Report and Transactions of The Devonshire Association for the Advancement of Science, Literature and Art.* (112), pp.185–213

5 Carter & Bonus submitted the tender on de Wolfe's behalf on 19 February, and the charter contract was signed on 23 March.

6   (1850, March 19). *The Times*, London, p.1

7   Brayshay, M. (1980, Dec) Government Assisted Emigration.

8   According to his death notice in *The North Australian* of 31 May 1864, p.2.

9   Great Britain. Royal Commission into the Condition of the Poorer Classes in Ireland. (1836). Condition of the poorer classes in Ireland: appendix E: baronial examination on food, cottages, clothing, furniture, etc. In: *Parliamentary Papers, Session 1836*, Vol. XXXII, p.221 [Retrieved from the Internet Archive]

10 *First Report from the Select Committee on Emigrant Ships* (P.P. 1854, XIII) c. 163 Minutes of Evidence Mr Sylvester Redmond, quoted in Brayshay, M. (1980)

11 (1875, Dec 13) *Western Daily Mercury* [Retrieved from 'The last port' http://www.historic-shipping.co.uk/Emigration/port.html]

12 Low, S. (1861). *The Charities of London*. London: Sampson Low, Son, and Marston [Retrieved from http://www.londonancestor. com/charity/british-female-emigration.htm]

13 The British Ladies' Female Emigration Society (1850). *The Emigrants' Penny Magazine*, 1 (2), pp.25–29

14 K. E. F. & Society for Promoting Christian Knowledge (Great Britain). Committee of General Literature and Education (1850). *Parting Words to Emigrant Parents*. London: Printed for the Society for Promoting Christian Knowledge

15 'Visits to emigrant ships'. (1850). In *The Emigrants' Penny Magazine*, 1 (1), p.20

16 (1850, Aug 17). *The Moreton Bay Courier*, p.2

17 This might have been Catherine Smith, who was the Kemp's servant in Liverpool according to the 1841 Census.

18 (1850, Aug 17). *The Moreton Bay Courier*, p.2

19 British Port Authorities did not need lists of all departing passengers, but they *were* required to submit to the government

the names of all those emigrants whose passage the government was funding. So only the assisted passengers were recorded on the embarkation list, but once they arrived in Australia, all passengers – whether assisted or not – had to be reported.

20 In 1849 the EES officially evolved into the British Ladies' Female Emigrant Society (BLFES) but in a note from the society in *The Emigrants' Penny Magazine* regarding their visit to the *Emigrant*, which took place 3 days before the BLFES' first annual meeting, they still refer to themselves as the EES.

21 This was probably Charlotte Hardwidge, a 19-year-old domestic servant from Long Ashton, Somerset.

22 The British Ladies' Female Emigration Society (1850). *The Emigrants' Penny Magazine*, 1 (1), p.20

23 Woolcock, H. R. (1986). *Rights of Passage : Emigration to Australia in the Nineteenth Century*. London: Tavistock Publications, p.194. The quote is from the diary of a voyage in 1862.

24 On embarkation, there were approximately 53 single women (i.e. women and girls 15 and over), 70 single men, eight married couples without children (i.e. 16 people) and 139 family members (parents and their children under the age of 15).

25 Ancestry.com. New South Wales, Australia, *Colonial Secretary's Papers, 1788–1856 [database on-line]*. Series: NRS 898; Reel or Fiche Numbers: Reels 6020–6040, 6070; Fiche 3260–3312

26 William was sentenced under the name of 'William Bramble' and continued to be known under that name in Australia, as are his descendants.

27 I.e. the crew's living quarters.

28 159 Irish, 113 English, two Scots and one of unknown origin (probably English) embarked, and another six were born on the voyage – one from an Irish family and five from English families.

PART 2

29 *A Parting Gift for an Emigrant Friend*. (1854). London: Harry Wooldridge, p.76 [Retrieved from the Internet Archive]

30 Domville-Fife, C. W. & Foulke, R. D. (2007). *Square Rigger Days: Autobiographies of Sail* (New ed). Sydney, NSW: UNSW Press, p.20

31 Steley, M. (1863). *OM71-14 Maria Steley Diary, 1863–1864*. This was a diary kept by Maria Steley during her voyage from England to Brisbane on board the *Ariadne*.

32 Davis, F. (1858). *[Diary kept during a voyage to Melbourne in the ship Conway, 1858]*. Cited in Hassam, Andrew (1994). *Sailing to Australia: Shipboard Diaries by Nineteenth-Century British Emigrants*. Manchester University Press, Manchester; New York

33 Melville, H. (1849). *Redburn: His First Voyage* [Retrieved from https://ebookcentral-proquest-com.ezproxy.usq.edu.au]

34 Davis, *[Diary kept during a voyage to Melbourne in the ship Conway, 1858]*, p.4

35 K. E. F. & Society for Promoting Christian Knowledge (Great Britain). Committee of General Literature and Education (1850). *A Letter to Young Female Emigrants Proceeding to Australia*. London: Printed for the Society for Promoting Christian Knowledge

36 Davis, *[Diary kept during a voyage to Melbourne in the ship Conway, 1858]*, p.4

37 (1850, Feb 28) *London Standard*, p.3

38 T.W.C. Murdoch and Frederic Rogers to H. Merivale, 9 May 1853, Enc. In no.3, in despatches from Newcastle to Latrobe, 15 May 1853, in 'Correspondence relating to emigration to the Australian colonies', BPP 1854 436, vol. XLVI, 123–4, quoted in Haines, R. (2005). *Doctors at Sea: Emigrant Voyages to Colonial Australia*. Basingstoke, England: Palgrave Macmillan, p.121

39 Neither Mrs Burberow's nor her daughter's names appear on the embarkation list. Mrs Burberow may have worked for her passage and her daughter may have paid for hers.

40 K. E. F. & Society for Promoting Christian Knowledge (Great Britain). Committee of General Literature and Education (1850). *Hints to Matrons of Emigrant Ships*. London: Printed for the Society for Promoting Christian Knowledge

41 State Records NSW: Immigration Agent; NRS 5239, Letters received 1846–97, Matron's Diary [9/6212-13], [Retrieved from www.records.nsw.gov.au/state-archives/digital-gallery/matrons-diary/complete-transcription]

42 Davis, *[Diary kept during a voyage to Melbourne in the ship Conway, 1858]*, p.13

43 Morton, G. (1852). *[Letters of George Morton] : [to his mother and sisters, 1852, during a voyage from Plymouth to Melbourne on the ship Blackwall, and after his arrival in Victoria]*.

44 The figures of 195 houses and 1043 inhabitants, as at 1837, are cited in Lewis, S. (1837) *A Topographical Dictionary of Ireland: Comprising the Several Counties, Cities, Boroughs, Corporate, Market, and Post Towns, Parishes, and Villages, with Historical and Statistical Descriptions . . . , Volume 2* [online].

45 A prison or reform school for petty offenders.

46 Lewis, S. (1837) *A Topographical Dictionary of Ireland: Comprising the Several Counties, Cities, Boroughs, Corporate, Market, and Post Towns, Parishes, and Villages, with Historical and Statistical Descriptions . . . , Volume 2* [online], p.65

47 'Cess' was a sort of tax, or rates, paid by land owners or lease holders and depended upon their incomes.

48 There may also have been another child, Robert, born around 1841; sources are unclear, however, whether this Robert Mitchell was a brother or a cousin to George.

49 *Irish miscellanea, chiefly from County Armagh*, FHL film 127354

50 Froggatt, P. (n.d.). *The Belfast Medical School, 1835–1985*. The Ulster Medical Society [Retrieved from http://www.ums.ac.uk/bmsch/bmsch_med.pdf]

51 Dixon, W.M. (1902). *Trinity College, Dublin*. London: F.E. Robinson, p.200 [Retrieved from Internet Archive]

52 According to Dixon: in 1864, out of 18,000 medical practitioners on the UK register, only 541 had degrees from Oxford, Cambridge or Dublin – i.e. only about 3% were university educated.

53 Bell, J. (1893). The Surgical Side of the Royal Infirmary of Edinburgh, 1854–1892: The Progress of a Generation. *Edinburgh Hospital Reports*, 1, p.22

54 Ibid

55 Bell, The Surgical Side of the Royal Infirmary of Edinburgh, pp.22–23. Note that the theatre described opened in 1853, some years after George Mitchell's attendance. George would have attended Syme's sessions in the old hospital building. In George's day, anaesthesia was yet to be used effectively in surgery, so the proceedings must also have differed somewhat; it can be assumed, however, that Dr Syme's character and habits and his ability to engage the rapt attention of his students were as much in evidence in the years that George Mitchell was a student.

56 Bell, The Surgical Side of the Royal Infirmary of Edinburgh, pp.27–28

57 Later Sir Robert Christison.

58 Cited in Roberts, S. (1993). *Sophia Jex-Blake: A Woman Pioneer in Nineteenth Century Medical Reform*. London: Routledge, p.86 [Retrieved from Google Books]

59 Professor Henderson, of Edinburgh. (1872). *The Medical Times And Gazette*, 1. (April 20), p.463 [Retrieved from Google Books]

60 According to Dr Alison, as reported in Creighton, C. (1894). *A History of Epidemics in Britain from A.D. 664 to the Extinction of Plague*, p.204.

61 According to Captain William Kemp in his letter to *The Moreton Bay Courier* on 5 October 1850, p 2, George was in the service of the 'Company' for four years. Given the timeframe, George could not have been at sea the whole time. He may have been engaged on isolated voyages when not working at the London Fever Hospital and on the 1849 voyage to Australia.

62 Captain Kemp wrote that George was employed at the hospital for 12 months prior to his voyage on the *Osprey*, which departed Plymouth in November 1849. George's name cannot be found anywhere in that hospital's records, however; perhaps he was in too junior a role, or employed for too short a time, to have rated a mention.

63 (1849, Mar 26). *Port Philip Gazette and Settler's Journal*, p.2

64 (1849, Nov 24). *Norfolk News*, p.3

65 (1849, Oct 20). *Oxford Chronicle and Reading Gazette*, p.2

66 (1849, March 23). *The Geelong Chronicle*, quoted in (2010) *The Draper and Sanders families of Enfield, M'Sex*. [Retrieved from http://drapersandsanders.blogspot.com.au/2010/10/my-great-great-great-grandmother-jane.html]

67 (1850, Oct 5) *The Moreton Bay Courier*, p.2

68 (1850, April 8). *Armagh Guardian*, pp.2–3

69 It is from travellers' journals that we have learned much of what we know about 19th-century shipboard life today. Many journals were written during similar voyages of the time but unfortunately no known journals from the *Emigrant's* passage still exist.

70 K. E. F. & Society for Promoting Christian Knowledge (Great Britain). Committee of General Literature and Education (1850).

A Letter to Young Female Emigrants Proceeding to Australia.
London: Printed for the Society for Promoting Christian
Knowledge

71 Haines, R. (2003). *Life and Death in the Age of Sail : The Passage
to Australia.* Sydney: University of New South Wales Press, p.141

72 MacKenzie, D. (1852). *Ten Years in Australia : Being the Results of
his Experience as a Settler During That Period.* London: William
S. Orr and Co.

73 Ibid

74 Ibid

75 *Australia: Who Should Go, How to Go, What to Do When There :
With a Map and Latest Information.* (1852). Liverpool : Gabriel
Thomson [Retrieved from http://nla.gov.au/nla.obj-80253536]

76 Australia (1850). In *The Emigrants' Penny Magazine,* 1(7),
pp.145–150

77 MacKenzie, *Ten Years in Australia*

78 1841 UK census

79 *A Parting Gift for an Emigrant Friend.* (1854). London, p.78.
[Retrieved from the Internet Archive]

80 Cited in Hassam, Andrew (1994). *Sailing to Australia: Shipboard
Diaries by Nineteenth-century British Emigrants.* Manchester
University Press, Manchester; New York, pp.163–164

81 Davis, F. (1858). *[Diary kept during a voyage to Melbourne in the
ship Conway, 1858].*

82 Prout, J.S. (1852). *An Illustrated Handbook of the Voyage to
Australia and a Visit to the Gold Fields : Descriptive of the New
Moving Panorama Exhibiting Daily at 309 Regent Street.* [London:
the author] [Retrieved from http://nla.gov.au/nla.obj-81151644]

83 Or possibly 8 May – accounts differ.

84 Huss, M. (1855). *Statistics and Treatment of Typhus and Typhoid
Fever.* London: Longman, Brown, Green, and Longmans, p.98

[Retrieved from the Internet Archive https://archive.org/details/statisticsandtr00hussgoog]

85 Graham, T.J. (1827). *Modern Domestic Medicine: A Popular Treatise* ... Stationer's Court, London: Simpkin & Marshall, p.515 [Retrieved from Google Books]

86 Upham, J. B. (1858). Illustrations of typhus fever in Great Britain : the result of personal observations made in the summer of 1853, with some remarks as to its origin, habits, symptoms, and pathology : to which is appended a brief account of the re-appearance of typhus in Boston in the winter of 1857–58. *The Boston Medical and Surgical Journal*, 58(24), pp.469–474

87 She had not been counted on the embarkation list.

88 Graham, T.J., *Modern Domestic Medicine*

89 Davis, *[Diary kept during a voyage to Melbourne in the ship Conway, 1858]*

90 Her name on the marriage register is recorded as Frances Jane Burberon.

91 (1852, Nov 27). *Moreton Bay Courier*, p.3

92 (1851). *The Emigrants' Penny Magazine*, 2(13), pp.109–110

93 Prout, *An Illustrated Handbook of the Voyage to Australia and a Visit to the Gold Fields*

94 (1851). *The Emigrants' Penny Magazine*, 2(13), pp.107–109

95 (1850, Sept 7). *The Moreton Bay Courier*, p.3

96 Captain Kemp gives the date of James Chapple's death as 15 July; Mrs Kemp 18 July.

97 Davis, *[Diary kept during a voyage to Melbourne in the ship Conway, 1858]*

98 Prout, *An illustrated handbook of the voyage to Australia and a visit to the gold fields*

99 In Captain Kemp's letter he names her 'Ann Connor'. In the embarkation list, only the 'head' of the family (i.e. her husband,

James) is named, and as she was not on the August arrival lists, she is not named there either. One of the two lists in existence that is dated 26 September – a list that was transcribed decades after the original list was written – gives her name as Mary Connor. This was the name used on the plaque at Dunwich cemetery.

100 (1851). *The Emigrants' Penny Magazine*, 2 (13) pp.109–110

101 Crew lists for the 1850 voyage of the *Emigrant* have not survived, but records from the 1849 voyage of the same vessel to Port Jackson give us an idea of the size, structure and employment conditions of the crew. On the 1849 passage, also commanded by William Henry Kemp, 39 men were engaged to convey government-assisted emigrants to Australia.

102 The National Archives of the UK. BT 98/2216, Port of Registry: Liverpool Ships Names: E, 1850

103 Her name on the embarkation list was 'Catherine', though Captain Kemp named her 'Caroline'. The name on the plaque at Dunwich is 'Caroline'.

104 Richard Watt's diary, cited in Fisher, R. & Brisbane History Group (2009). *Boosting Brisbane : Imprinting the Colonial Capital of Queensland.* Salisbury, Qld: Boolarong Press

105 There is some discrepancy about the date. The first page of the paperwork completed on Dr Ballow's inspection of the vessel is dated 9 August but subsequent pages are dated 10 August.

106 (1851). *The Emigrants' Penny Magazine*, 2(13), pp.107–109

PART 3

107 (1853, Dec 20). *Moreton Bay Free Press*, p.4

108 According to the 1846 NSW census.

109 (1850, July 29), *The Moreton Bay Courier* p.1

110 NSW Colonial Secretary's Office (1989). *Letters relating to*

Moreton Bay and Queensland, 1822–1860. Letters received 1851 and papers filed with them – Reel A2.21, p.685

111 NSW Colonial Secretary's Office *Letters Relating to Moreton Bay and Queensland*, pp.756–761

112 (1864, March 19). *Courier*, p.3

113 Great Britain. Colonial Office (1838). Great Britain. Colonial Office – New South Wales Governors' Despatches, 1813–1879, Call#A1218, p.272

114 (1838, Aug 30). *The Sydney Gazette and New South Wales Advertiser*, p.2

115 (1838, Sep 6). *The Sydney Gazette and New South Wales Advertiser*, p.2

116 Ibid

117 (1841, Jan 13). *Sydney Monitor and Commercial Advertiser*, p.2

118 Henry George Lewis. (n.d.) [Retrieved from http://www.medicalpioneers.com/cgi-bin/index.cgi?detail=1&id=2172]

119 (1840, Oct 17). *Australasian Chronicle*, p.3

120 (1840, Nov 5). *The Sydney Gazette and New South Wales Advertiser*, p.2

121 (1843, Jan 12). *Australasian Chronicle*, p.4

122 (1843, Jan 14). *Maitland Mercury and Hunter River General Advertiser*, p.2

123 (1842, April 1). *Sydney Morning Herald*, p.1

124 (1844, July 13). *Maitland Mercury and Hunter River General Advertiser*, p.3

125 (1845, May 31). *Morning Chronicle*, p.3

126 (1846, Jan 15). *Sydney Morning Herald*, p.3

127 (1846, Feb 11). *Morning Chronicle*, p.3

128 (1850, Oct 5). *Moreton Bay Courier*, p.2

129 NSW Colonial Secretary's Office *Letters Relating to Moreton Bay and Queensland*, pp.753–755

130 McConnel, M. (1905). *Memories of Days Long Gone By.* [Brisbane: the author]

131 QSA Item ID869682, *Register – court cases*

132 Harrison, J. (2005). Rigby, Hannah (1794–1853). *Australian Dictionary of Biography* [Retrieved from http://adb.anu.edu.au/ biography/rigby-hannah-13171]

133 QSA Agency ID11094, Moreton Bay Benevolent Society [Retrieved from http://www.archivessearch.qld.gov.au/Search/ AgencyDetails.aspx?AgencyId=11094]

134 (1840, Sept 2). *Sydney Herald*, p.2

135 (1846, Nov 25). *Cornwall Chronicle*, p.910

136 Rosamond Siemon alleges Mayne's guilt in her 1997 book *The Mayne Inheritance*. It should be noted, however, that no evidence of the alleged death-bed confession has ever come to light.

137 (1849, Oct 13). *Moreton Bay Courier*, p.2

138 One of Captain Wickham's letters states that Dr Ballow departed on 23 August; in another letter he states that Ballow reached the quarantine station on 24 August and took up his duties on that day.

139 (1853, Dec 20). *Moreton Bay Free Press*, p.4

140 (1895, Aug 20). *Queensland Times, Ipswich Herald and General Advertiser*, p.5

141 George Watson stated that 'James Halls' did the washing for the hospital. He probably meant 'Joseph Hall', who was listed as a passenger on the arrival list. Watson may have confused him with 'James Hall', a seaman on the *Emigrant*.

142 (1850, Aug 24). *The Moreton Bay Courier*, p.2–3

143 Like many of the passengers' details, Patrick's age is inconclusive. Some sources state that he was only three, but the arrival list, which gives his age as five, is probably correct.

144 (1898, March 5). *The Maitland Weekly Mercury*, p.10, and (1898, 2 March). Evening News, p.2

145 Reports are inconsistent, but from *The Moreton Bay Courier* reports of 7 and 14 Sept it seems that there were two deaths on 3 Sept, another two on 5 Sept and one on 6 Sept, all of unnamed adult males.

146 (1850, Aug 31). *The Moreton Bay Courier*, p.2

147 (1850, Sept 7). *The Moreton Bay Courier*, p.3

148 (1850, Sept 14). *The Moreton Bay Courier*, p.2

149 (1915, March 16). *The Brisbane Courier*, p.9. The newspaper reported that he had entered his ninety-fourth year but according to immigration records it would have been his 91st.

150 (1850, Sept 21). *The Moreton Bay Courier*, p.2

151 There is some confusion about the date. George Mitchell's grave, which was erected some time before the end of 1853, states that he died on 15 September. This date appears to be incorrect. In his daily returns for the quarantine station, Dr Ballow clearly gives Mitchell's (and Jane Syrett's) death as 19 September. An article in *The Moreton Bay Courier* of 21 September reports that on 18 September, Dr Mitchell was alive but his case was 'hopeless'.

152 The date is incorrect. He actually died on 19 September 1850.

153 The Earl of Charlemont's accounts; FHL BRITISH Film [1279331 Item 6]

154 Thanks to Elisabeth Mitchell, descendant of Alexander Mitchell, for sharing her family tree details.

155 NSW Colonial Secretary's Office, *Letters Relating to Moreton Bay and Queensland*, pp.681–683

156 (1850, Sept 28). *The Moreton Bay Courier*, p.2

157 (1850, Sept 28). *The Moreton Bay Courier*, p.3

158 (1850, Sept 28). *The Moreton Bay Courier*, p.2

159 No one died on 28 August. Joanna Dwyer died on 27 August but she was unmarried. During that time the deaths were coming

thick and fast, and it was not at all strange that Dr Mallon might have confused the dates.

160 (1850, Sept 28). *The Moreton Bay Courier*, p.3

161 (1850, Dec 7). *The Moreton Bay Courier*, p.1

162 McConnel, M. (1905). *Memories of Days Long Gone By*. M. McConnel, [Brisbane, QLD: the author]

163 Patrick, R., (1985). 'Death's *Emigrant*'. In: (ed), *Horsewhip the Doctor*. St Lucia, QLD: University of Queensland Press. pp.7–16 [Retrieved from UQ eSpace]

164 The child was unnamed by Dr Mallon, but may have been either Robert Chapple, or Hugh Reilly, the son of James and Bridget, from Dublin. These were the only one-year-old boys with living mothers in quarantine.

165 Or Julia, according to her death certificate.

166 Unfortunately no copies of the paper from those early days have survived.

167 (1850, Oct 5). *The Moreton Bay Courier*, p.2

168 Ibid

169 The only reference to the exact location of this plaque, cited in 1853, suggests that it was attached to the obelisk on Dr Mitchell's grave. The plaque is no longer there and no known record exists explaining its removal. An article in the *Queenslander* (1892, 8 Oct, p.699) suggests that it was still in Dunwich in 1892.

170 (1850, Oct 5). *The Moreton Bay Courier*, p.3

171 Ancestry.com. *New South Wales, Australia, Colonial Secretary's Papers, 1788–1856* [database on-line]. Provo, UT, USA: Ancestry.com Operations, Inc, 2010. NRS 983; Reel 750

172 (1850, Nov 18). *Moreton Bay Courier*, p.1

173 Fisher, R. & Brisbane History Group (2009). *Boosting Brisbane: Imprinting the Colonial Capital of Queensland*. Salisbury, QLD: Boolarong Press

PART 4

174 UK. Parliamentary Debates. House of Commons. 14 May 1852 vol 121 cc630–3 [Retrieved from http://hansard.millbanksystems. com/commons/1852/may/14/desertion-of-seamen-in-australia]

175 (1850, Nov 18). *Sydney Morning Herald*, p.3

176 (1852, July 10). *The Moreton Bay Courier*, p.2

177 (1852, Aug 31). *The Argus*, p.3

178 Different sources give conflicting ages. According to her marriage certificate she was 21 in June 1833 so would have turned 41 in 1853. Her death certificate states 37 and the newspaper notice 39.

179 NSW. Colonial Secretary's Office (1989). *Letters Relating to Moreton Bay and Queensland, 1822–1860*. W. & F. Pascoe, Balgowlah, NSW

180 *The Moreton Bay Courier* reported some months later that Mrs Ballow had been granted a gratuity of £300 (1852, Feb 7). *The Moreton Bay Courier*, p.3. This mysteriously large sum, which is much larger than the amount sought by Captain Wickham, is not mentioned in any of the colonial secretary's correspondence.

181 (1863, Sept 3) *The Brisbane Courier*, p.2

182 Gordon, D. (1969). Cannan, Kearsey (1815–1894). *Australian Dictionary of Biography* [Retrieved from http://adb.anu.edu.au/ biography/cannan-kearsey-3160]

183 Ibid

184 Ibid

185 (1850, Nov 18). *The Moreton Bay Courier*, p.1

186 (1852, Feb 14) *The Maitland Mercury and Hunter River General Advertiser*, p.2

187 Ibid

188 *The Maitland Mercury and Hunter River General Advertiser* reported on 25 January 1854 that he had married Angelina Harrison. This appears to have been journalistic error. According

to Dr Mallon's wife's death certificate, her mother's maiden name was Elizabeth Harris – and a witness at her wedding to Patrick Mallon was Elizabeth Harrison. Mrs Mallon (née Elizabeth Angela Wright) appears to have been known as Angela by her children (named as such on their death certificates). It seems that the journalist reporting the wedding mixed up the names of the bride and the witness, her mother.

189 (1859, Oct 24). *Sydney Morning Herald*, p.3

190 (1865, Feb 4). *The Maitland Mercury and Hunter River General Advertiser*, p.3

191 (1866, Oct 11). *Freeman's Journal*, p.16

192 (1874, Sept 18). *Sydney Morning Herald*, p.16

193 Now Bingara.

194 The immigration record that gives Margaret's age as 19 is incorrect.

195 (1864, May 31). *The North Australian*, p.2. The age of 103 was also recorded on his death certificate.

196 Patrick Maunsell gave evidence as a police constable in a number of trials from 24 November 1851. See QSA Item ID518885, *Register – depositions* (1850–1854).

197 (1855, Sept 29). *The Moreton Bay Courier*, p.3

198 (1857, Feb 14). *The Moreton Bay Courier*, p.1

199 (1860, Aug 2). *The Moreton Bay Courier*, p.3

200 (1867, Sep 19). *The Brisbane Courier*, p.1

201 (1867, Oct 1). *The Sydney Morning Herald*, p.3

202 (1873, Oct 7). *The Brisbane Courier*, p.2

203 (1875, April 17). *The Queenslander*, p.2

204 (1882, April 3). *The Telegraph*, p.3

205 Variously spelled as Bloxam, Bloxham, Bloxsam, Bloxsom.

206 (1900, Nov 1). *Morning Bulletin*, p.5

207 On his birth certificate, no father's name is recorded. According

to Walter's mother's death certificate, she was married twice: first to a 'Massey', to whom she bore a son, Walter Massey. The marriage is a fiction, but the child is not. Walter's death certificate muddies the waters, naming his father as John Tolman. John Tolman's admission record to Dunwich Benevolent Asylum and his death certificate claim Walter as his son.

208 (1889, Sept 11). *The Brisbane Courier*, p.5

209 Though her death certificate records her age as 42.

210 (1928, June 11). *The Brisbane Courier*, p.12

211 Rahemtula, A. (1988). Real, Patrick (1846–1928), *Australian Dictionary of Biography* [Retrieved from http://adb.anu.edu.au/biography/real-patrick-8169/text14281]

212 (1928, June 11). *The Brisbane Courier*, p.12

213 (1928, June 12). *The Brisbane Courier*, p.15

214 Ancestry.com. *New South Wales, Australia, Registers for the Randwick Asylum for Destitute Children, 1852–1915* [database on-line]. Provo, UT, USA: Ancestry.com Operations, Inc. State Archives NSW; Series: NRS 13362; Item: 7/3796; Roll: 1865

215 (1915, July 20). *Leader*, p.4

216 (1888, Oct 29). *Newcastle Morning Herald*

217 (1874, Dec 8). *The Maitland Mercury and Hunter River General Advertiser*, p.3

218 Edward may have died sometime between March 1866 and December 1868. Mary's death notice calls her 'widow of the late Edward Wheeler', although no death certificate for Edward can be found. He may have died in another colony or overseas.

219 (1899, June 21). *Brisbane Courier*, p.2

220 Ibid

221 It seems that her bereaved family didn't know her actual age. Emma's age at her death, given as 42, must have been calculated from her baptism certificate, which was dated 24 August 1834.

In fact, Emma had been ten years old when she was baptised, and was 51 when she died.

222 These were the passengers who departed Brisbane on 4 Dec, as listed in the *Moreton Bay Courier* on 7 Dec. However, the *Sydney Morning Herald* of 9 Dec reported the arrival of seven men, one lady, six orphan children, one matron, two invalids and 12 in steerage.

223 (1929, Feb 11). *The Voice of the North*, p.14

224 (1903, Sept 12). *Freeman's Journal*, p.26

225 (1855, Nov 19). *Sydney Morning Herald*, p.2

226 Ibid

227 Quoted in Ramsland, J. (1986). *Children of the Back Lanes: Destitute and Neglected Children in Colonial New South Wales.* Kensington, NSW: NSW University Press

228 (1868, Oct 22). *The Age*, p.3

229 Ramsland, J. *Children of the Back Lanes*, p.149

230 (1855, Nov 19). *Sydney Morning Herald*, p.2

231 (1852, March 18). *Sydney Morning Herald*, p.2

232 (1860, March 31). *Goulburn Chronicle and Southern Advertiser*, p.4

233 The Justice of the Peace who gave permission for the underage girl to marry was William Hilton Hovell, better known as the explorer who had teamed up with Hamilton Hume to explore the course of the western rivers of New South Wales.

234 (1902, Oct 10). *Albury Banner and Wodonga Express*, p.15

235 (1918, Feb 7). *Daily Advertiser*, p.2

236 (1903, Sept 12). *Freeman's Journal*, p.26

237 No immigrant record (nor any other record) can be found for a James Corkan at this time.

238 (1871, July 3). *The Age*, p.1

239 PROV. VPRS13579, P0001, Unit 4, David Hobbs (Teacher record number 1017)

240 (1881, May 20). *The Ballarat Star*, p.3

241 PROV, David Hobbs

242 (1867, Oct 19). *Illustrated News for Home Readers*, p.11

243 In this context, 'Infidel' this probably means lapsed Christian.

244 *New South Wales Government Gazettes*, 1889–1893

245 According to the admission register and his death certificate, he was 75 on admission, but this contradicts other records.

246 (1900, Dec 22). *The Queenslander*, p.1267

247 (1916, Aug 1). *The Brisbane Courier*, p.6

248 (1852, Feb 14). *The Shipping Gazette and Sydney General Trade List*, p.50

EPILOGUE

249 (1853, Dec 20). *Moreton Bay Free Press*, p.4

Index

Imagine
adjectives - bring reg p80   137 glittering sea   117

Suspenseful - hints of date ahead.

P59 eg P73 P84

120 1st mention of crypts

129: Tees up drama

182: Sense of excitement as grows in dr Mallon→
        guarantee cop

183 Overwrought? An earnest 27-yr old etc

R 186.7 Tender in writer devil of Ely Wade drawing
  . Little   positive to report

Too much detail on peripheral characters
   Expertly knitting facts together

Doctors fate - Mitchell, Mallon Ballow

186 Touching

189 Coffin Maker; important

207: Some Almost every hosp attendant fell ill

      Sobering tale
      How to keep pace with
         the marble gun frgf tragedies
           Conscripted ?
       Memorial to the dead

249: Number dead
        260 KPOf   funeral pyre burned
                      253   →Asylum   by young orphan

9 780648 650300